IN THE HEART OF WORDS

BY

Jenabe E. Caldwell

Reference: " The Hidden Words of Bahá'u'lláh"

In The Heart of Words

by
Jenabe E. Caldwell

Referencing The Hidden Words
of
Bahá'u'lláh

© Jenabe E. Caldwell
All Rights Reserved

Best Publisher
Wailuku, Hawaii

http://www.bestpublisher.org

ISBN 0-9762780-3-0

First edition 2008

Introduction

It was the year of my Lord, Bahá'u'lláh, 122BE that I once again mounted my charger of the love of God and hastened into the arena of service. This time my pioneering post was to be Mexico. I had been personally encouraged to do this by the beloved Hands of the Cause of God, Ugo Giachery and William Sears. As I was at this time financially independent, the National Spiritual Assembly of the Bahá'ís' of Mexico asked me to go to the state of Oaxaca. The goal of the Nine Year Plan was to have at least one Bahá'í in every state of Mexico.

From the hurricane force winds, snow, sleet, earthquakes and volcanoes of our Aleutian goal of the ten year Crusade, to the temperate ideal climate of Oaxaca was like coming into paradise. This city is in the high mountains of the Sierra Madres with beautiful blue skies, warm sunny days and cool comfortable nights. The cascades of bougainvillea flowers in oranges, whites, reds, pinks and purples lined the streets and avenues. The Zapotec Indians were a warm hearted, sensitive and happy people. Most of them were poor to the extreme. They would play music every evening in the town square, with a city orchestra playing a concert there on Sundays. Sometimes as you would walk down in the city you would find the people out dancing in the streets, happy, carefree and beautiful. I loved Oaxaca and I loved the people from my first day among them, and I still do. The Zapotec and Mixtec were the majority population; a people that struggled from dawn to dark to just stay alive by working an already overworked land.

So the goal of the Plan was won. With Elaine, the children and I now living in the state of Oaxaca all I had to do was sit in the sun, enjoy the music, people and climate. However, I decided with the help of Bahá'u'lláh to try and raise up just one Assembly during the remainder of the Nine Year Plan, so off I went to the villages: Zoquiappan, Ixtepeci, Santa Domingo Tamaltipec, La Fe and most of the other villages in and around Oaxaca. In just a few short years, because of the sweet open hearted reception of the people we had new Bahá'ís in around ninety-five villages. It wasn't that I wanted them. It was because Bahá'u'lláh did. I would go into a village where new Bahá'ís lived and someone else would become a Bahá'í. So I tried to just follow the following instructions:

"Those who declare themselves as Bahá'ís should become enchanted with the beauty of the Teachings; and touched by the love of Bahá'u'lláh. The declarants need not know all the proofs, history, laws, and principles of the Faith, but in the process of declaring themselves they must, in addition to catching the spark of faith, become basically informed about the Central Figures of the Faith, as well as the existence of laws they must follow and an administration they must obey. After declaration, the new believers must not be left to their own devices. Through correspondence and dispatch of visitors, through conferences and training courses, these friends must be patiently strengthened and lovingly helped to develop into full Bahá'í maturity." (Volume 2 COC, page 62)

This instruction clearly states, "After declaration, the new believers must not be left to their own devices." so off I went day after day, from dawn until after dark, trying to deepen these pure hearted souls in the Cause of God.

I made up felt boards, used slides and movies (carrying my own electric generator with me), and tried everything I could to follow the instructions. After over two years I still had not gotten any of the new friends strong enough to want to help me in forming the Local Spiritual Assemblies. What usually happened was that I would gather up these friends and we would all sit down and say prayers, which they loved to do. Then I no sooner would I start the deepening class than someone would come running in shouting, "Jose! Jose! the pig is caught in the fence." Everyone would jump up and run out and get the pig out of the fence. Then they had to talk about it and then they would disperse and go home. One time Grandfather fell down the well and drowned during one of my so called deepening classes. It seemed that even heaven was conspiring against me. I was truly overwhelmed and frustrated. Bahá'u'lláh says:

"He will never deal unjustly with any one, neither will He task a soul beyond its power." (Gleanings, page 106).

Yet I was sure that I had reached an insurmountable obstacle that I could not push out of the way, go around, go over, go under or go in another direction. I was sure that Bahá'u'lláh had given me a task in consolidating these souls that I was powerless to achieve. I felt I had an impossible task. I was indeed between a rock and a hard spot. I would go out all day every day and always more and more people would become Bahá'ís.

I found that the optimum time to visit was between four and six weeks. If I stayed away longer their interest would fall off and if I came back more often they became burdened. Now with about ninety-five villages, just to visit each place for one day would take up to ninety-five days. One village was a fifteen mile hike in and a fifteen mile hike out with Bahá'ís all along the trail in and out. You can understand my dilemma. I was heartsick and seemed to be tasked totally beyond my ability and capacity to obey and follow the instructions.

One day I received a letter from Hand of the Cause Ugo Giachery. He was giving me some information and right in the middle of his letter with no lead nor explanation he stated, "Jenabe, the answer lies in the institute." and went on with the other information. Now, I had no idea what an institute was nor how to do one, but because I was in a desperate situation I said OK. I consulted with the National Spiritual Assembly of the Bahá'ís of Mexico and they said to go ahead. As the Bahá'ís owned a piece of property outside of Puebla in San Raphael I was given permission to use it. I spent the next several months in building the Amelia Collins Institute. When I asked about what was an institute I was told to teach administration. The dictionary said an institute was "teacher training classes". As I was studying the Writings to make up an institute class, I found the following statement of 'Abdu'l-Bahá:

"He has written a book entitled the Hidden Words. The preface announces that it contains the essences of the words of the Prophets of the past, clothed in the garment of brevity, for the teaching and spiritual guidance of the people of the world. Read it that you may understand the true foundations of religion and reflect upon the inspiration of the Messengers of God. It is light upon light." (PUP, page 86)

Now as 'Abdu'l-Bahá said that the Hidden Words are the true foundations of religion. I logically thought that, OK, if we are going to have an institute to train teachers, we had better start with the Hidden Words. We would start by laying a good and solid foundation. Then I ran into the following statement of 'Abdu'l-Bahá on Prayer and Meditation:

"Prayer and Meditation, take much time for these two." (The Importance of Deepening, page 204)

That seemed like a very good idea so I added that to my institute program. Then a statement that Bahá'u'lláh made caught my eye:

"....a treatise that may well be regarded as His greatest mystical composition, designated as the Seven Valleys," (Shoghi Effendi: God Passes By, Page: 140)

"And further: The stages that mark the wayfarer's journey from the abode of dust to the heavenly homeland are said to be seven." (Seven Valleys and Four Valleys, page 4)

If we could truly get the new found friends from this abode of dust to a heavenly homeland, they would indeed be consolidated, so the Seven Valleys became part of my program. The last item on my agenda was from page 18 in the Advent of Divine justice to page 25, and designated by Shoghi Effendi as a "Spiritual Prerequisites" for all teaching plans:

"These requirements are none other that a high sense of moral rectitude in their social and administrative activities, absolute chastity in their individual lives, and complete freedom from prejudice in their dealings with peoples of a different race, class, creed or color." (Advent of Divine Justice page 18).

The new agenda for our trial institute was as follows:
    Wake up at 5:30 AM.
    Group prayers together 6:00 AM to 7:00 AM
    Breakfast from 7 AM to 8 AM
    Individual private prayer from 8 AM to 9 AM
    Classes from 9 AM to 12 Noon
    Lunch 12 to 1 PM
    Free time 1 PM to 2 PM
    Individual private prayer from 2 PM to 3 PM
    Classes from 3 PM to 6 PM
    Dinner from 6 PM to 7 PM
    Fun, singing & games from 7:30 Pm to 9:30 PM
    Lights out 10 PM

The other problem I faced was in how we were going to study. Again I went to the teachings and found some very clear advice on how to do this:

"It is my hope that you may put forth your most earnest endeavor to accomplish this end, that you may investigate and study the Holy Scriptures word by word so that you may attain knowledge of the mysteries hidden therein. Be not satisfied with words, but seek to understand the spiritual meanings hidden in the heart of the words." (Promulgation of Universal Peace, page 459)

"It hath been decreed by Us that the Word of God and all the potentialities thereof shall be manifested unto men in strict conformity with such conditions as have been fore ordained by Him

Who is the All-Knowing, the All-Wise. We have, moreover, ordained that its veil of concealment be none other except its own Self. Such indeed is Our Power to achieve Our Purpose." *(Gleanings, pages 76-77)*

It was decided to just do as Bahá'u'lláh said and study the teachings of these chosen books as He said to do, that is word by word trying to find the spiritual truth that was hidden in His holy Words. Also it was suggested to have the friends pray during the prayer times so that Bahá'u'lláh would open their minds and hearts to a better understanding of these Words. A word of caution in this line of study is to avoid insisting, or the friends insisting, that their understanding of His words is the right and only one. After all Bahá'u'lláh has said that His words are beyond the ordinary understanding of man:

"In like manner, those words that have streamed forth from the source of power and descended from the heaven of glory are innumerable and beyond the ordinary comprehension of man." (The Kitab-i-Iqan, page 5)

"He also saith: "We speak one word, and by it we intend one and seventy meanings; each one of these meanings we can explain." (The Kitab-i-Iqan, page 255)

In other places Bahá'u'lláh confirms that His words are inexhaustible:

"Know assuredly that just as thou firmly believest that the Word of God, exalted be His glory, endureth for ever, thou must, likewise, believe with undoubting faith that its meaning can never be exhausted." (Gleanings, page 175)

The following instructions are very important to understand when you are working with total class participation. The person conducting the class is not a teacher; he/she is only a coordinator, so this instruction is very important and significant:

"A clear distinction is made in our Faith between authoritative interpretation and the interpretation or understanding that each individual arrives at for himself from his study of its teachings. While the former is confined to the Guardian, the latter, according to the guidance given to us by the Guardian himself, should by no means be suppressed. In fact such individual interpretation is considered the fruit of man's rational power and conducive to a better understanding of the teachings, provided that no disputes or arguments arise among the friends and the individual himself understands and makes it clear that his views are merely his own. Individual interpretations continually change as one grows in comprehension of the teachings. As Shoghi Effendi explained: "To deepen in the Cause means to read the writings of Bahá'u'lláh and the Master so thoroughly as to be able to give it to others in its pure form. There are many who have some superficial idea of what the Cause stands for. They, therefore, present it together with all sorts of ideas that are their own. As the Cause is still in its early days we must be most careful lest we fall under this error and injure the Movement we so much adore. There is no limit to the study of the Cause. The more we read the Writings the more truths we can find in them and the more we will see that our previous notions were erroneous." So, although individual insights can be enlightening and helpful, they can also be misleading. The friends must therefore learn to listen to the views of others without being over-awed or allowing their faith to be shaken, and to express their own views without pressing them on their fellow Bahá'í s." (COC Volume 1, page 358)

The coordinator would do well to consider the above quote as well as this one:

"For it behooveth no man to interpret the holy words according to his own imperfect understanding, nor, having found them to be contrary to his inclination and desires, to reject and repudiate their truth." (The Kitab-i-Iqan, page 182)

"You shall not add to the word which I command you, nor take anything from it, that you may keep the commandments of the LORD your God which I command you." (Bible Deut 4:2)

The first institute was to be for two weeks, that is fourteen days, so with absolutely no experience in institutes and only a vague idea from the foregoing quotes, I set up my agenda and went back to Oaxaca. I went from village to village armed with pictures of our new Amelia Collins institute buildings and extended a heart-felt loving invitation to attend. The National Spiritual Assembly of the Bahá'ís of Mexico agreed to finance even the transportation and food for the participants. From all the villages I was able to recruit only 15 souls, and these were coming more for a paid vacation than for the classes.

All the classes were conducted with total class participation. The first session was on prayer. Why do we pray? When do we pray? What do we pray for? How do we pray? I let the students answer all the questions; all I did was to encourage them and attempt to draw them out. Thank God that my first institute was with the very vocal and very outgoing Zapotecs and Mixtecs. They responded with heart and soul. We then went into the Hidden Words and studied them word by word looking for that hidden spiritual meaning that was hidden in their depths. At the end of the third day one of the students with deep emotion and tears running down his face said, "Jenabe, I love Bahá'u'lláh so much that I want to give my life to Him."

Fifteen friends participated and each one of them at the end of the two weeks swore to heaven and Bahá'u'lláh that they would each take care of 30 villages. Now as you know I was unable to take care of ninety-five villages. In fifteen days by carefully studying these creative words of

Bahá'u'lláh with these new found friends, I theoretically could take care of 450 villages doing the institute and it only took two weeks, whereas previously, I was going from village to village, day after day from early morning until late at night. I read this following passage:

"Thus far ye have been untiring in your labors. Let your exertions henceforth increase a thousand fold." (Tablets of the Divine Plan, pages 43-44)

I wanted to sit down and cry when again I thought Bahá'u'lláh had given me an impossible task. Now my heart was put at peace with the power of the Creative Words of Bahá'u'lláh and the in depth study, I witnessed with my own eyes this transforming and creative spirit at work. I had found the key to true spiritual transformation.

As I write this it is now the year of my Lord, Bahá'u'lláh, 162 BE and I have never turned back. Bahá'u'lláh has allowed me to coordinate these most wonderful spiritual transformation institutes in seventy countries and I can truthfully say I have seen these creative words turn stones into warm and loving human beings. I have also seen new Bahá'ís in only one week become so intoxicated with this wine of the love of God, as to go out in the streets and become full time teachers of His Cause.

These writings and this spiritual transformation has nothing to do with worldly education. Some of the most advanced classes were held among primitive people that could not even read or write:

"The understanding of His words and the comprehension of the utterances of the Birds of Heaven are in no wise dependent upon human learning. They depend solely upon purity of heart, chastity of soul, and freedom of spirit." (The Kitab-i-Iqan, page 211)

In this book I will attempt to share with the reader just a few of the many insights I have gleaned from coordinating these classes. No two classes are ever the same and each human participant is as different as their fingerprints. I would most urgently plead with each and every one of you, now and in the far distant reaches of the future, to please give yourselves this most wonderful opportunity to submerge yourselves in the ocean of His Words. Experience for yourselves the true power of His Creative Words in your own souls. As stated above His words are inexhaustible and Bahá'u'lláh is the only one who really knows what these words mean. After years and years of classes and study I can only admit my complete and total ignorance in trying to understand even a glimmer of what these creative words mean.

    This book is in no way an attempt at interpretation. My sole purpose in writing it is to share with you some insights and to stimulate the reader to facilitate their own independent understanding of what it means. God forbid that such a creature as myself would even think that I can understand, even in a superficial way these profound teachings of Bahá'u'lláh. Quotes from the Holy Scriptures are used in the book, including the Holy Bible King James Version and the Holy Qur'án the translations by Yusif and Rodwell, to further help us in trying to understand.

"It hath been decreed by Us that the Word of God and all the potentialities thereof shall be manifested unto men in strict conformity with such conditions as have been foreordained by Him Who is the All-Knowing, the All-Wise. We have, moreover, ordained that its veil of concealment be none other except its own Self." (Gleanings, page 76)

". . . . haply the pure in heart may gain thereby a glimpse, be it as small as a needle's eye, of the mysteries of Thy Lord, the Almighty, the Omniscient, that lie concealed behind the veils." (The Kitab-i-Aqdas, page 83)

"I swear by the most sacred Essence of God that but one line of the Words uttered by Him is more sublime than the words uttered by all

that dwell on earth." (The Báb: Selections from the Báb, page 100)

"Thy word is a lamp unto my feet, and a light unto my path." (Bible Psalms 119:105)

"It is written, Man shall not live by bread alone, but by every word that proceedeth out of the mouth of God." (Bible Matthew 4:4)

"In the beginning was the Word, and the Word was with God, and the Word was God." (Bible John 1:1)

"That this is verily the word of an honored apostle; It is not the word of a poet: little it is ye believe! Nor is it the word of a soothsayer: little admonition it is ye receive. This is a Message sent down from the Lord of the Worlds." (Qur'án, The Sure Reality 40-43 Al-Haqqah)

Many of these quotes used throughout this compilation are repeated for different Hidden Words as they seemed to me to convey the message from Bahá'u'lláh that helped me to catch an idea of what might be meant.

HE IS THE GLORY OF GLORIES

"This is that which hath descended from the realm of glory, uttered by the tongue of power and might, and revealed unto the Prophets old. We have taken the inner essence thereof and clothed it in the garment of brevity, as a token of grace unto the righteous, that they may stand faithful unto the Covenant of God, may fulfill in their lives His trust, and in the realm of spirit obtain the gem of Divine virtue." (Arabic Hidden Words, page 1)

To study the Holy Words word by word is not to only to look up the word in the dictionary, as helpful as that might be. The instructions are to look for the spiritual meaning that lies hidden in the words. It seems that this makes us use that wonderful faculty of meditation. Often in the institutes the student would ask questions and I would respond with, "what do you think it means?" and they would come up with a most illumined idea.

In the foregoing passage, in the introduction to the Hidden Words of Bahá'u'lláh the first word is -**He**- The first question is, He who? Does this He mean God? Does this He refer to the Manifestation of God? As all the Manifestations are one, does this He refer to all of them? As God is Single, Alone and Unknowable, does this He refer to an Unknowable Essence? If this He does refer to the Unknowable Essence, how can we even contemplate an essence that is in effect unknowable? Does this He mean Bahá'u'lláh? Does this He mean Bahá'u'lláh and His revelation and manifestation? Does this He mean the Light and Voice of God as revealed through the person of Bahá'u'lláh which in effect is the Voice, Light and Pen of God or at least as close as we will ever come to that Infinite Source? Now in a class of fifteen or more just the discussion of this one word **HE** can open up vistas of light and understanding if we will listen to each other with open minds trying to understand how we all feel.

Let's now begin to string the pearls of understanding together and add the word -**is**-. Does this mean, He now is? Does it mean that He was when Bahá'u'lláh wrote it? Does this –**is**- mean reality, like it is a desk, or it is the sky? Does this –**is**- mean the beginning that has no beginning to the end that has no end? Does this –**is**- refer to the Alpha and the Omega? Does this –**is**- mean the ultimate Is of God is? Does this –**is**- refer to the Supreme Unknowable Essence meaning all that is, encompassing all, including all, surrounding all. Could it mean that when we say and think about **He** is all other words of is merge into nothingness?

Now let's add to our string one more pearl of divine revelation -**the**-. What is the significance of the? Does this –**the**- mean something very particular, such as, the garden as opposed to just garden? Is –**the**- only a grammatical word? By what stretch of our imaginations can we find a spiritual meaning to be hidden in this word?

Yet as we continue to string these brilliant jewels and add the word - **Glory**-, He IS THE GLORY, glory does give our hearts a special feeling. What does glory mean? Is glory a most brilliant display of light? Is glory something of exquisite beauty that takes our breath away? Does this glory as stated here by Bahá'u'lláh encompass all things of light and all other things? If He refers to the light, voice, pen and person of Bahá'u'lláh manifesting that unknowable essence God, could glory then mean the light and knowledge of God through His revelation of this Glory. Is Bahá'u'lláh saying here the greatest name "Ya Bahá'ul-Abhá"?

"Ya-Bahá'ul-Abhá" is an invocation meaning: "O Thou Glory of Glories!". (Aqdas: Notes, page 180).

The tiny two letter word -**of**-. Does this mean a part of something? Does – **of**- mean belonging to? When we say that we are creatures of God, it means that we were created by God and we are not, nor we can ever be part of Him.

"He, verily, is independent of all His creatures." (The Kitab-i-Aqdas, pages 41-42).
and in further reference to this,

"Beware, beware, lest thou be led to join partners with the Lord, thy God. He is, and hath from everlasting been, one and alone, without peer or equal, eternal in the past, eternal in the future, detached from all things, ever-abiding, unchangeable, and self-subsisting." (Gl, page 192)

"The Mighty One, God the LORD," (Bible PSA 50:1)

"God forgiveth not that partners should be set up with him; but He forgiveth anything else, to whom He pleaseth; to set up partners with

God is to devise a sin most heinous indeed." (Qur'án Women An-Nisa 48)

"*HE IS THE GLORY OF GLORIES*"

Let's put it all together. Bahá'u'lláh translated into English means the Glory of God. So couldn't it possibly mean that the Manifestation of God in this day is that Glory of all the previous Manifestations of God or Glories? Could it be referring to that Unknowable Essence as the He and His Glory as Manifested in Bahá'u'lláh as His Glory of Glories? Another thought we can ask is that the –**He-** and Glory of Glories all refer only to that Unknown Essence as the light of it shines upon man through Bahá'u'lláh?

"The Greatest Name is the Name of Bahá'u'lláh . "Yá Bahá'ul-Abhá" is an invocation meaning: "O Thou Glory of Glories!". "Alláh-u-Abhá" is a greeting which means: "God the All-Glorious." Both refer to Bahá'u'lláh . By Greatest Name is meant that Bahá'u'lláh has appeared in God's Greatest Name, in other words, that He is the supreme Manifestation of God." (Bahá'u'lláh: Aqdas: notes, page 180)

"But as truly as I live, all the earth shall be filled with the glory of the LORD." (Bible Numbers 14:21)

"For the earth shall be filled with the knowledge of the glory of the LORD, as the waters cover the sea." (Bible Habakkuk 2:14)

"And the Earth will shine with the glory of its Lord:" (Qur'án The Crowds 69 Az-Zumar)

"This is that which hath descended from the realm of glory, uttered by the tongue of power and might, and revealed unto the Prophets of old. We have taken the inner essence thereof and clothed it in the garment of brevity, as a token of grace unto the righteous, that they may stand faithful unto the Covenant of God, may fulfill in their lives His trust, and in the realm of spirit obtain the gem of Divine virtue." (Arabic Hidden Words, page 1)

-**THIS**- Doesn't –**this**- mean something that is near to me and -**THAT**- something that is further away? What is this? Is it the Hidden Words? Is it the revelation of Bahá'u'lláh? Is it the light and knowledge of Bahá'u'lláh's pen? Does –**this**- only mean this introduction? Doesn't the –**this**- followed by is give the –**this**- substance and a sense of reality? Could it possibly mean that –**this**- can only become a reality if it is made a part of my life and becomes is?

"Live thou in accord with the teachings of Bahá'u'lláh. Do not only read them. There is a vast difference between the soul who merely reads the words of Bahá'u'lláh and the one who tries to live them. Read thou "The Hidden Words". Ponder over their meanings and embody the behests into thy life...." (The Importance of Deepening, page 203)

"All who obey God and the Apostle are in the company of those on whom is the Grace of God, of the Prophets (who teach), the sincere (lovers of truth), the witnesses (who testify), and the righteous (who do good): ah! what a beautiful fellowship!." (Qur'án Women 69 An-Nisa)

"And he took the book of the covenant, and read in the audience of the people: and they said, All that the LORD hath said will we do, and be obedient." (Bible Exodus 24:7)

<u>This is that</u> if something is near to me like this house and something is far from me like that mountain, couldn't this is that mean the following?

"Considering what God hath revealed, that "We are closer to man than his life-vein," the poet hath, in allusion to this verse, stated that, though the revelation of my Best-Beloved hath so permeated my being that He is closer to me than my life-vein, yet, notwithstanding my certitude of its reality and my recognition of my station, I am still so far removed from Him." (Gleanings, page 185)

Which implies, this one or another one? This seems to imply a choice, a choice of what? Perhaps it could be replaced by that. In other words this is that which has descended. Could it mean that this is what has descended and that is what has descended? This is that which might mean the revelation of Bahá'u'lláh and specifically the Hidden Words which is the word of God in its purest form. Doesn't this maybe imply the following quote?

Even as He hath revealed: "The East and West are God's: therefore whichever way ye turn, there is the face of God."(1) (The Kitab-i-Iqan, pages 51-52)

"This is that which hath descended…."

Hath is a word that means has, and isn't the word has a present conditional that is something that takes place now or is in the process of taking place? Couldn't this hath then mean that these Hidden Words are taking place now? If Bahá'u'lláh used the word had that would put the words into the most definite past. For example couldn't we say that this divine revelation has now descended and the past revelation had descended from the same realm of glory?

Descended doesn't this imply that these words of God have come down from some high place? What about these verses?

"Verily, the hosts of revelation have descended with banners of inspiration from the heaven of the Tablet in the name of God, the powerful, the mighty!" (Bahá'í World Faith, page 204)

"In like manner, those words that have streamed forth from the source of power and descended from the heaven of glory are innumerable and beyond the ordinary comprehension of man." (The Kitab-i-Iqan, page 5)

"We sent down the (Qur'án) in Truth, and in Truth has it descended: and We sent thee but to give Glad Tidings and to warn (sinners)." (Qur'án Children of Israel 105 Al-Isra)

"Through the midst of them (all) descends His Command: that ye may know that God has power over all things, and that God comprehends all things in (His) Knowledge." (Qur'án The Divorce 12 At-Talaq)

"For the Lord Himself will descend from heaven with a shout, with the voice of an archangel, and with the trumpet of God." (Bible 1 Thessalonians 4:16)

Does this possibly mean that, <u>this is that which hath descended</u>? Somehow I get the feeling that although Bahá'u'lláh has allowed these words to descend, that we are going to have to do a lot of ascending to even dimly understand a glimmer of the greatness that lies hidden in the heart of His words.

<u>From</u> seems to give us the place of origin.

"All things proceed from God and unto Him they return. He is the source of all things and in Him all things are ended." (The Kitab-i-Aqdas, page 72)
"I am Alpha and Omega, the beginning and the ending, saith the

Lord, which is, and which was, and which is to come, the Almighty." (Bible Revelations 1:8)

"It is God Who begins (the process of) creation; then repeats it; then shall ye be brought back to Him." (Qur'án The Romans 11 Ar-Rum)

"Er-long will God raise up the treasures of the earth - men who will aid Thee through Thyself and through Thy Name, wherewith God hath revived the hearts of such as have recognized Him." (Epistle to the Son of the Wolf, page 21)

"The source of all bounty is derived, in this Day, from God, the One, the Forgiving!" (Gleanings, page 36)

The Doesn't this word indicate a particular subject? Doesn't it seem to imply that this isn't just any realm but the particular realm of glory?

Realm: "God hath, through His tongue that uttereth the truth, testified in all His Tablets to these words: "I am He that liveth in the Abhá Realm of Glory." (Gleanings, page 207)

"How could it, otherwise, have been possible for sheer nothingness to have acquired by itself the worthiness and capacity to emerge from its state of non-existence into the realm of being?" (Gleanings, page 65)

"The LORD hath prepared his throne in the heavens; and his kingdom ruleth over all." (Bible Psalms 103:19)

"And when thou lookest, it is there thou wilt see a Bliss and a Realm Magnificent." (Qur'án The Man 20. Al-Insan)

What is a realm? What is the difference between a kingdom and a realm? Could it be that if the realm is the realm of being brought into existence from nothingness, that the realm of glory would be all of God's creation? Could it be that the realm of glory signifies the Uncreated? Did these Holy and Sanctified Words descended from that placeless place of the court of Bahá'u'lláh?

Of means a part of something doesn't it? Doesn't it also mean belonging to? So we can think about it as the realm being part of glory. Also maybe we should meditate and think about the realm belonging to glory. If glory signifies Bahá'u'lláh isn't it possible that this belongs to and is part of Him?

Glory was discussed above in the Glory of Glories.

If **"*THIS IS THAT WHICH HATH DESCENDED FROM THE REALM OF GLORY*"** then this is quite a that don't you think? It seems that if we could only grasp an infinitesimal portion of the meaning that lies hidden in these creative words of Bahá'u'lláh our souls would be come so captivated that we would drink the ocean and still want more.

"**He drinketh the seven seas, but his heart's thirst is still unquenched, and he saith, 'Is there yet any more?'" (Seven Valleys and Four Valleys, page 10)**

"**Were men of insight to quaff their fill from the ocean of inner meanings which lie enshrined in these words and become acquainted therewith, they would bear witness to the sublimity and the excellence of this utterance." (Tablets of Bahá'u'lláh, page 167)**

"**Behold, the days come, saith the Lord GOD, that I will send a famine in the land, not a famine of bread, nor a thirst for water, but of hearing the words of the LORD:" (Bible Amos 8:11)**

"**But whosoever drinketh of the water that I shall give him shall never thirst; but the water that I shall give him shall be in him a well of water springing up into everlasting life." (Bible John 4:14)

"And He it is Who sends the Winds as heralds of glad tidings, going before His Mercy, and We send down purifying water from the sky - That with it We may give life to a dead land, and slake the thirst of things We have created,. . ." (Qur'án The Criterion 48-49 Al-Furqan)

Uttered

"No breeze can compare with the breezes of Divine Revelation, whilst the Word which is uttered by God shineth and flasheth as the sun amidst the books of men." (Epistle to the Son of the Wolf, pages 42-43)

"The LORD thundered from heaven, and the most High uttered his voice." (Bible 2 Samuel 22:14)

This word means to speak so what is the difference between utter and speak? Why didn't Bahá'u'lláh just say spoken by the tongue of power and might instead of Uttered? Why is this word in the past tense? Does this only refer to the Hidden Words?

"It is now incumbent upon them who are endowed with a hearing ear and a seeing eye to ponder these sublime words, in each of which the oceans of inner meaning and explanation are hidden, that haply the words uttered by Him Who is the Lord of Revelation may enable His servants to attain, with the utmost joy and radiance, unto the Supreme Goal and Most Sublime Summit -the dawning-place of this Voice." (Epistle to the Son of the Wolf, page 147)

"Every single letter proceeding out of the mouth of God is indeed a mother letter, and every word uttered by Him Who is the Well Spring of Divine Revelation is a mother word, and His Tablet a Mother

Tablet." (Gleanings, page 142)

"The Word of thy Lord doth find its fulfillment in truth and in justice: none can change His Words: for He is the one who heareth and knoweth all." (Qur'án The Cattle 115 Al-Anam)

"I will open My mouth in parables; I will utter things which have been kept secret from the foundation of the world." (Bible Matthew 13:35)

Utter also signifies totality like "utter destruction" or the most distant like utter most parts of the earth.

"Hearken unto the voice of this Wronged One, and be not of them that are in utter loss." (Bahá'u'lláh: Epistle to the Son of the Wolf, Page: 173)

"Our purpose in revealing these convincing and weighty utterances is to impress upon the seeker that he should regard all else beside God as transient, and count all things save Him, Who is the Object of all adoration, as utter nothingness." (Bahá'u'lláh: Gleanings, Page: 266)

By is a very important word because it tells us who is the originator of what is being said. Who is speaking? Who is revealing? Who is writing what is being revealed? The this is that which hath descended by who?

The Refer to (The) above.

Tongue Doesn't this refer to the language one speaks? For example, my native tongue is English. Following through on this idea it would seem that this is the language of God. The following quotes can give us a glimpse of some of the hidden meanings of tongue:

"God hath, through His tongue that uttereth the truth, testified in all

His Tablets to these words: "I am He that liveth in the Abhá Realm of Glory." (Gleanings, page 207)

"From my pen floweth only the summons which Thine own exalted pen hath voiced, and my tongue uttereth naught save what the Most Great Spirit hath itself proclaimed in the kingdom of Thine eternity." (Prayers and Meditations, page 108)

"...and His tongue the fountain-head of the waters of Thy praise and the well-spring of the soft-flowing streams of Thy wisdom, ..." (Prayers and Meditations, page 131)

"This is a Tablet wherein the Pen of the Unseen hath inscribed the knowledge of all that hath been and shall be -a knowledge that none other but My wondrous Tongue can interpret." (Tablets of Bahá'u'lláh, page 149)

"We have moreover given thee to drink the choice wine of utterance from the chalice of the heavenly bestowals of thy merciful Lord, which is none other than this Tongue of holiness - a Tongue that, as soon as it was unloosed, quickened the entire creation, set in motion all beings and caused the Nightingale to pour forth its melodies." (Tablets of Bahá'u'lláh, page 195)

"The Spirit of the LORD spake by me, and his word was in my tongue." (Bible 2 Samuel 23:2)

Of seems to mean the one it belongs to in other words this tongue of God is the reality of Bahá'u'lláh. He is in truth a special creation of God. Created to be the physical tongue of our Creator.

"I know not what the water is with which Thou hast created me, or what the fire Thou hast kindled within me, or the clay wherewith

Thou hast kneaded me." (Prayers and Meditations, page 12)

"THE substance wherewith God hath created Me is not the clay out of which others have been formed. He hath conferred upon Me that which the worldly-wise can never comprehend, nor the faithful discover ..." (Selections from the Báb, page 11)

"It is He who has sent His Apostle with Guidance and the Religion of Truth, to proclaim it over all religion: and enough is God for a Witness." (Qur'án The Victory 28 Al-Fath)

<u>Power</u> seems to mean a force, a power house is a place where power is generated.

"God, verily, enricheth whomsoever He willeth through both heavenly and earthly means, and He, in truth, hath power over all things." (The Kitab-i-Aqdas, page 42)

"He is God, exalted be He, the Lord of majesty and power!" (Aqdas: Questions and Answers, page 139)

"They constitute the word "Be", which, he states, "means the creative Power of God Who through His command causes all things to come into being" and "the power of the Manifestation of God, His great spiritual creative force". (Aqdas: Notes, page 247)

"All life is of Thee, and all power lieth within the grasp of Thine omnipotence." (Epistle to the Son of the Wolf, page 9)

"They, verily, are the manifestations of the power of God, and the sources of His authority, and the repositories of His knowledge, and the daysprings of His commandments." (Epistle to the Son of the Wolf, page 90)

"For there is no power but of God; the powers that be are ordained of God." (Epistle to the Son of the Wolf, page 91)

"And then shall appear the sign of the Son of man in heaven: and then shall all the tribes of the earth mourn, and they shall see the Son of man coming in the clouds of heaven with power and great glory." (Bible Matthew 24:30)

"For to God belongeth the dominion of the heavens and the earth, and all that is between. He createth what He pleaseth. For God hath power over all things."(The Table Spread 19 Al-Maidah)

"How immensely exalted are the wondrous testimonies of His almighty sovereignty, a glimmer of which, if it but touched them, would utterly consume all that are in the heavens and in the earth! How indescribably lofty are the tokens of His consummate power, a single sign of which, however inconsiderable, must transcend the comprehension of whatsoever hath, from the beginning that hath no beginning, been brought into being, or will be created in the future till the end that hath no end." (Gleanings, page 61)

From the above quotes we can get a better understanding of this power as the creative force of all that is. As Bahá'u'lláh is the tongue and voice of God, He proclaims and manifests this power in this world of being. As the last quote states this power is far and away above our poor ability of comprehension.

<u>*Might*</u> What is the difference between power and might? A man may have power and be weak in body and mind, this is a position of power. For example history shows many examples of idiots or mental cases having power over the masses. Where a man of might would have strength in body and mind. Might seems to have more of a meaning of strength.

"He is, in very truth, the God of might and power." (The Kitab-i-Aqdas, page 65)

"Sanctified be the Lord of all mankind, at the mention of Whose name all the atoms of the earth have been made to vibrate, and the Tongue of Grandeur hath been moved to disclose that which had been wrapt in His knowledge and lay concealed within the treasury of His might. He, verily, through the potency of His name, the Mighty, the All-Powerful, the Most High, is the ruler of all that is in the heavens and all that is on earth." (Gleanings, pages 16-17)

"The mightiest of men are abased before the revelations of Thy glory, and they who are endued with strength tremble when faced with the evidences of Thy might." (Prayers and Meditations, page 138)
Who is this King of glory? The LORD strong and mighty, the LORD mighty in battle." (Bible Psalms 24:8)

"Every other perfection is as naught in face of His consummate perfection, and every other display of might is as nothing before His absolute might." (Selections from the Báb, page 157)

"Behold, God is mighty, but despises no one; He is mighty in strength of understanding." (Bible Job 36:5)

Another meaning of might is may, I might do it or I might not. Which could mean that God does what ever God wants to do. In other words He might or He might not.

"He it is Who is the manifestation of "God doeth whatsoever He pleaseth", and abideth upon the throne of "He ordaineth whatsoever He chooseth". (The Kitab-i-Aqdas, page 76)

"Verily God doeth whatsoever He willeth, and ordaineth whatsoever He pleaseth." (The Kitab-i-Iqan, page 97)

"But what could tell thee but that perchance he might Grow (in spiritual understanding)?" (Qur'án He Frowned 3 (Abasa))

and means that something is to follow. More is to come.

Revealed makes something known that was unknown. Bring a thing from the invisible into the visible.

"He that was hidden from mortal eyes is come! His all-conquering sovereignty is manifest; His all-encompassing splendor is revealed." (Gleanings, page 16)

"Therefore do not fear them. For there is nothing covered that will not be revealed, and hidden that will not be known. (Bible Matthew 10:26)

"Who brings to light what is hidden in the heavens and the earth," (Qur'án The Ant 25 An-Nam)

"Say: This is the Paradise on whose foliage the wine of utterance hath imprinted the testimony: 'He that was hidden from the eyes of men is revealed, girded with sovereignty and power!' This is the Paradise, the rustling of whose leaves proclaims: 'O ye that inhabit the heavens and the earth! There hath appeared what hath never previously appeared. He Who, from everlasting, had concealed His Face from the sight of creation is now come.'" (Gleanings, page 31)

"Through their appearance the Revelation of God is made manifest, and by their countenance the Beauty of God is revealed." (Gleanings, page 53)

"Blessed is the people that know the joyful sound: they shall walk, O LORD, in the light of thy countenance." (Bible Psalms 89:15)

"This He hath accomplished through the agency of but one Letter of His Word, revealed by His Pen - a Pen moved by His directing Finger -His Finger itself sustained by the power of God's Truth." (Gleanings, page 104)

"Through the might of God and His power, and out of the treasury of His knowledge and wisdom, I have brought forth and revealed unto you the pearls that lay concealed in the depths of His everlasting ocean." (Gleanings, page 327)

"Through His potency everything that hath, from time immemorial, been veiled and hidden, is now revealed." (Tablets of Bahá'u'lláh, page 50)

As far as revealed goes Bahá'u'lláh makes a fantastic statement about knowledge. All knowledge consists of 20 and 7 letters and up until the coming of the Báb only 2 letters had been revealed. Now all 27 letters have been revealed. Since the coming of this revelation we have seen such advances in knowledge and science as can not help but amaze even the most skeptical.

"Consider; He hath declared Knowledge to consist of twenty and seven letters, and regarded all the Prophets, from Adam even unto the "Seal," as Expounders of only two letters thereof and of having been sent down with these two letters. He also saith that the Qa'im will reveal all the remaining twenty and five letters." (The Kitab-i-Iqan, pages 243-244)

Unto this seems to refer to who has received this revelation. The recipient of what hath descended from the realm of glory, uttered by the tongue of power and might.

"In unfolding these mysteries, We have, in Our former Tablets which were addressed to a friend in the melodious language of Hijaz, cited a few of the verses revealed unto the Prophets of old." (The Kitab-i-Iqan, page 19)

The prophets of old is all inclusive. It is all the prophets of the past from Adam up to and including the Báb. This does not make a distinction between the major and minor prophets.

"The Prophets and Messengers of God have been sent down for the sole purpose of guiding mankind to the straight Path of Truth." (Gleanings, pages 156-157)

"We gave Moses the Book and followed him up with a succession of Apostles; We gave Jesus the son of Mary clear (Signs) and strengthened him with the holy spirit." (Qur'án The Cow 87 Al-Baqarah)

"Each one (of them) believeth in God, His angels, His books, and His Apostles "We make no distinction (they say) between one and another of His Apostles."(Qur'án The Cow 285 Al-Baqarah)

"These Prophets and chosen Ones of God are the recipients and revealers of all the unchangeable attributes and names of God. They are the mirrors that truly and faithfully reflect the light of God. Whatsoever is applicable to them is in reality applicable to God, Himself, Who is both the Visible and the Invisible." (The Kitab-i-Iqan, page 142)

HE IS THE GLORY OF GLORIES
This is that which hath descended from the realm of glory, uttered by the tongue of power and might, and revealed unto the Prophets of old.

As one can see, these words and letters of Bahá'u'lláh are indeed inexhaustible. We have just barely scratched the surface in trying to understand this first sentence and it has taken us many pages.

"How can feeble reason encompass the Qur'án, Or the spider snare a phoenix in his web?" (Seven Valleys and Four Valleys, page 33)

Second sentence
"We have taken the inner essence thereof and clothed it in the garment of brevity, as a token of grace unto the righteous, that they may stand faithful unto the Covenant of God, may fulfill in their lives His trust, and in the realm of spirit obtain the gem of Divine virtue."

We - this is the kingly pronoun as explained in the following quote:

"When Bahá'u'lláh uses the plural -'We', 'Our' etc.- He is merely using a form which is regal and has greater power than the singular 'I'. We have the same usage in English, when the King says 'we'. The Pope does the same thing." (Lights of Guidance page 471-472)

As all the manifestations of God are considered one and the same, this Kingly - **We** - of Bahá'u'lláh's could have a greater meaning than that used by a King. It seems that we must be careful not to join partners with God. Although a Manifestation of God is a creation far above our ability to understand, yet Bahá'u'lláh tells us that He is still a creation of that Unknowable Essence.

"And now concerning thy reference to the existence of two Gods. Beware, beware, lest thou be led to join partners with the Lord, thy

God. He is, and hath from everlasting been, one and alone, without peer or equal, eternal in the past, eternal in the future, detached from all things, ever-abiding, unchangeable, and self-subsisting." (Gleanings, page 192)

"Certain ones among you have said: 'He it is Who hath laid claim to be God.' By God! This is a gross calumny. I am but a servant of God Who hath believed in Him and in His signs, and in His Prophets and in His angels. My tongue, and My heart, and My inner and My outer being testify that there is no God but Him, that all others have been created by His behest, and been fashioned through the operation of His Will." (Gleanings, pages 227-228)

"Muhammad is no more than an Apostle:" (Qur'án The Family of Imran 144 (Al-Imran)

"I and my Father are one." (Bible John 10:30)

"For I have not spoken of myself; but the Father which sent me, he gave me a commandment, what I should say, and what I should speak." (Bible John 12:49)

"He Who is the Father is come, and the Son (Jesus), in the holy vale, crieth out: `Here am I, here am I, O Lord, My God!'" (Bahá'u'lláh: Proclamation of Bahá'u'lláh, page 27)

Have taken What does it mean to take? Isn't have taken an action just completed? Bahá'u'lláh doesn't say "We have revealed," but rather it is clear that He has taken these Hidden Words that were already there. What did He take?

"Know thou that he is truly learned who hath acknowledged My Revelation, and drunk from the Ocean of My knowledge, and soared in the atmosphere of My love, and cast away all else besides Me, and taken firm hold on that which hath been sent down from the Kingdom of My wondrous utterance." (Tablets of Bahá'u'lláh, pages 207-208)

<u>Inner Essence Thereof</u> Bahá'u'lláh took all the revelations of the past and the knowledge of all the Prophets of the past and squeezed them down to their most fundamental truth. He then took this central core of truth and went right to the very heart of these teachings. When one goes to the Library of Congress in the United States and into the religious section, thousands of books are there about the religions of the past. Bahá'u'lláh has, through the meaning of inner essence, condensed this and more, down to this small book. We can refer back to "This is that" is so big that the mind can't cope with it.

"So perfect and comprehensive is Thy proof, O my God, that its inner essence transcendeth the description of any soul and so abundant are the outpourings of Thy gifts that no faculty can appraise their infinite range." (Selections from the Báb, page 204)

"The door of the knowledge of the Ancient of Days being thus closed in the face of all beings, the Source of infinite grace, according to His saying, 'His grace hath transcended all things; My grace hath encompassed them all,' hath caused those luminous Gems of Holiness to appear out of the realm of the spirit, in the noble form of the human temple, and be made manifest unto all men, that they may impart unto the world the mysteries of the unchangeable Being, and tell of the subtleties of His imperishable Essence." (Gleanings, page 47)

<u>Clothed</u> What is the purpose of clothes? Don't we clothe ourselves to protect our bodies? Don't clothes not only cover up but also make us beautiful? Clothes also hide from view what is underneath and couldn't this add to a better understanding of why this book is called "The Hidden

Words?"

"By "angels" is meant those who, reinforced by the power of the spirit, have consumed, with the fire of the love of God, all human traits and limitations, and have clothed themselves with the attributes of the most exalted Beings and of the Cherubim." (The Kitab-i-Iqan, pages 78-79)

<u>Garment of Brevity</u> What kind of clothes are used to cover up, protect, make beautiful and hide these "Hidden Words?" The word garment seems to lend an added beauty. A garment is more than just ordinary everyday clothes. The word brevity means brief and adds support to the inner essence mentioned above. It seems that in order for us to even catch a lightening glimpse of understanding, we will have to do some unwrapping.

"As the body of man needeth a garment to clothe it, so the body of mankind must needs be adorned with the mantle of justice and wisdom. Its robe is the Revelation vouchsafed unto it by God." (Gleanings, page 81)

"I put on righteousness, and it clothed me: my judgment was as a robe and a diadem." (Bible Job 29:14)

"A salient characteristic is their brevity. They constitute the kernel of a vast range of law that will arise in centuries to come. This elaboration of the law will be enacted by the Universal House of Justice under the authority conferred upon it by Bahá'u'lláh Himself." (Aqdas: Other Sections, page 4)

<u>Token</u> Token is just a sign or an emblem. For example, I love you with all my heart, so I send you a bouquet of flowers. These roses are not my love; my love is so big and intense that it can never be expressed, only felt. The flowers are just a token, an expression, a sign of my love. It must be the

same with God's grace.

"Thou, in truth, art He Whose grace is infinite." (The Kitab-i-Aqdas, page 65)

"Whatever duty Thou hast prescribed unto Thy servants of extolling to the utmost Thy majesty and glory is but a token of Thy grace unto them, that they may be enabled to ascend unto the station conferred upon their own inmost being, the station of the knowledge of their own selves." (Gleanings, pages 4-5)

"All the favors of God have been sent down, as a token of His grace." (Gleanings, page 34)

"The door of the knowledge of the Ancient of Days being thus closed in the face of all beings, the Source of infinite grace, according to His saying, 'His grace hath transcended all things; My grace hath encompassed them all,' hath caused those luminous Gems of Holiness to appear out of the realm of the spirit, in the noble form of the human temple, and be made manifest unto all men, that they may impart unto the world the mysteries of the unchangeable Being, and tell of the subtleties of His imperishable Essence." (Gleanings, page 47)

<u>Unto the Righteous</u>   Only through God's grace we can attain unto righteousness, as no truly righteous man exists except, of course, 'Abdu'l-Bahá. Couldn't this also mean the one who wants to be right, act right, live right and do right?

"Be pure, O people of God, be pure; be righteous, be righteous.... Say: O people of God! That which can ensure the victory of Him Who is the Eternal Truth, His hosts and helpers on earth, have been set down in the sacred Books and Scriptures, and are as clear and manifest as the sun. These hosts are such righteous deeds, such conduct and character, as are acceptable in His sight." (Gleanings, page 287)

"For the righteous LORD loveth righteousness; his countenance doth behold the upright." (Bible Psalms 11:7)

"Let there arise out of you a band of people inviting to all that is good, enjoining what is right, and forbidding what is wrong; they are the ones to attain felicity." (The Family of Imran 104 (Al-Imran))

"Righteous men of learning who dedicate themselves to the guidance of others and are freed and well guarded from the promptings of a base and covetous nature are, in the sight of Him Who is the Desire of the world, stars of the heaven of true knowledge." (Tablet's of Bahá'u'lláh, pages 96-97)

"Not by the force of numbers, not by the mere exposition of a set of new and noble principles, not by an organized campaign of teaching - no matter how worldwide and elaborate in its character - not even by the staunchness of our faith or the exaltation of our enthusiasm, can we ultimately hope to vindicate in the eyes of a critical and sceptical age the supreme claim of the Abhá Revelation. One thing and only one thing will unfailingly and alone secure the undoubted triumph of this sacred Cause, namely, the extent to which our own inner life and private character mirror forth in their manifold aspects the splendor of those eternal principles proclaimed by Bahá'u'lláh." (Shoghi Effendi: Bahá'í Administration, page 66)

"The wrong in the world continues to exist just because people talk only of their ideals, and do not strive to put them into practice. If actions took the place of words, the world's misery would very soon be changed into comfort." ('Abdu'l-Bahá: Paris Talks*, page 16)

Stand This means to get up doesn't it? At least it doesn't mean to sit idle. It seems to require some kind of action. Also Bahá'u'lláh uses this term to indicate strength.

"We cherish the hope that men of piety may illumine the world through the radiant light of their conduct, and We entreat the Almighty - glorified and exalted is He - to grant that everyone may in this Day remain steadfast in His love and stand firm in His Cause." (Tablets of Bahá'u'lláh, page 91)

"God loves those who are firm and steadfast." (Qur'án The Family of Imran 46 (Al-Imran))

"Therefore, my beloved brethren, be ye steadfast, unmoveable, always abounding in the work of the Lord, forasmuch as ye know that your labour is not in vain in the Lord." (Bible 1 Corinthians 15:58)

"I entreat Thee, O Lord of the Kingdom of eternity, by the shrill voice of the Pen of Glory, and by the Burning Fire which calleth aloud from the verdant Tree, and by the Ark which Thou hast specially chosen for the people of Bahá, to grant that I may remain steadfast in my love for Thee, be well pleased with whatsoever Thou hast prescribed for me in Thy Book and may stand firm in Thy service and in the service of Thy loved ones." (Tablets of Bahá'u'lláh, pages 116-117)

"Blessed are the steadfast; blessed are they that stand firm in His Faith." (Tablets of Bahá'u'lláh, page 123)

". . . to remain firm and immovable as the mountain in His Cause." (Gleanings, page 59)

Faithful What is the meaning of faithful? It seems to me that it is an indication of being entirely full of faith, not half full. When one starts on a spiritual journey the first step is doubt; then one begins to believe. This is followed by faith, and the final step is absolute certitude.

For example, a man comes into a room of people that have lived their whole lives in a world of darkness and tries to explain about the sun. As no one has experienced the sun the teacher faces a most difficult task. However, if even one person believes the teacher and has faith in his teachings and follow his instructions that person will find the door and come out into the radiant sunshine.

He won't then go back into the dark house and say, "I believe the sun is shining," nor will he say, "I have faith that the sun is shining." He knows the sun is shining and that is certitude.

Faithful also means being strong and secure in my teacher and his teachings. A faithful spouse is a spouse who is true and honest and truthful with their mate. Wouldn't a faithful lover of Bahá'u'lláh be one that is strong, true, honest and truthful to Him?

"The soul that hath remained faithful to the Cause of God, and stood unwaveringly firm in His Path shall, after his ascension, be possessed of such power that all the worlds which the Almighty hath created can benefit through him." (Gleanings, page 161)

"Among them is this saying: 'Earth and heaven cannot contain Me; what can alone contain Me is the heart of him that believeth in Me, and is faithful to My Cause.'" (Gleanings, page 186)

"Happy is the faithful one who is attired with the vesture of high endeavour and hath arisen to serve this Cause." (Tablets of Bahá'u'lláh, page 257)

"Therefore stand firm (in the straight path) as thou art commanded -thou and those who with thee turn (unto God); and transgress not (from the Path): for He seeth well all that ye do." (Qur'án Hud 112 Hud)

Covenant of God There is the Most Great Covenant and in this day, the Lesser Covenant. What is a covenant? It is a firm and binding agreement between two parties. In this case it refers to the firm and binding agreement between God and man.

"Call ye to mind that covenant ye have entered into with Me upon Mount Paran, situate within the hallowed precincts of Zaman." (Persian Hidden Words, page 71)

The first part is the ancient, eternal and everlasting covenant of God, is God's promise, and His part of the Covenant which was that He would never leave mankind without help. Mankind's part of this covenant is that we must seek out that help in our day and obey it.

"Thou didst establish His covenant with every one who hath been created in the kingdoms of earth and heaven and in the realms of revelation and of creation." (Prayers and Meditations, page 36)

"The Lord of the universe hath never raised up a prophet nor hath He sent down a Book unless He hath established His covenant with all men, calling for their acceptance of the next Revelation and of the next Book; inasmuch as the outpourings of His bounty are ceaseless and without limit." (Selections from the Báb, page 87)

"Whenever My laws appear like the sun in the heaven of Mine utterance, they must be faithfully obeyed by all, though My decree be such as to cause the heaven of every religion to be cleft asunder." (Gleanings, page 333)

"He, truly, is to be obeyed in whatsoever He commandeth, and decreeth, and revealeth, and is to be loved in everything He, through His sovereignty, enjoineth, and, through His power, ordaineth."

(Prayers and Meditations, page 286)

"For He hath, through irrefutable Texts, entered into a binding Covenant with us all, requiring us to act in accordance with His sacred instructions and counsels." (Selections `Abdu'l-Baha, page 71)

"The Covenant of God is like unto a vast and fathomless ocean. A billow shall rise and surge therefrom and shall cast ashore all accumulated foam." (Selections ... 'Abdu'l-Bahá, page 223)

"But this shall be the covenant that I will make with the house of Israel; After those days, saith the LORD, I will put my law in their inward parts, and write it in their hearts; and will be their God, and they shall be my people." (Bible Jeremiah 31:33)

The Lesser Covenant established the Center of the Covenant, 'Abdu'l-Bahá, and laid the foundation of our present Administration. This covenant is unique and peerless. No prior revelation had established such a covenant.

"He likewise, with His Supreme Pen, entered into a great Covenant and Testament with all the Bahá'ís whereby they were all commanded to follow the Center of the Covenant after His departure, and turn not away even to a hair's breadth from obeying Him." (Bahá'í World Faith*, page 358)

"In accordance with the explicit text of the Kitab-i-Aqdas Bahá'u'lláh hath made the Center of the Covenant the Interpreter of His Word - a Covenant so firm and mighty that from the beginning of time until the present day no religious Dispensation hath produced its like." (The Covenant, page 116)

This is a most wondrous statement, that this little book of the Hidden

Words is going to help me in fulfilling my part of the Covenant of God and allow me to stand firm and strong in the promise I have made to God to seek out, in this day, His Manifestation and to obey Him.

"That which beseemeth you is the love of God, and the love of Him Who is the Manifestation of His Essence, and the observance of whatsoever He chooseth to prescribe unto you, did ye but know it." (Bahá'u'lláh: Gleanings, pages 304-305)

"So will I sing praise unto thy name for ever, that I may daily perform my vows." (Bible Psalms 61:8)

Fulfill in Their Lives Doesn't this seem to indicate that if we study, understand and apply these Hidden Words to our lives that we will live a full and productive life?

"How lofty is the station which man, if he but choose to fulfill his high destiny, can attain!" (Gleanings, page 206)

"Aid me to do what Thou desirest, and to fulfill what Thou pleasest." (Prayers and Meditations, page 22)

His Trust What is a trust and what does it mean? A trust account is money that we give to a financial institution to take care of for us. It doesn't belong to us; we just take care of it for God. In reality, our life, our spirit and soul all belong to God.

"The wisdom of the appearance of the spirit in the body is this: the human spirit is a Divine Trust, and it must traverse all conditions, for its passage and movement through the conditions of existence will be the means of its acquiring perfections." (`Abdu'l-Baha: Some Answered Questions, page 200)

"Verily, we are God's, and to Him shall we return." (Gleanings, page 345)

If we are the property of God surely we should want His property to be returned clean and beautiful and refined with all the divine virtues, don't you think? Are we going to return this gift to Him dirty and defiled, worn and ugly? I would even like this body, which is nothing more than the wrapping, to be pretty and clean and tied with a pretty ribbon.

Bahá'u'lláh said that by my bad conduct I stain His snow-white robe and this pains Him. Don't you think that Bahá'u'lláh has indeed suffered enough? Even after I know this with an absolute certitude, I still pick up a handful of mud and fling it onto His snow-white robe. The pain of this action is intensified by His love and forgiveness.

" **We have admonished all the loved ones of God to take heed lest the hem of Our sacred vesture be smirched with the mire of unlawful deeds, or be stained with the dust of reprehensible conduct.**" **(Gleanings, page 240)**

"That which can harm Me is the conduct of those who love Me, who claim to be related to Me, and yet perpetrate what causeth My heart and My pen to groan." (Aqdas: Notes, page 250)

<u>In The Realm of Spirit</u> Bahá'u'lláh says that the realm of the spirit is the City of God.

"Shouldst thou soar in the holy realm of the spirit, thou wouldst recognize God manifest and exalted above all things, in such wise that thine eyes would behold none else but Him." (The Kitab-i-Iqan, page 91)

". . . that he may enter the realm of the spirit, which is the City of

God." (Seven Valleys and Four Valleys, page 7)

If we can attain this most exalted station we would see the face of our Beloved manifest in all created things.

"Whichever way ye turn, there is the face of God." (Aqdas: Questions and Answers, page 111)

"From their knowledge, the knowledge of God is revealed, and from the light of their countenance, the splendour of the Face of God is made manifest." (The Kitab-i-Iqan, page 142)

"Therefore, whosoever, and in whatever Dispensation, hath recognized and attained unto the presence of these glorious, these resplendent and most excellent Luminaries, hath verily attained unto the "Presence of God" Himself, and entered the city of eternal and immortal life." (The Kitab-i-Iqan, page 143)

"He Who is the Eternal Truth is the one Power Who exerciseth undisputed sovereignty over the world of being, Whose image is reflected in the mirror of the entire creation." (Gleanings, page 166)

"These Tabernacles of holiness, these primal Mirrors which reflect the light of unfading glory, are but expressions of Him Who is the Invisible of the Invisibles." (The Kitab-i-Iqan, page 103)

"Magnified be Thy name, O my God, for that Thou hast manifested the Day which is the King of Days, the Day which Thou didst announce unto Thy chosen Ones and Thy Prophets in Thy most excellent Tablets, the Day whereon Thou didst shed the splendor of the glory of all Thy names upon all created things." (Prayers and Meditations, page 117)

In this "realm of the spirit" all things merge into nothingness and Bahá'u'lláh alone is seen, felt and experienced.

"And of all men, the most accomplished, the most distinguished and the most excellent are the Manifestations of the Sun of Truth. Nay, all else besides these Manifestations, live by the operation of their Will, and move and have their being through the outpourings of their grace. "But for Thee, I would have not created the heavens." Nay, all in their holy presence fade into utter nothingness, and are a thing forgotten." (Bahá'u'lláh: The Kitab-i-Iqan, page 103)

<u>**Obtain**</u> To obtain something is to have it. This also could mean that we must do some work to get it. In order to obtain the thing I want, I must strive with heart and soul until I obtain my goal.

"Arise, therefore, and, with the whole enthusiasm of your hearts, with all the eagerness of your souls, the full fervor of your will, and the concentrated efforts of your entire being, strive to attain the paradise of His presence, and endeavor to inhale the fragrance of the incorruptible Flower, to breathe the sweet savors of holiness, and to obtain a portion of this perfume of celestial glory." (Gleanings, page 321)

"How great the felicity that awaiteth the man that forsaketh all he hath in a desire to obtain the things of God! Such a man, We testify, is among God's blessed ones." (Gleanings, page 214)

"I the LORD search the heart, I try the reins, even to give every man according to his ways, and according to the fruit of his doings." (Bible Jeremiah 17:10)

Every soul on earth wants to be happy and free and here Bahá'u'lláh is telling us how to find felicity; in other words, how to be happy and not just 'happy' but <u>great</u> happiness. Then He gives us an added bounty of becoming a blessed one.

"Then those who have believed and worked righteous deeds, shall be made happy in a Mead of Delight." (Qur'án The Romans 15 (Ar-Rum)

<u>*The Gem*</u> Isn't a gem something very rare and of the greatest value? It is also hard or very difficult to get. We must search for it and even after we find the mine we must dig and discard the debris that hides the gems. Separate the rock from the jewels. Bahá'u'lláh tells us where this mine is and how to extract these gems.

"The purpose of the one true God, exalted be His glory, hath been to bring forth the Mystic Gems out of the mine of man" (Epistle to the Son of the Wolf, page 13)

"The Great Being saith: Regard man as a mine rich in gems of inestimable value. Education can, alone, cause it to reveal its treasures, and enable mankind to benefit therefrom." (Gleanings, page 260)

"A divine Mine only can yield the gems of divine knowledge, and the fragrance of the mystic Flower can be inhaled only in the ideal Garden, and the lilies of ancient wisdom can blossom nowhere except in the city of a stainless heart." (The Kitab-i-Iqan, page 191)

<u>*of Divine virtue.*</u> The gem we are to obtain is no ordinary gem, but is the gem of Divine virtue. What is the meaning of virtue? What is Divine? Then what does it mean to "obtain the gem of Divine virtue?" Why is Divine capitalized? Virtue means goodness, morality, rectitude, chastity, innocence, purity, virginity, value, excellence, worth, merit, strength, force, efficacy, potency and power. Divine means celestial, Godly,

heavenly, excellent, marvelous, sublime, wonderful, hallowed, holy, religious, sacred and spiritual. When we combine these two elements "Divine virtue" with these meanings it truly becomes a wonderful thing to want to possess.

These Manifestations of God, the heaven sent Teachers to mankind, have through the pen of Bahá'u'lláh referred to themselves as Gems of Divine Virtue.

"**These Tabernacles of Holiness, these Primal Mirrors which reflect the light of unfading glory, are but expressions of Him Who is the Invisible of the Invisibles. By the revelation of these Gems of Divine virtue all the names and attributes of God, such as knowledge and power, sovereignty and dominion, mercy and wisdom, glory, bounty, and grace, are made manifest.**" (Gleanings, pages 47-48)

This preamble, written by Bahá'u'lláh, to His book of the Hidden Words explains that this is no ordinary book.

First He tells us where this book came from. Then He explains who said it. He then goes on to explain that what is written in this book was what had been revealed to all the Prophets of the past by God. By taking the inner essence He gives these truths to us in their very purest form. If one takes these Hidden Words of Bahá'u'lláh and studies them, understands them and applies them to one's life, such a person will receive the grace of God, be faithful to the Covenant of God, fulfill his purpose of being created and grow to become a gem of Divine virtue.

1. O SON OF SPIRIT!
My first counsel is this: Possess a pure, kindly and radiant heart, that thine may be a sovereignty ancient, imperishable and everlasting.

O- We use this to give an added feeling. For example, if I say, "My darling, my love, my sweetheart", this sounds good but if I say, "O! My darling, O! My love. O! My sweetheart," it sounds a lot better than just good - it sounds great!

"O" also is a letter without beginning or end and it seems when Bahá'u'lláh says, "O" Son, it adds that love and oneness.

"Thus it is evident and clear that although the beings exist, in relation to God and to the Word of God they are nonexistent. This is the beginning and the end of the Word of God, Who says: "I am Alpha and Omega"; for He is the beginning and the end of Bounty." ('Abdu'l-Bahá : Some Answered Questions, page 281)

"I am Alpha and Omega, the beginning and the ending, saith the Lord, which is, and which was, and which is to come, the Almighty." (Bible Revelations 1:8)

Son- A son is an offspring of a father or mother and in Arabic it is not gender specific. It indicates a child that was born from this mother and father, so it would appear that Bahá'u'lláh is talking more specifically to those that are of Him and belong to Him. However, He has indicated that all Creation is His.

"Having created the world and all that liveth and moveth therein, He, through the direct operation of His unconstrained and sovereign Will, chose to confer upon man the unique distinction and capacity to know Him and to love Him - a capacity that must needs be regarded as the generating impulse and the primary purpose underlying the whole of creation...." (Gleanings, page 65)

"There is none other God besides Him. His is all creation and its empire." (Gleanings, page 150)

"In the Name of God, the Compassionate, the Merciful
1. SAY: He is God alone:
2. God the eternal!
3. He begetteth not, and He is not begotten;
4. And there is none like unto Him." (Qur'án The Purity of Faith SURA 112. - THE UNITY MECCA. - 4 Verses Rodwell Al-Ikhlas)

<u>*OF SPIRIT!*</u>- It is not just any son, but the son of the spirit or the offspring of His Spirit:

"**And when the hour at which Thy resistless Faith was to be made manifest did strike, Thou didst breathe a breath of Thy spirit into Thy Pen, and lo, the entire creation shook to its very foundations, unveiling to mankind such mysteries as lay hidden within the treasuries of Him Who is the Possessor of all created things." (Gleanings, page 15)**

"Thou sendest forth thy spirit, they are created: and thou renewest the face of the earth." (Bible Psalms 104:30)

Spirit, as stated above, is the breath that is breathed into the pen of Bahá'u'lláh, meaning His words and His revelation. Also He states that the Spirit that moved in Him was the Divine Spirit.

"**The Breathings of the Divine Spirit awoke Him, and bade Him arise and proclaim His Revelation." (Gleanings, page 99)**

A good point of interest is that every-time Bahá'u'lláh mentions the name of Jesus Christ He refers to Him as the Spirit. So it would seem that this opening phrase of the first Hidden Word could have a very special meaning for those of a Christian background.

"**Jesus answered, Verily, verily, I say unto thee, Except a man be born** of water and of the Spirit, he cannot enter into the kingdom of God. That which is born of the flesh is flesh; and that which is born of the Spirit is spirit." (Bible John 3:5-6)

Man without the human spirit, which is the spirit of the heart and the emotional side of man, is less than an animal. It is that spirit that makes man a true man.

"The spirit that animateth the human heart is the knowledge of God, and its truest adorning is the recognition of the truth that "He doeth whatsoever He willeth, and ordaineth that which He pleaseth." *(Gleanings, page 291)*

"Wert thou to attain to but a dewdrop of the crystal waters of divine knowledge, thou wouldst readily realize that true life is not the life of the flesh but the life of the spirit." (The Kitab-i-Iqan, page 120)

<u>*My first counsel is this:*</u>- My seems to refer to the voice of God as heard through the Manifestation, Bahá'u'lláh.

"The first station, which is related to His innermost reality, representeth Him as One Whose voice is the voice of God Himself..." (Aqdas: Notes, page 233)

"As a token of His mercy, however, and as a proof of His loving-kindness, He hath manifested unto men the Day Stars of His divine guidance, the Symbols of His divine unity, and hath ordained the knowledge of these sanctified Beings to be identical with the knowledge of His own Self. Whoso recognizeth them hath recognized God. Whoso hearkeneth to their call, hath hearkened to the Voice of God, and whoso testifieth to the truth of their Revelation, hath testified to the truth of God Himself. Whoso turneth away from them, hath turned away from God, and whoso disbelieveth in them, hath disbelieved in God. Every one of them is the Way of God that connecteth this world with the realms above, and the Standard of His Truth unto every one in the kingdoms of earth and heaven. They are the Manifestations of God amidst men, the evidences of His Truth, and the signs of His glory." (Gleanings, pages 49-50)

From the above statement of Bahá'u'lláh it is clear that all the heavenly Manifestations from Adam to Bahá'u'lláh and all those Manifestations of the future are the "My" referred to in this phrase.

The first means that which comes before anything else, and the Hidden Words was one of the first books revealed by Bahá'u'lláh and the first counsel of this first book is what is to follow. A counsel is more than just advice; it is the advice of an expert in one's field. When I need help in any facet of life I will go to a counsellor and pay for this expert's opinion. In this case this expert advice is given to man freely. Another aspect is that this seems to imply a freedom of choice or free will. I can follow the counseling received or I can ignore it. However, if it is the advice of an expert I would be foolish indeed to ignore it.

"Shouldst thou accept this counsel, thou wilt have acted to thine own behoof; and shouldst thou reject it, thy Lord, verily, can well dispense with thee, and with all those who, in manifest delusion, have followed thee." (The Kitab-i-Aqdas, page 87)

"This is the Counsel of God; would that thou mightest heed it! This is the Bounty of God; would that thou mightest receive it! This is the Utterance of God; if only thou wouldst apprehend it! This is the Treasure of God; if only thou couldst understand!" (The Kitab-i-Aqdas, page 87)

"Heed, therefore, My counsel, and hearken thou, with the hearing of thine heart, unto My speech, and be not careless of My words, nor be of them that reject My truth." (Gleanings, page 226)

Possess- What is it that man really possesses? Even man's soul is a divine trust that belongs to God and will be returned to Him.

"What thou dost possess is naught but husks which We have left to thee as bones are left to dogs." (The Kitab-i-Aqdas, page 31)

"Exultest thou over the treasures thou dost possess, knowing they shall perish? Rejoicest thou in that thou rulest a span of earth, when the whole world, in the estimation of the people of Bahá, is worth as much as the black in the eye of a dead ant." (Epistle to the Son of the Wolf, page 124)

"Say: Rejoice not in the things ye possess; tonight they are yours, tomorrow others will possess them." (The Kitab-i-Aqdas, page 33)

The only real possessions that one can have are the Divine virtues and the knowledge and the worship of God. To gain these lasting possessions an effort needs to be made on our part.

"All that which ye potentially possess can, however, be manifested only as a result of your own volition." (Gleanings, page 149)

"For every one of you his paramount duty is to choose for himself that on which no other may infringe and none usurp from him. Such a thing - and to this the Almighty is My witness - is the love of God, could ye but perceive it." (Gleanings, page 261)

Pure- What is pure? Pure gold would be 100% gold with no impurities in it. Pure water would be 100% water. Thus it would seem that a pure heart would be 100% heart. It is noted that Bahá'u'lláh did not say an empty heart. A heart filled with love and Divine virtue may be what is meant. In the following passage Baha'u'llah tells us that the way to purify the heart is through love and severance.

"A pure heart is as a mirror; cleanse it with the burnish of love and severance from all save God, that the true sun may shine within it and the eternal morning dawn." (Seven Valleys and Four Valleys, page 21)

"Exert thyself night and day until spiritual powers may penetrate thy heart and soul. Abandon the body and the material, until the merciful powers may become manifest; because not until the soil is become pure will it develop through the heavenly bounty; not until the heart is purified, will the radiance of the Sun of Truth shine therein. I beg of God that thou wilt day by day increase the purity of thy heart, the cheerfulness of thy soul, the light of thy insight and the search for Truth." ('Abdu'l-Bahá : Bahá'í World Faith*, page 362)

"Thus purge thou thine ear that thou mayest hear no mention besides God, and purge thine eye that it behold naught except God, and thy conscience that it perceive naught other than God, and thy tongue that it proclaim nothing but God, and thy hand to write naught but the words of God, and thy knowledge that it comprehend naught except God, and thy heart that it entertain no wish save God, and in like manner purge all thine acts and thy pursuits that thou mayest be nurtured in the paradise of pure love, and perchance mayest attain the presence of Him Whom God shall make manifest, adorned with a purity which He highly cherisheth, and be sanctified from whosoever hath turned away from Him and doth not support Him. Thus shalt thou manifest a purity that shall profit thee." (Selections from the Báb, page 98)

For love of God and spiritual attraction do cleanse and purify the human heart and dress and adorn it with the spotless garment of holiness; and once the heart is entirely attached to the Lord, and bound over to the Blessed Perfection, then will the grace of God be revealed. (Selections ... 'Abdu'l-Bahá , pages 202-203)

These teachings are the way for us to get a pure heart. One other thing we can do to achieve this in our lives is to pray.

"Create in me a pure heart, O my God, and renew a tranquil conscience within me, O my Hope!" (Prayers and Meditations, page 248)

"Create in me a clean heart, O God; and renew a right spirit within me." (Bible Psalms 51:10)

"We have indeed created man in the best of molds," (Qur'án Fig Al-Tin 4.)

"O God! Refresh and gladden my spirit. Purify my heart. Illumine my powers. I lay all my affairs in Thy hand. Thou art my Guide and my Refuge. I will no longer be sorrowful and grieved; I will be a happy and joyful being. O God! I will no longer be full of anxiety, nor will I let trouble harass me. I will not dwell on the unpleasant things of life.
O God! Thou art more friend to me than I am to myself. I dedicate myself to Thee, O Lord." (Bahá'í Prayers (US edition), page 152)

<u>Kindly</u>- To have a pure heart one might be able to do this secluded in a cave and isolated from all human contact. To be kindly, however, forces one out of seclusion, for in order to be really kind there must be someone to be kind to. Even a pure heart, if we think about it more deeply, requires love and love needs someone to express that love to.

"In this Day, however, let them give up the life of seclusion and direct their steps towards the open world and busy themselves with that which will profit themselves and others." (Tablets of Bahá'u'lláh, page 24)

Kindly seems to imply the nature of a gentle, sweet and caring person. If a baby is falling in front of a train and the only way to save the child is to throw the baby out of the way even if this means using force, this would be kind. Kindly, therefore does not necessarily mean gentle.

"The friends of God must be adorned with the ornament of justice, equity, kindness and love." (Women, page 379)

"Emulate God. Consider how kindly, how lovingly He deals with all, and follow His example. You must treat people in accordance with the divine precepts - in other words, treat them as kindly as God treats them, for this is the greatest attainment possible for the world of humanity." (Promulgation of Universal Peace*, page 291)

"Therefore, to you my first admonition is this: Associate most kindly with all; be as one family; pursue this same pathway. Let your intentions be one that your love may permeate and affect the hearts of others so that they may grow to love each other and all attain to this condition of oneness." (Promulgation of Universal Peace*, pages 336-337)

"Love is heaven's kindly light, the Holy Spirit's eternal breath that vivifieth the human soul." (Selections ... `Abdu'l-Baha, page 27)

"Be kindly affection one to another with brotherly love; in honour preferring one another;" (Bible Romans 12:10)
"for God loveth those who are kind." (Qur'án The Table Spread 14 Al-Maidah)

<u>*Radiant*</u>- The sun is radiant, so man must be like the sun that is giving off

heavenly light, heat, warmth, and life giving rays. A radiant heart seems to be a pure heart and a kindly heart in action, and then it would become a radiant heart.

"Let the flame of the love of God burn brightly within your radiant hearts. Feed it with the oil of Divine guidance, and protect it within the shelter of your constancy." (Gleanings, page 325)

"Worship none but God, and, with radiant hearts, lift up your faces unto your Lord, the Lord of all names." (Proclamation of Bahá'u'lláh, page 5)

"We cherish the hope that men of piety may illumine the world through the radiant light of their conduct, and We entreat the Almighty - glorified and exalted is He - to grant that everyone may in this Day remain steadfast in His love and stand firm in His Cause." (Tablets of Bahá'u'lláh, page 91)

"In truth, religion is a radiant light and an impregnable stronghold for the protection and welfare of the peoples of the world, for the fear of God impelleth man to hold fast to that which is good, and shun all evil." (Tablets of Bahá'u'lláh, page 125)

"Blessed is he who hath rent the intervening veils asunder and is illumined by the radiant light of divine Revelation." (Tablets of Bahá'u'lláh, pages 255-256)

"And God said, Let there be light: and there was light." (Bible Genesis 1:3)

"For with thee is the fountain of life: in thy light shall we see light." (Bible Psalms 36:9)

"If thy whole body therefore be full of light, having no part dark, the whole shall be full of light, as when the bright shining of a candle doth give thee light." (Bible Luke 11:36)

"There hath come to you from God a (new) Light and a perspicuous Book. Wherewith God guideth all who seek His good pleasure to ways of peace and safety, and leadeth them out of darkness, by His Will, unto the light, guideth them to a Path that is Straight." (Qur'án The Table Spread 17 & 18 Al-Maidah)

These passages quoted above can give us an idea of what a radiant heart is and how to possess it. It will come into being through our love of God, through following His teachings and seeking to understand the spiritual reality within His teachings. Our conduct must be the conduct of a Bahá'í.

<u>*That thine may be a sovereignty*</u>- This is a beautiful example of the covenant. If I will possess a pure, kindly and radiant heart then God will bestow upon me a sovereignty. The first part is mine to do and the second part is His to give. In both cases I am the winner. To be able to have a pure, kindly and radiant heart would be the most wonderful gift anyone could possibly have and then to also gain a sovereignty ancient, imperishable and everlasting is adding gifts to gifts.

"It is Thine to command, and all sovereignty belongeth to Thee, and the realm of might boweth before Thy behest." (Epistle to the Son of the Wolf, page 10)

"This sovereignty, however, is not the sovereignty which the minds of men have falsely imagined." (The Kitab-i-Iqan, page 106)

"Nay, by sovereignty is meant that sovereignty which in every dispensation resideth within, and is exercised by, the person of the Manifestation, the Day-star of Truth. That sovereignty is the spiritual ascendancy which He exerciseth to the fullest degree over all that is in heaven and on earth, and which in due time revealeth itself to the world in direct proportion to its capacity and spiritual receptiveness, even as the sovereignty of Muhammad, the Messenger of God, is today apparent and manifest amongst the people." (The Kitab-i-Iqan, pages 107-108)

"Thou bestowest sovereignty on whom Thou willest and dost withhold it from whom Thou desirest." (Selections from the Báb, page 202)

Ancient- This seems to imply eternal in the past, the term of reference to Bahá'u'lláh as the Ancient Beauty or the Beauty that has always existed.

"Consider these days in which He Who is the Ancient Beauty hath come in the Most Great Name, that He may quicken the world and unite its peoples." (Epistle to the Son of the Wolf, page 63)

"The Most Great Law is come, and the Ancient Beauty ruleth upon the throne of David. Thus hath My Pen spoken that which the histories of bygone ages have related." (Proclamation of Bahá'u'lláh, page 89)

"Consider these days in which the Ancient Beauty, He Who is the Most Great Name, hath been sent down to regenerate and unify mankind." (Peace, page 157)

Imperishable- This is something that is now in existence and has always been in existence.

"Imperishable dominion hath exclusively pertained unto the One true God and His loved ones and will continue to pertain unto them everlastingly." (Tablets of Bahá'u'lláh, page 259)

"If ye follow in His way, His incalculable and imperishable blessings will be showered upon you." (Gleanings, page 9)

"God grant that through His gracious and invisible assistance, thou mayest divest thy body and soul of the old garment, and array thyself with the new and imperishable attire." (The Kitab-i-Iqan, page 158)

Everlasting- This is something that will last forever. We have in the Ancient, Imperishable and Everlasting a sovereignty that has always existed, is now in existence and will always be in existence. It is like a description of the Garden of Eden. The door is once more open and a loving Lord is giving us a loving invitation to come back in. To re-enter this Paradise requires a pure, kindly and radiant heart.

"Their recompense with their Lord shall be gardens of Eden, 'neath which the rivers flow, in which they shall abide for evermore." (Qur'án Clear Evidence 7 (Al-Bayyinah))

"This is the food that conferreth everlasting life upon the pure in heart and the illumined in spirit." (The Kitab-i-Iqan, pages 22-23)

"My sole purpose in revealing to thee these words is to sanctify thee from the transitory things of the earth, and aid thee to enter the realm of everlasting glory, that thou mayest, by the leave of God, be of them that abide and rule therein...." (Proclamation of Bahá'u'lláh, page 52)

"Beseech ye God - magnified be His glory - to grant that His loved ones may be privileged to take a portion from the ocean of His good-pleasure, for this would serve as the means for the salvation of mankind, and may of their own accordance carry out that which would purify them and cause them to attain everlasting life..." (Huququ'llah, page 495)

2. O SON OF SPIRIT!

The best beloved of all things in My sight is Justice; turn not away therefrom if thou desirest Me, and neglect it not that I may confide in thee. By its aid thou shalt see with thine own eyes and not through the eyes of others, and shalt know of thine own knowledge and not through the knowledge of thy neighbor. Ponder this in thy heart; how it behooveth thee to be. Verily justice is My gift to thee and the sign of My loving-kindness. Set it then before thine eyes.

Justice- According to the dictionary justice is equal treatment under the law. Bahá'u'lláh's definition goes far beyond this. For example, if I have a pie and I have four people normally I would divide the pie into four pieces and each person would get an equal share of the pie. Now, under the teachings of Bahá'u'lláh, if one person had a special need, we would all willingly and gladly give this needy one the whole pie.

Bahá'u'lláh has given us some very interesting definitions of justice:

"**Know verily that the essence of justice and the source thereof are both embodied in the ordinances prescribed by Him Who is the Manifestation of the Self of God amongst men, if ye be of them that recognize this truth.**" (Gleanings, page 175)

"**Everything Thou doest is pure justice, nay, the very essence of grace.**" (Epistle to the Son of the Wolf, page 10)

"**The Word of thy Lord doth find its fulfillment in truth and in justice: none can change His Words: for He is the one who heareth and knoweth all.**" (Qur'án The Cattle 115 Al-Anam)

"**And if thine eyes be turned towards justice, choose thou for thy neighbor that which thou choosest for thyself.**" (Epistle to the Son of the Wolf, page 30)

"Justice is a powerful force. It is, above all else, the conqueror of the citadels of the hearts and souls of men, and the revealer of the secrets of the world of being, and the standard-bearer of love and bounty." (Epistle to the Son of the Wolf, page 32)

"The purpose of justice is the appearance of unity among men. The ocean of divine wisdom surgeth within this exalted word, while the books of the world cannot contain its inner significance." (Tablets of Bahá'u'lláh, page 67)

"The essence of all that We have revealed for thee is Justice," (Tablets of Bahá'u'lláh, page 157)

From the above quotes it seems that the very essence of Justice is obedience to God's commands. Then it further states that the essence of all that Bahá'u'lláh has revealed is no more or no less than justice. So this word justice in its broadest meaning is the total revelation of Bahá'u'lláh, and can never hope to be defined or understood by mere man.

Bahá'u'lláh explains that justice is built on the foundation of reward and punishment. Our present system of what is termed justice is primarily concerned only with punishment.

"That which traineth the world is Justice, for it is upheld by two pillars, reward and punishment. These two pillars are the sources of life to the world." (Aqdas: Other Sections, page 91)

"Justice hath a mighty force at its command. It is none other than reward and punishment for the deeds of men." (Tablets of Bahá'u'lláh, page 164)

"To do justice and judgment is more acceptable to the LORD than sacrifice." (Bible Proverbs 21:3)

"***The best beloved of all things in My sight is Justice***" Above everything else in the sight of Bahá'u'lláh, He loves justice most of all and He then goes on to tell us to ***"turn not away therefrom if thou desirest Me."*** In other words if we desire to know and love God then we had best try with heart and soul to obey Him and be just. "***and neglect it not that I may confide in thee.***" When one person confides in another it is a very beautiful thing; that is, to take another into your confidence means one that you have confidence in and they have confidence in you.

"In these planes, the nightingale of the heart hath other songs and secrets, which make the heart to stir and the soul to clamor, but this mystery of inner meaning may be whispered only from heart to heart, confided only from breast to breast." (Seven Valleys and Four Valleys, page 30)

"1. Whatever is in the heavens and on earth, doth declare the Praises and Glory of God: to Him belongs Dominion, and to Him belongs Praise: and He has power over all things.
2. It is He Who has created you; and of you are some that are Unbelievers, and some that are Believers: and God sees well all that ye do.
3. He has created the heavens and the earth in just proportions, and has given you shape, and made your shapes beautiful: and to Him is the final Goal.
4. He knows what is in the heavens and on earth: and He knows what ye conceal and what ye reveal: yes, God knows well the (secrets) of (all) hearts." (Qur'án The Loss and Gain 1-4 At-Taghabun)

"Put your whole trust and confidence in God, Who hath created you, and seek ye His help in all your affairs." (Gleanings, page 251)

"By its aid thou shalt see with thine own eyes and not through the eyes of others, and shalt know of thine own knowledge and not through the knowledge of thy neighbor." Individual investigation of the truth is one of the most fundamental teachings in this Cause of God. Here Bahá'u'lláh stresses this principle in His second Hidden Word.

"The first teaching of Bahá'u'lláh is the duty incumbent upon all to investigate reality. What does it mean to investigate reality? It means that man must forget all hearsay and examine truth himself, for he does not know whether statements he hears are in accordance with reality or not. Wherever he finds truth or reality, he must hold to it, forsaking, discarding all else; for outside of reality there is naught but superstition and imagination." (Promulgation of Universal Peace*, page 62)

"And God said unto him, Because thou hast asked this thing, and hast not asked for thyself long life; neither hast asked riches for thyself, nor hast asked the life of thine enemies; but hast asked for thyself understanding to discern judgment;" (Bible 1 Kings 3:11)

"In this day man must investigate reality impartially and without prejudice in order to reach the true knowledge and conclusions." (Promulgation of Universal Peace*, page 75)

"So shall the knowledge of wisdom be unto thy soul: when thou hast found it, then there shall be a reward, and thy expectation shall not be cut off." (Bible Proverbs 24:14)

"Another new principle revealed by Bahá'u'lláh is the injunction to investigate truth - that is to say, no man should blindly follow his ancestors and forefathers. Nay, each must see with his own eyes, hear with his own ears and investigate the truth himself in order that he may follow the truth instead of blind acquiescence and imitation of ancestral beliefs." (Promulgation of Universal Peace*, page 454)

"Verily in this is a Message for any that has a heart and understanding or who gives ear and earnestly witnesses (the truth)." (Qur'án Qaf 37)

"Ponder this in thy heart; how it behooveth thee to be." The heart is the spiritual organ of feeling and sensitivity, to ponder in thy heart would mean to think so deeply on the subject that it becomes felt. In this case, a just or unjust action would be felt as well as understood.

"Were any man to ponder in his heart that which the Pen of the Most High hath revealed and to taste of its sweetness, he would, of a certainty, find himself emptied and delivered from his own desires, and utterly subservient to the Will of the Almighty." (Gleanings, page 343)

"Ponder a while those holy words in your heart, and, with utter detachment, strive to grasp their meaning." (The Kitab-i-Iqan, page 5)

"It is now incumbent upon them who are endowed with a hearing ear and a seeing eye to ponder these sublime words, in each of which the oceans of inner meaning and explanation are hidden, that haply the words uttered by Him Who is the Lord of Revelation may enable His servants to attain, with the utmost joy and radiance, unto the Supreme Goal and Most Sublime Summit -the dawning-place of this Voice." (Epistle to the Son of the Wolf, page 147)

"(Here is) a Book which We have sent down unto thee, full of blessings, that they may meditate on its Signs, and that men of understanding may receive admonition." (Qur'án 29 Sad)

"But his delight is in the law of the LORD; and in his law doth he meditate day and night." (Bible Psalms 1:2)

The word behooveth conveys something that would be to our own best interest, so it follows that if we do ponder these Holy verses in our hearts and act accordingly it will be to our own best interest.

"Therefore it behooveth you, O creatures of God, to help your own selves and to believe in the Verses revealed by Me..." (Selections from the Báb, page 102)

"Say: "No reward do I ask of you: it is (all) in your interest: my reward is only due from God: and He is Witness to all things." (Qur'án Sheba 47 Saba))

<u>*"Verily justice is My gift to thee and the sign of My loving-kindness."*</u>- This is a new idea of justice; justice as a gift and justice to be associated with love and kindness. I, for one, can say that I fear the justice of God. I know if He were to deal with me with justice I would be of the lost, so I desire His grace, love and mercy. With all my heart I seek His forgiveness of what I have done and for what I should have done and didn't do.

"Should God punish men for their perverse doings, He would not leave on earth a moving thing! But to an appointed term doth He respite them...." (Bahá'u'lláh : Seven Valleys and Four Valleys, Page: 21)

"The essence of wisdom is the fear of God, the dread of His scourge and punishment, and the apprehension of His justice and decree." (Tablets of Bahá'u'lláh, page 155)

"Wherefore, hearken ye unto My speech, and return ye to God and repent, that He, through His grace, may have mercy upon you, may wash away your sins, and forgive your trespasses. The greatness of His mercy surpasseth the fury of His wrath, and His grace encompasseth all who have been called into being and been clothed with the robe of life, be they of the past or of the future." (Gleanings, page 130)

"Every good gift and every perfect gift is from above, and cometh down from the Father of lights, with whom is no variableness, neither shadow of turning." (Bible James 1:17)

God, teaching us through His Manifestation, Bahá'u'lláh, is the greatest gift from God to man. Then our teaching other souls the divine teachings is our greatest gift to them.

"Of all the gifts of God the greatest is the gift of Teaching." (Will and Testament, page 25)

"For I long to see you, that I may impart unto you some spiritual gift, to the end ye may be established;" (Bible Romans 1:11)

"But teach (thy Message): for teaching benefits the Believers." (Qur'án The Winds 55 Adh-Dhariyat)

<u>**"Set it then before thine eyes."**</u> This seems to be telling us to never ever lose sight of justice and it also implies to be steadfast. As justice is the very essence of all that Bahá'u'lláh has revealed to us this means a firmness in our obedience to Him; firm in the covenant of God.

"Gazing with the eye of God, he will perceive within every atom a door that leadeth him to the stations of absolute certitude." (The Kitab-i-Iqan, page 196)

"With the ear of God he heareth, with the eye of God he beholdeth the mysteries of divine creation." (Seven Valleys and Four Valleys, page 17)

"But this thing commanded I them, saying, Obey my voice, and I will be your God, and ye shall be my people: and walk ye in all the ways that I have commanded you, that it may be well unto you." (Bible Jeremiah 7:23)

3. O SON OF MAN!
Veiled in My immemorial being and in the ancient eternity of My essence, I knew My love for thee; therefore I created thee, have engraved on thee Mine image and revealed to thee My beauty.

O SON OF MAN! This is a new title. It seems that in the first two Hidden Words Bahá'u'lláh was addressing our spiritual nature. This one seems to be addressing us individually and collectively as man and mankind.

"And now, concerning thy question regarding the creation of man. Know thou that all men have been created in the nature made by God, the Guardian, the Self-Subsisting. Unto each one hath been prescribed a pre-ordained measure, as decreed in God's mighty and guarded Tablets. All that which ye potentially possess can, however, be manifested only as a result of your own volition." (Bahá'u'lláh: Gleanings, page 149)

"And those who strive in Our (Cause), We will certainly guide them to Our Paths: for verily God is with those who do right." (Qur'án The Spider 69 Al-Ankabut)

"Whoso maketh efforts for Us," he shall enjoy the blessings conferred by the words: "In Our Ways shall We assuredly guide him." (Bahá'u'lláh: Gleanings, Pages: 266-267)

"Man is, therefore, superior to all the creatures below him, the loftiest and most glorious being of creation." ('Abdu'l-Bahá : Promulgation of Universal Peace*, page 69)

"So God created man in his own image, in the image of God created he him; male and female created he them." (Bible Genesis 1:27)

In the first Hidden Word He told us to prepare ourselves; what to do and how to do it. Then in the second one He tells us to be just and see with our own eyes and know of our own knowledge; in other words to open our minds to individual investigation of the truth. In this one He does not ask anything from us but just makes a statement of fact - that He loves me even before He created me, the individual, He loved me. Even before He created mankind He loved mankind. He wants us to really know this and understand it with a pure heart.

"The purpose of the creation of man is the attainment of the supreme virtues of humanity through descent of the heavenly bestowals." (''Abdu'l-Bahá: Promulgation of Universal Peace*, page 4)

<u>Veiled in My immemorial being and in the ancient eternity of My essence,</u>-Veiled is an interesting word. We know something is there but it is still hidden from us.

"And when this process of progressive Revelation culminated in the stage at which His peerless, His most sacred, and exalted Countenance was to be unveiled to men's eyes, He chose to hide His own Self behind a thousand veils, lest profane and mortal eyes discover His glory." (Gleanings, page 75)

"And when the set time of concealment was fulfilled, We sent forth, whilst still wrapt within a myriad veils, an infinitesimal glimmer of the effulgent Glory enveloping the Face of the Youth, and lo, the entire company of the dwellers of the Realms above were seized with violent commotion and the favored of God fell down in adoration before Him." (Gleanings, page 75)

"The secret things belong unto the LORD our God: but those things which are revealed belong unto us and to our children for ever, that we may do all the words of this law." (Bible Deuteronomy 29:29)

We get something of the feeling of the unknowable Essence of God. He is Single, Alone and Unknowable. He sees and knows all, even man's inmost secret thoughts, yet He is inscrutable even to His Manifestation.

"To every discerning and illuminated heart it is evident that God, the unknowable Essence, the Divine Being, is immensely exalted beyond every human attribute, such as corporeal existence, ascent and descent, egress and regress. Far be it from His glory that human tongue should adequately recount His praise, or that human heart comprehend His fathomless mystery. He is, and hath ever been, veiled in the ancient eternity of His Essence, and will remain in His Reality everlastingly hidden from the sight of men. "No vision taketh in Him, but He taketh in all vision; He is the Subtile, the All-Perceiving."... (Gleanings, pages 46-47)

"So perfect and comprehensive is His creation that no mind nor heart, however keen or pure, can ever grasp the nature of the most insignificant of His creatures; much less fathom the mystery of Him Who is the Day Star of Truth, Who is the invisible and unknowable Essence. The conceptions of the devoutest of mystics, the attainments of the most accomplished amongst men, the highest praise which human tongue or pen can render are all the product of man's finite mind and are conditioned by its limitations. Ten thousand Prophets, each a Moses, are thunderstruck upon the Sinai of their search at His forbidding voice, "Thou shalt never behold Me!"; whilst a myriad

Messengers, each as great as Jesus, stand dismayed upon their heavenly thrones by the interdiction, "Mine Essence thou shalt never apprehend!" From time immemorial He hath been veiled in the ineffable sanctity of His exalted Self, and will everlastingly continue to be wrapt in the impenetrable mystery of His unknowable Essence. Every attempt to attain to an understanding of His inaccessible Reality hath ended in complete bewilderment, and every effort to approach His exalted Self and envisage His Essence hath resulted in hopelessness and failure." (Gleanings, pages 62-63)

"Does not God know best all that is in the hearts of all Creation?" (Qur'án 10 The Spider (Al-Ankabut)

"But the falcon of the mystic heaven hath many a wondrous carol of the spirit in His breast, and the Persian bird keepeth in His soul many a sweet Arab melody; yet these are hidden, and hidden shall remain." (Seven Valleys and Four Valleys, page 29)

"Were all the things that lie enshrined within the heart of Bahá, and which the Lord, His God, the Lord of all names, hath taught Him, to be unveiled to mankind, every man on earth would be dumbfounded." (Gleanings, page 176)

"How great the multitude of truths which the garment of words can never contain! How vast the number of such verities as no expression can adequately describe, whose significance can never be unfolded, and to which not even the remotest allusions can be made!" (Gleanings, page 176)

"Howbeit when he, the Spirit of truth, is come, he will guide you into all truth: for he shall not speak of himself; but whatsoever he shall hear, that shall he speak: and he will shew you things to come." (Bible John 16:13)

My immemorial being – This seems to signify the time before memory existed, at least as we know it. Bahá'u'lláh was veiled and hidden from the eyes of men before memory was created and at that period of creation He already confessed His love for us. Not only did He love us but this love was known by Him.

"I testify that Thou wast a hidden Treasure wrapped within Thine immemorial Being and an impenetrable Mystery enshrined in Thine own Essence." (Bahá'u'lláh: Aqdas: Notes, page 175)

"For where your treasure is, there will your heart be also." (Bible Mathew 6:21)

"And I will give thee the treasures of darkness, and hidden riches of secret places, that thou mayest know that I, the LORD, which call thee by thy name, am the God of Israel." (Bible Isaiah 45:3)

I knew My love for thee; therefore I created thee; - Here in this third Hidden Word of Bahá'u'lláh's, God tells us in no uncertain terms why we were created. Each and every one of us was created because God loved us. It is very important to realize that in any love relationship someone has to make the first step.

"The living waters of My mercy, O Ali, are fast pouring down, and Mine heart is melting with the heat of My tenderness and love. At no time have I been able to reconcile Myself to the afflictions befalling My loved ones, or to any trouble that could becloud the joy of their hearts." (Gleanings, page 308)

"They that surround thee love thee for their own sakes, whereas this Youth loveth thee for thine own sake, and hath had no desire except to draw thee nigh unto the seat of grace, and to turn thee toward the right-hand of justice." (Proclamation of Bahá'u'lláh, page 58)

"The fragrances of Thy love have thereby been wafted over Thy cities and have encompassed all the dwellers of Thy realm." (Prayers and Meditations, page 31)

"Thou art most dear to Us; and, as We love thee, so love We all in whom may be perceived the goodly adornments of trustworthiness and uprightness, and such qualities of virtue and integrity as have been enjoined upon men in the Book of God, the Lord of the Mighty Throne." (Trustworthiness, page 333)

__have engraved on thee Mine image__ -Something that is engraved indicates that it is cut deeply into it. This image of Bahá'u'lláh's then is not just a surface thing that can be easily erased. It seems to go right to the heart of His creation.

"So God created man in his own image, in the image of God created he him; male and female created he them." (Bible: Gen 1:27)

"The spirit of God hath made me, and the breath of the Almighty hath given me life." (Bible Job 33:4)

"God has created all earthly things under a law of progression in material degrees, but He has created man and endowed him with powers of advancement toward spiritual and transcendental kingdoms. He has not created material phenomena after His own image and likeness, but He has created man after that image and with potential power to attain that likeness. He has distinguished man above all other created things." (Promulgation of Universal Peace*, page 302)

"He hath chosen out of the whole world the hearts of His servants, and made them each a seat for the revelation of His glory. Wherefore, sanctify them from every defilement, that the things for which they were created may be engraven upon them. This indeed is a token of God's bountiful favor." (Gleanings, page 297)

"Nay, enrich Thyself increasingly, in the kingdom of creation, with the incorruptible vestures of Thy God, that the beauteous image of the Almighty may be reflected through Thee in all created things and the grace of Thy Lord be infused in the plenitude of its power into the entire creation." (Gleanings, page 283)

<u>*and revealed to thee My beauty.*</u> -Not only did God create us because He loved us and engraved His image in us, He also gave us the priceless treasure of getting an infinitesimal glimpse of the reality of His beauty.

"Suffer not yourselves to be shut out as by a veil from God after He hath revealed Himself." (Epistle to the Son of the Wolf, pages 154-155)

"He that was hidden from mortal eyes is come! His all-conquering sovereignty is manifest; His all-encompassing splendor is revealed." (Gleanings, page 16)

"Say: This is the Paradise on whose foliage the wine of utterance hath imprinted the testimony: "He that was hidden from the eyes of men is revealed, girded with sovereignty and power!" (Gleanings, page 31)

"Through their appearance the Revelation of God is made manifest, and by their countenance the Beauty of God is revealed." (Gleanings, page 53)

"The measure of the favors of God hath been filled up, His Word hath been perfected, the light of His countenance hath been revealed, His sovereignty hath encompassed the whole of creation, the glory of His Revelation hath been made manifest, and His bounties have rained upon all mankind." (Gleanings, page 259)

"I testify that through Thee the sovereignty of God and His dominion, and the majesty of God and His grandeur, were revealed, and the Day-Stars of ancient splendor have shed their radiance in the heaven of Thine irrevocable decree, and the Beauty of the Unseen hath shone forth above the horizon of creation." (Prayers and Meditations, pages 310-311)

The beauty that God reveals to us is evident in all creation. The sun, moon, stars, sky, rainbow, sunrise, sunset and every created thing reveals to us the beauty of God. The greatest beauty, of course, is the Divine Manifestation. This is revealed to us in His person and in His teachings.

"Consider how all created things eloquently testify to the revelation of that inner Light within them." (The Kitab-i-Iqan, page 140)

"Upon the inmost reality of each and every created thing He hath shed the light of one of His names, and made it a recipient of the glory of one of His attributes. Upon the reality of man, however, He hath focused the radiance of all of His names and attributes, and made it a mirror of His own Self. Alone of all created things man hath been singled out for so great a favor, so enduring a bounty." (Gleanings, page 65)

These attributes and names of God and the reflection of God in man lie within man as, in the winter, the apple lies hidden in the apple tree. First man must put forth his own effort, and then the wise gardener can bring the tree of man into fruition, and this 'gardener' is God's Manifestation in the day in which we live.

"These energies with which the Day Star of Divine bounty and Source of heavenly guidance hath endowed the reality of man lie, however, latent within him, even as the flame is hidden within the candle and the rays of light are potentially present in the lamp. The radiance of these energies may be obscured by worldly desires even as the light of the sun can be concealed beneath the dust and dross which cover the mirror. Neither the candle nor the lamp can be lighted through their own unaided efforts, nor can it ever be possible for the mirror to free itself from its dross. It is clear and evident that until a fire is kindled the lamp will never be ignited, and unless the dross is blotted out from the face of the mirror it can never represent the image of the sun nor reflect its light and glory. Since there can be no tie of direct intercourse to bind the one true God with His creation, and no resemblance whatever can exist between the transient and the Eternal, the contingent and the Absolute, He hath ordained that in every age and dispensation a pure and stainless Soul be made manifest in the kingdoms of earth and heaven. Unto this subtle, this mysterious and ethereal Being He hath assigned a twofold nature; the physical, pertaining to the world of matter, and the spiritual, which is born of the substance of God Himself." (Gleanings, pages 65-66)

"These Essences of Detachment, these resplendent Realities are the channels of God's all-pervasive grace. Led by the light of unfailing guidance, and invested with supreme sovereignty, They are commissioned to use the inspiration of Their words, the effusions of Their infallible grace and the sanctifying breeze of Their Revelation for the cleansing of every longing heart and receptive spirit from the dross and dust of earthly cares and limitations. Then, and only then, will the Trust of God, latent in the reality of man, emerge, as resplendent as the rising Orb of Divine Revelation, from behind the veil of concealment, and implant the ensign of its revealed glory upon the summits of men's hearts." (Gleanings, page 67)

"There can be no doubt whatever that, in consequence of the efforts which every man may consciously exert and as a result of the exertion of his own spiritual faculties, this mirror can be so cleansed from the dross of earthly defilements and purged from satanic fancies as to be able to draw nigh unto the meads of eternal holiness and attain the courts of everlasting fellowship." (Gleanings, page 262)

"Success or failure, gain or loss, must, therefore, depend upon man's own exertions. The more he striveth, the greater will be his progress." (Gleanings, pages 81-82)

"O ye who believe! do your duty to God, seek the means of approach unto Him, and strive with might and main in His cause: that ye may prosper." (Qur'án The Table Spread 38 Maidah)

"Strive to enter in at the strait gate: for many, I say unto you, will seek to enter in, and shall not be able." (Bible Luke 13:24)

4. O SON OF MAN!

I loved thy creation, hence I created thee. Wherefore, do thou love Me, that I may name thy name and fill thy soul with the spirit of life.

<u>I loved thy creation, hence I created thee.</u> This seems to imply that God loved the very act of creating; creating me the individual, mankind in its totality, the beautiful world and the universe. As the last hidden word explained, the reason God created us was because He loved us, but this one gives us another reason why we were created. We were created because God loved doing it.

"Wishing to reveal Thyself, Thou didst call into being the Greater and the Lesser Worlds, and didst choose Man above all Thy creatures, and didst make Him a sign of both of these worlds, O Thou Who art our Lord, the Most Compassionate!" (Prayers and Meditations, page 49)

"Having created the world and all that liveth and moveth therein, He, through the direct operation of His unconstrained and sovereign Will, chose to confer upon man the unique distinction and capacity to know Him and to love Him - a capacity that must needs be regarded as the generating impulse and the primary purpose underlying the whole of creation...." (Gleanings, page 65)

"The purpose of God in creating man hath been, and will ever be, to enable him to know his Creator and to attain His Presence." (Gleanings, page 70)

"God created the heavens and the earth for just ends, and in order that each soul may find the recompense of what it has earned, and none of them be wronged." (Qur'án Bowing the Knee 22 Al-Jathiyah)

"The supreme cause for creating the world and all that is therein is for man to know God." (Tablets of Bahá'u'lláh, page 268)

The following quote is referring to this Hidden Word as stated in the Aqdas.

"'Abdu'l-Bahá, in His commentary on the above-cited tradition, wrote: O wayfarer in the path of the Beloved! Know thou that the main purpose of this holy tradition is to make mention of the stages of God's concealment and manifestation within the Embodiments of Truth, They who are the Dawning-places of His All-Glorious Being." (Bahá'u'lláh: Aqdas: Notes, Page: 175)

"Should a man wish to adorn himself with the ornaments of the earth, to wear its apparels, or partake of the benefits it can bestow, no harm can befall him, if he alloweth nothing whatever to intervene between him and God, for God hath ordained every good thing, whether created in the heavens or in the earth, for such of His servants as truly believe in Him." (Gleanings, page 276)

"Thou shalt worship the Lord thy God, and him only shalt thou serve." (Bible Mathew 4:10)

<u>*Wherefore, do thou love Me*</u>- This "wherefore" is an interesting word. It means cause or why but it also is a continuing action. Therefore, it is not an action solely completed in the past. In other words we cannot say to God. "I love you God" and so that is now finished. It means that I must love Him now, tomorrow, next week, next month, next year and always. I must continuously love Him.

Bahá'u'lláh said in the previous Hidden Word, that He loved us. Again in this Hidden Word He not only confirms His love for us but assures us that He even loved creating us and the creation around us. After two affirmations of His love He then asks us to love Him. For love to be complete it must be two-way. One-sided love is an unfulfilled love. For love to be true love it must be given and returned.

God's love for man is so intense that we are taught that if His love were to be stopped for one split second, that everything in the universe would vanish.

"Were this revelation to be withdrawn, all would perish." (Gleanings, page 190)

"There can be no doubt whatever that if for one moment the tide of His mercy and grace were to be withheld from the world, it would completely perish." (Gleanings, page 68)

"I can have no doubt that should the holy breaths of Thy loving-kindness and the breeze of Thy bountiful favor cease, for less than the twinkling of an eye, to breathe over all created things, the entire creation would perish, and all that are in heaven and on earth would be reduced to utter nothingness." (Prayers and Meditations, page 90)

"If it were His will, He could destroy you, O mankind, and create another race: for He hath power this to do." (Qur'án Women 133 (An-Nisa)

that I may name thy name- This may imply that Bahá'u'lláh will call me by my name. It could also mean that God would bestow upon me a new name that would befit the station of one who loves God with all his heart, all his soul and all his being. In any event, the condition for receiving this name is to truly love our Creator.

"Let your joy be the joy born of My Most Great Name, a Name that bringeth rapture to the heart, and filleth with ecstasy the minds of all who have drawn nigh unto God." (The Kitab-i-Aqdas, page 38)

"Every name hath been created by His Word, and every cause is dependent on His irresistible, His mighty and wondrous Cause." (The Kitab-i-Aqdas, page 80)

Say: "Call upon God, or call upon Rahman: by whatever name ye call upon Him, (it is well): for to Him belong the Most Beautiful Names." (Qur'án Children of Israel 110 (Al-Isra)

"I ask Thee, O Lord of all being and King of the seen and unseen, by Thy power, Thy majesty and Thy sovereignty, to grant that my name may be recorded by Thy pen of glory among Thy devoted ones, them whom the scrolls of the sinful hindered not from turning to the light of Thy countenance, O prayer-hearing, prayer-answering God!" (Bahá'í Prayers (US), page 164)

"Attire thy temple with the ornament of My Name, and thy tongue with remembrance of Me, and thine heart with love for Me, the Almighty, the Most High." (Proclamation of Bahá'u'lláh, pages 18-19)

"A good name is rather to be chosen than great riches, and loving favour rather than silver and gold." (Bible Proverbs 22:1)

"He beholdeth in his own name the name of God; to him, "all songs are from the King," and every melody from Him." (Seven Valleys and Four Valleys, page 18)

"This is the day whereon nothing amongst all things, nor any name amongst all names, can profit you save through this Name which God hath made the Manifestation of His Cause and the Dayspring of His Most Excellent Titles unto all who are in the kingdom of creation." (Tablets of Bahá'u'lláh, page 211)

<u>*and fill thy soul with the spirit of life.*</u>- It seems that if one does not love God, then that person's soul would be empty of life.

"Wert thou to attain to but a dewdrop of the crystal waters of divine knowledge, thou wouldst readily realize that true life is not the life of the flesh but the life of the spirit. For the life of the flesh is common to both men and animals, whereas the life of the spirit is possessed only by the pure in heart who have quaffed from the ocean of faith and partaken of the fruit of certitude. This life knoweth no death, and this existence is crowned by immortality." (The Kitab-i-Iqan, page 120)

"But Jesus said unto him, Follow me; and let the dead bury their dead." (Bible: Mat 8:22)

5. O SON OF BEING!
Love Me, that I may love thee. If thou lovest Me not, My love can in

no wise reach thee. Know this, O servant.

O SON OF BEING- This is a new title. We have had "Son of Spirit" and "Son of Man." "Being" means something that exists. Bahá'u'lláh says He joins together the letters B and E and then "it is." In the following passage, Announcer, refers to the Báb.

"Whom Thou hast appointed as the Announcer of the One through Whose name the letter B and the letter E have been joined and united," (Bahá'u'lláh: Prayers and Meditations, Page: 85)

"Shoghi Effendi, in letters written on his behalf, has explained the significance of the "letters B and E". They constitute the word "Be", which, he states, "means the creative Power of God Who through His command causes all things to come into being" and "the power of the Manifestation of God, His great spiritual creative force." The imperative "Be" in the original Arabic is the word "kun", consisting of the two letters "kaf" and "nun". They have been translated by Shoghi Effendi in the above manner. This word has been used in the Qur'án as God's bidding calling creation into being." (Aqdas: Notes, page 247)

"Verily, when He intends a thing, His command is, "Be," and it is!" (Qur'án Ya-Sin 82 (Ya-Sin)

Love Me,- Twice, Bahá'u'lláh has said that God loves us and that this is the primary reason for creation. The next reason and purpose for creation is to return that love and love Him.

"Having created the world and all that liveth and moveth therein, He, through the direct operation of His unconstrained and sovereign Will, chose to confer upon man the unique distinction and capacity to know Him and to love Him - a capacity that must needs be regarded as the generating impulse and the primary purpose underlying the whole of creation...." (Gleanings, page 65)

"I bear witness, O my God, that Thou hast created me to know Thee and to worship Thee." (Aqdas: Other Sections, page 100)

"And the scribe said unto him, Well, Master, thou hast said the truth: for there is one God; and there is none other but He: And to love Him with all the heart, and with all the understanding, and with all the soul, and with all the strength, and to love his neighbour as himself, is more than all whole burnt offerings and sacrifices." (Bible Mark 12:32 & 33)

<u>that I may love thee. If thou lovest Me not, My love can in no wise reach thee.</u>- If we want to receive the love of God, we must first open up our hearts and souls by being lovers of Him. God created us, so He surely knows how He put us together and one of the gifts that He gave us was free will to love Him if we <u>want</u> to, not because we <u>have</u> to.

Say: "If ye do love God, follow me: God will love you, and forgive you your sins, for God is Oft-Forgiving, Most Merciful." (Qur'án The Family of Imran 31 (Al-Imran))

"He that hath my commandments, and keepeth them, he it is that loveth me: and he that loveth me shall be loved of my Father, and I will love him, and will manifest myself to him." (Bible John 14:21)

"Success or failure, gain or loss, must, therefore, depend upon man's own exertions. The more he striveth, the greater will be his progress." (Gleanings, pages 81-82)

Love, to be true love, must be freely given. Since God is Single, Alone and Unknowable, it is impossible for us to love something that we can't relate to. So God created a very special creation that walks upon the earth and seems to have all the limitations of man. This Divine Being is the Manifestation and in this day it is Bahá'u'lláh, the Revealer of these Hidden Words. He shines with the Light of God and is a mirror of that glorious Essence. He speaks with the very words and authority of God.

"The substance wherewith God hath created Me is not the clay out of which others have been formed." (Shoghi Effendi, The Promised Day is Come, p. 43)

"This is why God has created me out of a clay from which no one else has been created." (Shoghi Effendi, The Dawn-Breakers)

"The Person of the Manifestation hath ever been the representative and mouthpiece of God. He, in truth, is the Day Spring of God's most excellent Titles, and the Dawning-Place of His exalted Attributes." (Gleanings, page 70)

"O mankind! the Apostle hath come to you in truth from God: believe in him: it is best for you." (Qur'án Women 170 (An-Nisa)

"For I have not spoken of myself; but the Father which sent me, he gave me a commandment, what I should say, and what I should speak. And I know that his commandment is life everlasting: whatsoever I speak therefore, even as the Father said unto me, so I speak." (Bible John 12:49 & 50)

It is Him that we can love, and it is through Him that we can send our love to that Unknowable Essence, our Creator. Another way we can love God is by loving His creation and most especially, by loving our fellow men. The Baha'is asked 'Abdu'l-Bahá how it was possible for him to love everyone so much. He said that in every face he saw his Father's face.

"He "saw the Face of His Heavenly Father in every face" and

reverenced the soul behind it." ('Abdu'l-Bahá, page 233)

Know this O servant- What do we really know? To know something is to study it, understand it and apply it to our lives. Bahá'u'lláh tells us what would happen if we really knew.

"Know ye from what heights your Lord, the All-Glorious, is calling? Think ye that ye have recognized the Pen wherewith your Lord, the Lord of all names, commandeth you? Nay, by My life! Did ye but know it, ye would renounce the world, and would hasten with your whole hearts to the presence of the Well-Beloved. Your spirits would be so transported by His Word as to throw into commotion the Greater World - how much more this small and petty one!" (The Kitab-i-Aqdas, page 39)

"Know thou that he is truly learned who hath acknowledged My Revelation, and drunk from the Ocean of My knowledge, and soared in the atmosphere of My love, and cast away all else besides Me, and taken firm hold on that which hath been sent down from the Kingdom of My wondrous utterance." (Epistle to the Son of the Wolf, page 83)

"Strive to know Him through His own Self and not through others. For no one else besides Him can ever profit thee." (Gleanings, page 148)

"Every attempt which, from the beginning that hath no beginning, hath been made to visualize and know God is limited by the exigencies of His own creation - a creation which He, through the operation of His own Will and for the purposes of none other but His own Self, hath called into being. Immeasurably exalted is He above the strivings of human mind to grasp His Essence, or of human tongue to describe His mystery." (Gleanings, page 318)

To know something is to follow the instructions given in the second Hidden Word, where Bahá'u'lláh tells us about justice.

"By its aid thou shalt see with thine own eyes and not through the eyes of others, and shalt know of thine own knowledge and not through the knowledge of thy neighbor." (Arabic Hidden Words, page 2)

Again Bahá'u'lláh calls us by our true station; that is, the station of servitude.

"That one indeed is a man who, today, dedicateth himself to the service of the entire human race." (Gleanings, page 250)

"For we, the followers of the Blessed Beauty, should all be engaged in the service of the Cause of God, and become sources of guidance to humanity." (Prominent People, page 268)

6. O SON OF BEING!
Thy Paradise is My love; thy heavenly home, reunion with Me. Enter therein and tarry not. This is that which hath been destined for thee in Our kingdom above and Our exalted Dominion.

<u>*Thy Paradise is My love;*</u>- What is paradise? Where is paradise? How do we attain paradise? Bahá'u'lláh tells us that paradise is His love. Love exsists in the heart so paradise can only be found in the heart of His lovers. To attain paradise is to open our hearts to the love of God.

"They say: `Where is Paradise, and where is Hell?' Say: `The one is reunion with Me; the other thine own self," (Epistle to the Son of the Wolf, page 132)

"Whoso hath recognized the Day Spring of Divine guidance and entered His holy court hath drawn nigh unto God and attained His

Presence, a Presence which is the real Paradise, and of which the loftiest mansions of heaven are but a symbol." (Gleanings, page 70)

The way to enter into this paradise of the love of God is to obey Him with heart and soul. This implies recognition of the Manifestation's divine authority.

"Enter, then, the holy paradise of the good-pleasure of the All-Merciful. Sanctify your souls from whatsoever is not of God, and taste ye the sweetness of rest within the pale of His vast and mighty Revelation, and beneath the shadow of His supreme and infallible authority." (Gleanings, page 143)

"As to Paradise: It is a reality and there can be no doubt about it, and now in this world it is realized through love of Me and My good-pleasure." (Tablets of Bahá'u'lláh, page 189)

"All who obey God and the Apostle are in the company of those on whom is the Grace of God, of the Prophets (who teach), the sincere (lovers of truth), the witnesses (who testify), and the righteous (who do good): ah! what a beautiful fellowship!." (Qur'án Women 69 (An-Nisa)

"Not every one that saith unto me, Lord, Lord, shall enter into the kingdom of heaven; but he that doeth the will of my Father which is in heaven." (Bible Mathew 7:21

thy heavenly home,- Home is a place of safety, security, happiness which is free from the cares and anxieties of life. It is a place of warmth and comfort. A house is where one lives, but a home is where one is loved. This, of course, is no ordinary home but it is a heavenly home.

"Wherefore, O friend, give up thy self that thou mayest find the

Peerless One, pass by this mortal earth that thou mayest seek a home in the nest of heaven." (Seven Valleys and Four Valleys, pages 9-10)

"For thus the Master of the house hath appeared within His home, and all the pillars of the dwelling are ashine with His light." (Seven Valleys and Four Valleys, page 22)

"Those who patiently persevere, seeking the countenance their Lord; establish regular prayers; spend, out of (the gifts) We have bestowed for their sustenance, secretly and openly; and turn off Evil with good: for such there is the final attainment of the (Eternal) Home." -(Qur'án The Thunder 22 (Ar-Rad)

reunion with Me.- Reunion means to be united with Bahá'u'lláh once again. This also means that we have been there before, so this heavenly home is like the Garden of Eden and God is inviting us to come home where we belong. Muhammad, when he explained man's eviction from the garden of Eden, said it was only for a time and the time is now over.

"The Garden of Eden, which the God of Mercy hath promised to his servants, though yet unseen: for his promise shall come to pass:" (Qur'án Mary 62 (Maryam)

"And the LORD God took the man, and put him into the garden of Eden to dress it and to keep it." (Bible Genesis 2:15)

"On earth will be your dwelling-place and your means of livelihood, for a time." (Qur'án The Heights 24 (Al-Araf)

"And I will give them an heart to know me, that I am the LORD: and they shall be my people, and I will be their God: for they shall return unto me with their whole heart." (Bible JER 24:7)

"Before long you will see that new bounties and divine teachings will illuminate this dark world and will transform these sad regions into the paradise of Eden." (Some Answered Questions, page 163)

"The Lord of all mankind hath fashioned this human realm to be a Garden of Eden, an earthly paradise. If, as it must, it findeth the way to harmony and peace, to love and mutual trust, it will become a true abode of bliss, a place of manifold blessings and unending delights. Therein shall be revealed the excellence of humankind, therein shall the rays of the Sun of Truth shine forth on every hand." (Selections ... 'Abdu'l-Bahá , page 275)

This also is a confirmation of the fact that we have all come from God and to Him we will return.

"Verily, we are God's, and to Him shall we return." Gleanings, page 345)

"ALL men have proceeded from God and unto Him shall all return." (Selections from the Báb page 157)

<u>*Enter therein and tarry not.*</u>- The message here is to hurry up and not to be slow. Bahá'u'lláh taught us that He is nearer to us than our own life vein and we can reach Him if we really want to, but this must be done in the realm of the spirit.

"O My servants! The one true God is My witness! This most great, this fathomless and surging Ocean is near, astonishingly near, unto you. Behold it is closer to you than your life-vein! Swift as the twinkling of an eye ye can, if ye but wish it, reach and partake of this imperishable favor, this God-given grace, this incorruptible gift, this most potent and unspeakably glorious bounty." (Gleanings, page 326)

"Take thou the step of the spirit, so that, swift as the twinkling of an eye, thou mayest flash through the wilds of remoteness and bereavement, attain the Ridván of everlasting reunion, and in one breath commune with the heavenly Spirits." (The Kitab-i-Iqan, page 43)

"A man that hath friends must shew himself friendly: and there is a friend that sticketh closer than a brother." (Bible Proverbs 18:24)

"The Prophet is closer to the Believers than their own selves," (Qur'án The Confederates 6 Al-Ahzab)

Even knowing of this nearness and even knowing how to attain to Him, the amazing thing is that we put ourselves at such a great distance from Him.

"Meditate on what the poet hath written: "Wonder not, if my Best-Beloved be closer to me than mine own self; wonder at this, that I, despite such nearness, should still be so far from Him."... Considering what God hath revealed, that "We are closer to man than his life-vein," the poet hath, in allusion to this verse, stated that, though the revelation of my Best-Beloved hath so permeated my being that He is closer to me than my life-vein, yet, notwithstanding my certitude of its reality and my recognition of my station, I am still so far removed from Him. By this he meaneth that his heart, which is the seat of the All-Merciful and the throne wherein abideth the splendor of His revelation, is forgetful of its Creator, hath strayed from His path, hath shut out itself from His glory, and is stained with the defilement of earthly desires." (Gleanings, page 185)

"It was We who created man and We know what dark suggestions his soul makes to him: for We are nearer to him than (his) jugular vein." (Qur'án Qaf 16 (Qaf)

This is that which hath been destined for thee in Our kingdom above and Our exalted Dominion - When we were created our Creator prepared for us a very wonderful spiritual destiny, and this destiny is paradise, a heavenly home and reunion with God. God's "kingdom above" and "exalted Dominion" puts it at the very highest point.

"O My servants! Sorrow not if, in these days and on this earthly plane, things contrary to your wishes have been ordained and manifested by God, for days of blissful joy, of heavenly delight, are assuredly in store for you. Worlds, holy and spiritually glorious, will be unveiled to your eyes. You are destined by Him, in this world and hereafter, to partake of their benefits, to share in their joys, and to obtain a portion of their sustaining grace." (Gleanings, page 329)

We should not only strive to achieve our destiny but should be content and happy with what happens to us in this transitory and swiftly passing world.

"Be thou satisfied with what God hath destined for thee." (Prayers and Meditations, page 11)

"High indeed is the station We have destined for thee." (Tablets of Bahá'u'lláh, page 253)

"The people of God should not be grieved. By the righteousness of God, that which is destined for them is far beyond the power of reckoners to reckon." (Huqúqu'lláh, page 501)

"Send down upon them that which will bring comfort to their minds, will rejoice their inner beings, will impart assurance to their hearts and tranquillity to their bodies and will enable their souls to ascend to the presence of God, the Most Exalted, and to attain the supreme Paradise and such retreats of glory as Thou hast destined for men of

true knowledge and virtue." (Selections from the Báb , page 179)

7. O SON OF MAN!
If thou lovest Me, turn away from thyself; and if thou seekest My pleasure, regard not thine own; that thou mayest die in Me and I may eternally live in thee.

"*If*" is that small word with a big meaning. If again implies free will. I must use that free will to turn away from my greedy and selfish self to the point where my very life and existence is moved and motivated by His Divine will and pleasure. I, me, mine, my, personal desire and will no longer even exist. Only the will and pleasure of Bahá'u'lláh would then motivate one.

"Do thou sacrifice the thing which Thou lovest most in the path of God, even as Husayn, peace be upon him, hath offered up his life for My sake." (The Kitab-i-Iqan, page 232)

"Suffer us not to rely on aught else besides Thee, and vouchsafe unto us, through Thy bounty, that which Thou lovest and desirest and well beseemeth Thee." (Selections from the Báb, page 177)

If one is to love Bahá'u'lláh, then we must show and prove our love for Him by loving creation and most especially by loving our fellow men.

"Thou canst best praise Him if thou lovest His loved ones, and dost safeguard and protect His servants from the mischief of the treacherous, that none may any longer oppress them." (Gleanings, page 234)

"Thou shalt love thy neighbour as thyself." (Bible Matthew 19:19)

We have to examine what are our pleasures? Then, what is God's pleasure for us? He has already told us where He wants us to go and that is to our heavenly home, paradise, and exalted dominion, and what he wants us to do - fill our souls with the spirit of life. Anything that I might want in comparison with what God wants for me is as different as night and day.

Let us imagine a beautiful mountain and I am at its base digging in the mud for bitter, stringy roots to eat. Someone comes along and tells me that at the top of the mountain is a banquet of all the most delicious food set on a table with flowers and a white tablecloth. Everyone is invited and it is a permanent invitation. However, my response is that I dare not go for if I leave someone else will get my root patch.

This is an example of what my pleasure is and what God's pleasure is for me. My pleasure is the bitter roots and His pleasure is the banquet on a beautiful mountain top.

To die in God and in return to live in God is better explained by Bahá'u'lláh in the following passages.

"It behoveth the people of Bahá to die to the world and all that is therein, to be so detached from all earthly things that the inmates of Paradise may inhale from their garment the sweet smelling savor of sanctity, that all the peoples of the earth may recognize in their faces the brightness of the All-Merciful, and that through them may be spread abroad the signs and tokens of God, the Almighty, the All-Wise." (Gleanings, page 100)

"I beseech Thee, O my God, by Thy Beauty that shineth forth above the horizon of eternity, a Beauty before which as soon as it revealeth itself the kingdom of beauty boweth down in worship, magnifying it in ringing tones, to grant that I may die to all that I possess and live to whatsoever belongeth unto Thee." (Prayers and Meditations, page 290)

As stated, this life God is offering us in Him, is life eternal.

"I have turned to Thee, forsaking mine own will and desire, that Thy holy will and pleasure may rule within me and direct me according to that which the pen of Thy eternal decree hath destined for me." (Bahá'í Prayers (US), page 149)

"In like manner, whosoever partook of the cup of love, obtained his portion of the ocean of eternal grace and of the showers of everlasting mercy, and entered into the life of faith - the heavenly and everlasting life." (The Kitab-i-Iqan, page 114)

The spiritual meaning of life and death seems to have little or nothing to do with physical life and death.

"By the terms "life" and "death," spoken of in the scriptures, is intended the life of faith and the death of unbelief." (The Kitab-i-Iqan, page 114)

8. O SON OF SPIRIT!
There is no peace for thee save by renouncing thyself and turning unto Me; for it behooveth thee to glory in My name, not in thine own; to put thy trust in Me and not in thyself, since I desire to be loved alone and above all that is.

<u>*There is no peace for thee save by renouncing thyself and turning unto Me:*</u> -Peace is something that all mankind wants; peace within one's heart, peace in one's family, peace in one's country and, of course, peace on earth. Peace within me requires that I give up my ego and selfishness. Peace in one's family is to think more of the family than of one's own desires. Peace in the nation requires world thought and undertakings. Peace in the world would follow.

"Thus have We illuminated the heavens of utterance with the splendours of the Sun of divine wisdom and understanding, that thy heart may find peace, that thou mayest be of those who, on the wings of certitude, have soared unto the heaven of the love of their Lord, the All-Merciful." (The Kitab-i-Iqan, page 61)

"For unto us a child is born, unto us a son is given: and the government shall be upon his shoulder: and his name shall be called Wonderful, Counsellor, The mighty God, The everlasting Father, The Prince of Peace." (Bible ISA 9:6)

"If the learned and worldly-wise men of this age were to allow mankind to inhale the fragrance of fellowship and love, every understanding heart would apprehend the meaning of true liberty, and discover the secret of undisturbed peace and absolute composure." (Tablets of Bahá'u'lláh, page 162)

"It is incumbent upon all the peoples of the world to reconcile their differences, and, with perfect unity and peace, abide beneath the shadow of the Tree of His care and loving-kindness." (Gleanings, page 6)

"Our world has entered the dark heart of an age of fundamental change beyond anything in all of its tumultuous history. Its peoples, of whatever race, nation, or religion, are being challenged to subordinate all lesser loyalties and limiting identities to their oneness as citizens of a single planetary homeland. In Bahá'u'lláh's words: "The well-being of mankind, its peace and security, are unattainable unless and until its unity is firmly established." (Aqdas: Other Sections, page 11)

"God is He, than whom there is no other god - the sovereign, the Holy

One, the Source of Peace (and Perfection). The Guardian of Faith, the Preserver of Safety, the Exalted in Might, the Irresistible, the Supreme: Glory to God! (high is He) above the partners they attribute to Him." (Qur'án The Gathering 23 Al-Hashr)

<u>for it behooveth thee to glory in My name, not in thine own;</u> -This tells us that the real glory is in the Glory of God as reflected in the human being. Whose creation is it? It is God's, of course. What name would be better for us than to be called by His Name?

"He seeth in himself neither name nor fame nor rank, but findeth his own praise in praising God. He beholdeth in his own name the name of God; to him, "all songs are from the King," and every melody from Him." (Seven Valleys and Four Valleys, page 18)

"And further We said: "We make mention of thee for the sake of God, and desire that thy name may be exalted through thy remembrance of God, the Creator of earth and of heaven." (Epistle to the Son of the Wolf, page 60)

"Cast away, in My name that transcendeth all other names, the things ye possess, and immerse yourselves in this Ocean in whose depths lay hidden the pearls of wisdom and of utterance, an ocean that surgeth in My name, the All-Merciful." (Gleanings, page 33)

This command of God to give up everything, even your life, property and name must be understood in the context of detachment. Bahá'u'lláh has said that all good things have been created for the benefit of man, but not to be attached to or worshiped.

"Should a man wish to adorn himself with the ornaments of the earth, to wear its apparels, or partake of the benefits it can bestow, no harm can befall him, if he alloweth nothing whatever to intervene between him and God, for God hath ordained every good thing, whether created in the heavens or in the earth, for such of His servants as truly believe in Him. Eat ye, O people, of the good things which God hath allowed you, and deprive not yourselves from His wondrous bounties." (Gleanings, page 276)

<u>*to put thy trust in Me and not in thyself,*</u>- To trust God is easy when everything is going the way we want it. It is much more difficult when things God has ordained for us seem to be going opposite to what we think we want. The most important aspect of this command is to know with an absolute certitude that God truly loves us. If we do know this then, and only then, can we knowingly trust God to do what is the best for us no matter how difficult it may seem.

"I implore Thee, O Thou that turnest darkness into light, and revealest Thy mysteries on the Sinai of Thy Revelation, to aid me, at all times, to put my trust in Thee, and to commit mine affairs unto Thy care. Make me, then, O my God, content with that which the finger of Thy decree hath traced, and the pen of Thy ordinance hath written." (Epistle to the Son of the Wolf, page 8)

"He that giveth up himself wholly to God, God shall, assuredly, be with him; and he that placeth his complete trust in God, God shall, verily, protect him from whatsoever may harm him, and shield him from the wickedness of every evil plotter." (Gleanings, page 233)

It is important to understand that putting our trust wholly in God means to use our intelligence and strive with heart and soul. It does not mean to sit and wait for God to guide and help me. It is only when I am in motion that God will redirect me into the right path and His way.

"Concerning the means of livelihood, thou shouldst, while placing thy whole trust in God, engage in some occupation." (Tablets of

Bahá'u'lláh, page 268)

"Then, when thou hast taken a decision, put thy trust in God. For God loves those who put their trust (in Him)." (Qur'án The Family of Imran 159 Al-Imran)

"As for God, his way is perfect; the word of the LORD is tried: he is a buckler to all them that trust in him." (Bible 2SA 22:31)

" For therefore we both labour and suffer reproach, because we trust in the living God, who is the Saviour of all men, specially of those that believe." (Bible 1TI 4:10)

"O Lord! Whether traveling or at home, and in my occupation or in my work, I place my whole trust in Thee." (Selections from the Báb, page 193)

To trust God is to obey with heart and soul the commands of Bahá'u'lláh. Then, and only then, can we secure the victory.

"Arise in His name, put your trust wholly in Him, and be assured of ultimate victory." (Compilation of Compilations Volume 2, page 207)

<u>*since I desire to be loved alone and above all that is.*</u>- *A* young woman of today when she thinks of marriage might be thinking, "Now, what can this man do for me?" "Well he is rich, good-looking, he has a good education and he will do such and such and so and so for me." This is not love but selfishness. The same thing happens with the young man. He might think, "She will cook for me, clean my house, snuggle with me and so on and so on." Again this is pure selfishness.

Now we take another woman and man and they say. "O God my God, my Beloved, my Heart's Desire! I love Thee so, I love Thee so, Beloved.

"What can I do for You? How can I serve You this day." Then Bahá'u'lláh tells us to think more of others than we think of ourselves; to be kind, to be loving, to be gentle, to be sweet, to be giving, to be forgiving, to be faithful to our spouses and to take loving care of our families. Now by loving God first and above all that is, this woman has become a princess and the man has become a prince and it all happens because they are loving God alone and above all that is. It is like a pyramid and the point at the top is the love of God and everything else fits into place underneath this. When we place anything else above the love of God the whole pyramid crumbles.

Isaiah saith: "The Lord alone shall be exalted in that Day." (Epistle to the Son of the Wolf, page 146)

"For I know that the LORD is great, and that our Lord is above all gods." (Bible PSA 135:5)

"No God is there beside Thee, Thou alone art my Beloved in this world and in the world which is to come. Thou alone art the Desire of all them that have recognized Thee." (Prayers and Meditations, page 179)

9. O SON OF BEING!
My love is My stronghold; he that entereth therein is safe and secure, and he that turneth away shall surely stray and perish.

A stronghold is like a fortress, a place to go in times of danger. This stronghold is also paradise because the sixth Hidden Word stated that "Paradise is My love" and "My love is My stronghold." Not only is it a place of safety but it is also our security. In these days everyone is worried about their security and they put away money and buy property and make investments for their security, only to have it all gone in a few seconds with an earthquake, tidal wave, fire, or flood.

"The first word which the Abhá Pen hath revealed and inscribed on the first leaf of Paradise is this: Verily I say: The fear of God hath ever been a sure defence and a safe stronghold for all the peoples of the world. It is the chief cause of the protection of mankind, and the supreme instrument for its preservation." (Epistle to the Son of the Wolf, page 27)

"Indeed His ordinances constitute the mightiest stronghold for the protection of the world and the safeguarding of its peoples . . ." (Tablets of Bahá'u'lláh, page 50)

"Wherewith God guideth all who seek His good pleasure to ways of peace and safety, and leadeth them out of darkness, by His Will, unto the light, guideth them to a Path that is Straight." (Qur'án The Table Spread 18 Al-Maidah)

"And he said, The LORD is my rock, and my fortress, and my deliverer; The God of my rock; in him will I trust: he is my shield, and the horn of my salvation, my high tower, and my refuge, my Saviour; thou savest me from violence." (Bible 2SA 22:2)

The alternative that Bahá'u'lláh gives us to entering His stronghold is to stray and perish. Stray means to lose our way and perish means to rot and disintegrate.

"The days of your life shall roll away, and all the things with which ye are occupied and of which ye boast yourselves shall perish, and ye shall, most certainly, be summoned by a company of His angels to appear at the spot where the limbs of the entire creation shall be made to tremble, and the flesh of every oppressor to creep." (Gleanings, page 125)

"And call not, besides God, on another god. There is no god but He. Everything (that exists) will perish except His own Face. To him belongs the Command, and to him will ye (all) be brought back." (Qur'án The Narrations 88 Al-Qasas)

"For the LORD knoweth the way of the righteous: but the way of the ungodly shall perish." (Bible PSA 1:6)

"In all these journeys the traveler must stray not the breadth of a hair from the "Law," for this is indeed the secret of the "Path" and the fruit of the Tree of "Truth"; and in all these stages he must cling to the robe of obedience to the commandments, and hold fast to the cord of shunning all forbidden things, that he may be nourished from the cup of the Law and informed of the mysteries of Truth." (Seven Valleys and Four Valleys, pages 39-40)

"Say: O ye that have strayed and lost your way! The Divine Messenger, Who speaketh naught but the truth, hath announced unto you the coming of the Best-Beloved. Behold, He is now come." (Gleanings, page 168)

10. O SON OF UTTERANCE!
Thou art My stronghold; enter therein that thou mayest abide in safety. My love is in thee, know it, that thou mayest find Me near unto thee.

O SON OF UTTERANCE! -This is a new title and follows the ninth Hidden Word. Nine in numerology means unity and so we have completed one unit of the Hidden Words. To utter is to speak and Bahá'u'lláh is the voice of God to humankind. A son would speak what his father would speak.

"To read but one of the verses of My Revelation is better than to peruse the Scriptures of both the former and latter generations. This is the Utterance of the All-Merciful, would that ye had ears to hear!" (The Kitab-i-Aqdas, page 69)

"This is the Counsel of God; would that thou mightest heed it! This is the Bounty of God; would that thou mightest receive it! This is the Utterance of God; if only thou wouldst apprehend it! This is the Treasure of God; if only thou couldst understand!" (The Kitab-i-Aqdas, page 87)

"The Lord GOD hath given me the tongue of the learned, that I should know how to speak a word in season to him that is weary: he wakeneth morning by morning, he wakeneth mine ear to hear as the learned." (Bible ISA 50:4)

This seems to mean a follower of Bahá'u'lláh. A Bahá'í who obeys the teachings of Bahá'u'lláh must be the stronghold for all mankind. Also, referring back to the sixth and ninth Hidden Words, it would seem that a follower would also be His love and His paradise.

"Unsheathe the sword of your tongue from the scabbard of utterance, for therewith ye can conquer the citadels of men's hearts." (Epistle to the Son of the Wolf, page 25)

"Be patient under all conditions, and place your whole trust and confidence in God. Aid ye your Lord with the sword of wisdom and of utterance. This indeed well becometh the station of man." (Gleanings, page 296)

As our Creator, He created us and he put His love within our proper selves. Here again action is needed to reach within ourselves and find this love and in turn find Bahá'u'lláh in our own hearts. Once again we are advised to know and to know with a true knowledge.

"The first Taraz and the first effulgence which hath dawned from the horizon of the Mother Book is that man should know his own self and recognize that which leadeth unto loftiness or lowliness, glory or abasement, wealth or poverty." (Tablets of Bahá'u'lláh, pages 34-35)

"That thou mightest know the certainty of those things, wherein thou hast been instructed." (Bible LUK 1:4)

"We ask thee to reflect upon that which hath been revealed, and to be fair and just in thy speech, that perchance the splendors of the day-star of truthfulness and sincerity may shine forth, and may deliver thee from the darkness of ignorance, and illumine the world with the light of knowledge." (Epistle to the Son of the Wolf, page 11)

11. O SON OF BEING!
Thou art My lamp and My light is in thee. Get thou from it thy radiance and seek none other than Me. For I have created thee rich and have bountifully shed My favor upon thee.

Thou art My lamp and My light is in thee. -The purpose of a lamp is to give light. You can have the most beautiful lamp in the world, but it is useless unless it gives light. As Bahá'u'lláh said it is His light that is in us and that light is His love.

"For example, look at this lamp: is not the light within it superior to the lamp which holds it? However beautiful the form of the lamp may be, if the light is not there its purpose is unfulfilled, it is without life - a dead thing. The lamp needs the light, but the light does not need the lamp." ('Abdu'l-Bahá: Paris Talks*, Page: 86)

"The utterance of God is a lamp, whose light are these words: Ye are the fruits of one tree, and the leaves of one branch. Deal ye one with another with the utmost love and harmony, with friendliness and fellowship. He Who is the Day-Star of Truth beareth Me witness! So powerful is the light of unity that it can illuminate the whole earth. The One true God, He Who knoweth all things, Himself testifieth to the truth of these words." (Bahá'u'lláh : Epistle to the Son of the Wolf, Page: 14)

"Deprive not yourselves of the unfading and resplendent Light that shineth within the Lamp of Divine glory." (Gleanings, page 325)

"In brief, let each one of you be as a lamp shining forth with the light of the virtues of the world of humanity. Be trustworthy, sincere, affectionate and replete with chastity. Be illumined, be spiritual, be divine, be glorious, be quickened of God, be a Bahá'í." ('Abdu'l-Bahá : Promulgation of Universal Peace*, Page: 453)

"For thou art my lamp, O LORD: and the LORD will lighten my darkness." (Bible 2SA 22:29)

"Thy word is a lamp unto my feet, and a light unto my path." (Bible PSA 119:105)

"For the commandment is a lamp; and the law is light; and reproofs of instruction are the way of life:" (Bible PRO 6:23)

"God is the Light of the heavens and the earth. The parable of His Light is as if there were a Niche and within it a lamp: the Lamp enclosed in Glass: the glass as it were a brilliant star: lit from a blessed Tree, an Olive, neither of the East nor of the West, whose Oil is well-nigh luminous, though fire scarce touched it: Light upon Light! God doth guide whom He will to His Light. God doth set forth Parables for men: and God doth know all things." (Qur'án The Light 35 An-Nur)

Get thou from it thy radiance and seek none other than Me.- *We* will get this radiance within our own hearts as that is where the love of God is to be found.

"Let the flame of the love of God burn brightly within your radiant hearts. Feed it with the oil of Divine guidance, and protect it within the shelter of your constancy." (Gleanings, page 325)

In order to get the light, even with the lamp, the light bulb and the connection, one must still turn on the switch to get any radiance. We turn on our switch by trying to obey the commands of God.

"Know assuredly that My commandments are the lamps of My loving providence among My servants, and the keys of My mercy for My creatures." (Gleanings, page 332)

"The sincere among His servants will regard the precepts set forth by God as the Water of Life to the followers of every faith, and the Lamp of wisdom and loving providence to all the denizens of earth and heaven." (The Kitab-i-Aqdas, page 29)

Also there is a warning not to go looking for another light when the sun of Bahá'u'lláh has come up.

"At this hour the morn of knowledge hath arisen and the lamps of wayfaring and wandering are quenched." (Seven Valleys and Four Valleys, page 16)

Radiance is not just light. For example, the radiance of the sun is heat, light, gamma rays, beta rays, ultra violet light rays, etc. For us to get God's radiance that He has placed within the human heart, that heart must reflect in all its glory all the divine attributes of God as revealed to us by His Manifestation.

"In the Name of God, the Compassionate, the Merciful
1. BY the heaven, and by the NIGHT-COMER!
2. But who shall teach thee what the night-comer is?
3. 'Tis the star of piercing radiance." (Qur'án SURA The Morning Star 86 At-Tariq)

"But when the stunning trumpet-blast shall arrive. There shall be faces on that day radiant Laughing and joyous:" (Qur'án He Frowned 33 Abasa)

"The Sun of Divine Utterance can never set, neither can its radiance be extinguished. These sublime words have, in this day, been heard from the Lote-Tree beyond which there is no passing: `I belong to him that loveth Me, that holdeth fast My commandments, and casteth away the things forbidden him in My Book." (Bahá'u'lláh: Epistle to the Son of the Wolf, Page: 25)

"Upon the reality of man, however, He hath focused the radiance of all of His names and attributes, and made it a mirror of His own Self. Alone of all created things man hath been singled out for so great a favor, so enduring a bounty." (Bahá'u'lláh: Gleanings, Page: 65)

"Indeed every light is generated by God through the power of His behest. He of a truth is the Light in the kingdom of heaven and earth and whatever is between them. Through the radiance of His light God imparteth illumination to your hearts and maketh firm your steps, that perchance ye may yield praise unto Him." (Selections from the Báb, Pages: 154-155)

".....not until the heart is purified, will the radiance of the Sun of Truth shine therein." ('Abdu'l-Bahá: Bahá'í World Faith*, Page: 362)

"Illumine my face with the radiance of the orb of Thy bounty, and graciously aid me in ministering at Thy holy threshold." ('Abdu'l-Bahá: Bahá'í Prayers (US edition), Page: 30)

<u>*For I have created thee rich and have bountifully shed My favor upon thee.*</u>- The riches which Bahá'u'lláh refers to cannot be the riches of the world because when we come into this world we don't even own one piece of clothing. These are spiritual riches and the human soul. What favor is more bountiful than the gift of the human soul? Without it we would just be another animal.

"The essence of wealth is love for Me; whoso loveth Me is the possessor of all things, and he that loveth Me not is indeed of the poor and needy. This is that which the Finger of Glory and Splendour hath revealed." (Tablets of Bahá'u'lláh, Page: 156)

"By `riches' therefore is meant independence of all else but God, and by `poverty' the lack of things that are of God." (Bahá'u'lláh: The Kitab-i-Iqan, Page: 132)

"The soul of man is the sun by which his body is illumined, and from which it draweth its sustenance, and should be so regarded." (Gleanings, page 155)

"Thou hast asked Me concerning the nature of the soul. Know, verily, that the soul is a sign of God, a heavenly gem whose reality the most learned of men hath failed to grasp, and whose mystery no mind, however acute, can ever hope to unravel. It is the first among all created things to declare the excellence of its Creator, the first to recognize His glory, to cleave to His truth, and to bow down in adoration before Him." (Gleanings, pages 158-159)

This favor is life and the whole of creation; te sun that shines, the rain that falls and the very air we breathe.

"Gentle zephyrs are set in motion, wafting and fragrant; flowers bloom; the trees are in blossom, the air temperate and delightful; how pleasant and beautiful become the mountains, fields and meadows." (Promulgation of Universal Peace*, page 38)

"The Sun of Reality dawned, the cloud of mercy poured down its rain, the breezes of providence moved, the world became a new world, mankind reflected an extraordinary radiance, souls were educated, minds were developed, intelligence became acute, and the human world attained a new freshness of life, like unto the advent of spring." ('Abdu'l-Bahá: Promulgation of Universal Peace*, Pages: 54-55)

12. O SON OF BEING!
With the hands of power I made thee and with the fingers of strength I created thee; and within thee have I placed the essence of My light. Be thou content with it and seek naught else, for My work is perfect and My command is binding. Question it not, nor have a doubt thereof.

Power is like a king. He has power although he may not be very strong. The real power is the power of God.

"Think not that We have revealed unto you a mere code of laws. Nay, rather, We have unsealed the choice Wine with the fingers of might and power." (The Kitab-i-Aqdas, page 21)

"God, verily, enricheth whomsoever He willeth through both heavenly and earthly means, and He, in truth, hath power over all things." (The Kitab-i-Aqdas, page 42)

"All life is of Thee, and all power lieth within the grasp of Thine omnipotence." **(Epistle to the Son of the Wolf, page 9)**

"The lamp is Thine, and the glass is Thine, and all things in the heavens and on earth are in the grasp of Thy power." (Epistle to the Son of the Wolf, page 104)

"A wise man is strong; yea, a man of knowledge increaseth strength." (Bible PRO 24:5)

If a king is strong it is in the strength of his army and the strength of others. Strength is usually referred to as physical strength. This is like a potter's wheel on which the clay is shaped with a very strong and steady hand and then the detail is added with the fingers.

"Behold the Lord God will come with strong hand, and His arm shall rule for Him." (Proclamation of Bahá'u'lláh, page 90)

Before He said that His light was within us and now He says that the very essence of His light is within us. Essence is the most basic and fundamental part of a thing and in this case it could be the essence of love.

"The essence of love is for man to turn his heart to the Beloved One, and sever himself from all else but Him, and desire naught save that which is the desire of his Lord." (Tablets of Bahá'u'lláh, page 155)

Light has also been likened to knowledge. From the knowledge of God comes all knowledge.

"The source of all learning is the knowledge of God, exalted be His Glory, and this cannot be attained save through the knowledge of His Divine Manifestation." (Tablets of Bahá'u'lláh, page 156)

**"The Essence of knowledge exclaimeth and saith: Lo! He Who is the

Object of all knowledge is come and through His advent the sacred Books of God, the Gracious, the Loving, have been embellished." (Tablets of Bahá'u'lláh, page 245)

"To read but one of the verses of My Revelation is better than to peruse the Scriptures of both the former and latter generations. This is the Utterance of the All-Merciful, would that ye had ears to hear! Say: This is the essence of knowledge, did ye but understand." (Bahá'u'lláh: The Kitab-i-Aqdas, Page: 69)

"The source of all learning is the knowledge of God, exalted be His Glory, and this cannot be attained save through the knowledge of His Divine Manifestation." (Bahá'u'lláh: Tablets of Bahá'u'lláh, Page: 156)

"It is He who hath created for you all things that are on earth; moreover His design comprehended the heavens, for He gave order and perfection to the seven firmaments; and of all things he hath perfect knowledge." (Qur'án The Cow 29 Al-Baqarah)

"According as his divine power hath given unto us all things that pertain unto life and godliness, through the knowledge of him that hath called us to glory and virtue:" (Bible 2PE 1:3)

Bahá'u'lláh then tells us to be content because we are made with power and strength and the essence of light is created in us. He assures us that we are perfectly created the way God wanted us to be and He is All Knowing and All Wise.

"The source of all good is trust in God, submission unto His command, and contentment with His holy will and pleasure." (Bahá'u'lláh: Tablets of Bahá'u'lláh, Page: 155)

"The source of all glory is acceptance of whatsoever the Lord hath bestowed, and contentment with that which God hath ordained." (Bahá'u'lláh: Tablets of Bahá'u'lláh, Page: 155)

"So perfect and comprehensive is His creation that no mind nor heart, however keen or pure, can ever grasp the nature of the most insignificant of His creatures; much less fathom the mystery of Him Who is the Day Star of Truth, Who is the invisible and unknowable Essence." (Gleanings, page 62)

"Man, the noblest and most perfect of all created things, excelleth them all in the intensity of this revelation, and is a fuller expression of its glory." (Gleanings, page 179)

Although His work is perfect, we mess it up. What we do with His perfect creation is pretty bad.

"Regard the world as the human body which, though at its creation whole and perfect, hath been afflicted, through various causes, with grave disorders and maladies." (Epistle to the Son of the Wolf, page 62)

Then Bahá'u'lláh says that His work is not only perfect but His commands are binding. This means two things; first, we should be content with God's will, and second, we should obey His commands. Then we must not question the whys and wherefores of God nor have any doubts about what He is doing or what He has done.

"In all these journeys the traveler must stray not the breadth of a hair from the "Law," for this is indeed the secret of the "Path" and the fruit of the Tree of "Truth"; and in all these stages he must cling to the robe of obedience to the commandments, and hold fast to the cord of shunning all forbidden things, that he may be nourished from the cup of the Law and informed of the mysteries of Truth." (Seven Valleys and Four Valleys, pages 39-40)

"The Prophets of God should be regarded as physicians whose task is to foster the well-being of the world and its peoples, that, through the spirit of oneness, they may heal the sickness of a divided humanity. To none is given the right to question their words or disparage their conduct, for they are the only ones who can claim to have understood the patient and to have correctly diagnosed its ailments." (Gleanings, page 80)

"He chooseth; and none may question His choice. Whatsoever He, the Well-Beloved, ordaineth, the same is, verily, beloved." (Gleanings, page 333)

"He who obeys the Apostle, obeys God:" (Qur'án Women 80 An-Nisa)

"A blessing, if ye obey the commandments of the LORD your God, which I command you this day:" (Bible DEU 11:27

"Obey my voice, and do them, according to all which I command you: so shall ye be my people, and I will be your God:" (Bible JER 11:3)

13. O SON OF SPIRIT!
I created thee rich, why dost thou bring thyself down to poverty? Noble I made thee, wherewith dost thou abase thyself? Out of the essence of knowledge I gave thee being, why seekest thou enlightenment from anyone beside Me? Out of the clay of love I molded thee, how dost thou busy thyself with another? Turn thy sight unto thyself, that thou mayest find Me standing within thee, mighty, powerful and self-subsisting.

It seems that Bahá'u'lláh is asking us to question ourselves as to why we do the things we shouldn't and don't do the things we should.

"Should God punish men for their perverse doings, He would not leave on earth a moving thing!" (Seven Valleys and Four Valleys, page 21)

I created thee rich, why dost thou bring thyself down to poverty? -As pointed out before, this richness is spiritual richness and it then follows that the poverty is spiritual poverty.

"Having acknowledged my poverty, and recognized Thy wealth, suffer me not to be deprived of the glory of Thy riches." (Gleanings, page 134)

"By `riches' therefore is meant independence of all else but God, and by `poverty' the lack of things that are of God." (The Kitab-i-Iqan, page 132)

Noble I made thee, wherewith dost thou abase thyself? - A noble man is a truly humble man, not proud or arrogant. The word noble in my mind conjures up a true human being not one that is animalistic.

"Man, the noblest and most perfect of all created things, excelleth them all in the intensity of this revelation, and is a fuller expression of its glory. And of all men, the most accomplished, the most distinguished, and the most excellent are the Manifestations of the Sun of Truth." (Gleanings, page 179)

Man abases himself with alcohol, drugs and all forms of disobedience to the commands of a loving Creator.

"Say: Honesty, virtue, wisdom and a saintly character redound to the exaltation of man, while dishonesty, imposture, ignorance and hypocrisy lead to his abasement." (Tablets of Bahá'u'lláh, page 57)

"We cherish the hope that the Hand of Divine power may lend its assistance to mankind, and deliver it from its state of grievous abasement." (Gleanings, page 93)

"In the name of God, Most Gracious, Most Merciful. We have indeed created man in the best of molds, Then do We abase him (to be) the lowest of the low, Except such as believe and do righteous deeds: for they shall have a reward unfailing." (Qur'án The Fig 4-6 At-Tin)

"Yet I had planted thee a noble vine, wholly a right seed: how then art thou turned into the degenerate plant of a strange vine unto me?" (Bible JER 2:21)

<u>*Out of the essence of knowledge I gave thee being,*</u> -Once again Bahá'u'lláh turns us towards individual investigation of the truth. From the knowledge of God comes all knowledge.

"For the Word of God is collective wisdom, absolute knowledge and eternal truth." (Promulgation of Universal Peace*, page 154)

"This is the Utterance of the All-Merciful, would that ye had ears to hear! Say: This is the essence of knowledge, did ye but understand." (Bahá'u'lláh: The Kitab-i-Aqdas, Page: 69)

"This is the Day in which the Ocean of knowledge hath lifted up its Voice and hath brought forth its pearls. Would that ye knew it! The heaven of the Bayan hath been raised up in truth at the behest of God, the Help in Peril, the Self-Subsisting. I swear by God! The Essence of knowledge exclaimeth and saith: Lo! He Who is the Object of all knowledge is come and through His advent the sacred Books of God, the Gracious, the Loving, have been embellished." (Tablets of Bahá'u'lláh, Page: 245)

"The beginning of all things is the knowledge of God, and the end of all things is strict observance of whatsoever hath been sent down from the empyrean of the Divine Will that pervadeth all that is in the heavens and all that is on the earth." (Bahá'u'lláh: Gleanings, Page: 5)

<u>*why seekest thou enlightenment from anyone beside Me?*</u> -

"Is it not astonishing that although man has been created for the knowledge and love of God, for the virtues of the human world, for spirituality, heavenly illumination and eternal life, nevertheless, he continues ignorant and negligent of all this? Consider how he seeks knowledge of everything except knowledge of God." (Promulgation of Universal Peace*, pages 226-227)

".... that which is the cause of everlasting life, eternal honor, universal enlightenment, real salvation and prosperity is, first of all, the knowledge of God. It is known that the knowledge of God is beyond all knowledge, and it is the greatest glory of the human world." ('Abdu'l-Bahá: Some Answered Questions, Page: 300)

"Yet there is among men such a one as disputes about God, without knowledge, without guidance, and without a Book of Enlightenment" (Qur'án The Pilgrimage 8 Al-Hajj)

"The statutes of the LORD are right, rejoicing the heart: the commandment of the LORD is pure, enlightening the eyes." (Bible PSA 19:8)

Out of the clay of love I molded thee, -The reality of man is not molded out of water and earth. He was molded out of the clay of love. We were made to be lovers, why don't we just be ourselves?

"Methinks they have been moulded from the clay of infinite knowledge, and kneaded with the water of divine wisdom." (The Kitab-i-Iqan, page 46)

"I know not what the water is with which Thou hast created me, or what the fire Thou hast kindled within me, or the clay wherewith Thou hast kneaded me." (Prayers and Meditations, page 12)

"And the LORD God formed man of the dust of the ground, and breathed into his nostrils the breath of life; and man became a living soul." (Bible GEN 2:7)

"Behold! thy Lord said to the angels: "I am about to create man, from sounding clay, from mud molded into shape;   "When I have fashioned him (in due proportion) and breathed into him of My spirit, fall ye down in obeisance unto him."   So the angels prostrated themselves all of them together:" (Qur'án The Rocky Tract 28-30 Al-Hijr)

how dost thou busy thyself with another? -We will all live and we will all die and no one can escape. We should not busy ourselves with anyone else except Bahá'u'lláh, not even our own concerns.

 "Hasten ye then (at once) to God: I am from Him a warner to you, clear and open!   And make not another an object of worship with God: I am from Him a Warner to you, clear and open!" (Qur'án The Winds 50-51 Adh-Dhariyat)

"And it shall be, if thou do at all forget the LORD thy God, and walk after other gods, and serve them, and worship them, I testify against you this day that ye shall surely perish." (Bible DEU 8:19)

"And Jesus answered and said unto him, Get thee behind me, Satan: for it is written, Thou shalt worship the Lord thy God, and him only shalt thou serve." (Bible Luk 4:8)

"In one of the Tablets these words have been revealed: O people of God! Do not busy yourselves in your own concerns; let your thoughts be fixed upon that which will rehabilitate the fortunes of mankind and sanctify the hearts and souls of men. This can best be achieved through pure and holy deeds, through a virtuous life and a goodly behavior. Valiant acts will ensure the triumph of this Cause, and a saintly character will reinforce its power. Cleave unto righteousness, O people of Bahá! This, verily, is the commandment which this wronged One hath given unto you, and the first choice of His unrestrained Will for every one of you." (Bahá'u'lláh: Gleanings, Pages: 93-94)

"The days of your life shall roll away, and all the things with which ye are occupied and of which ye boast yourselves shall perish, and ye shall, most certainly, be summoned by a company of His angels to appear at the spot where the limbs of the entire creation shall be made to tremble, and the flesh of every oppressor to creep." (Gleanings, page 125)

"Night hath succeeded day, and day hath succeeded night, and the hours and moments of your lives have come and gone, and yet none of you hath, for one instant, consented to detach himself from that which perisheth. Bestir yourselves, that the brief moments that are still yours may not be dissipated and lost. Even as the swiftness of lightning your days shall pass, and your bodies shall be laid to rest beneath a canopy of dust. What can ye then achieve? How can ye atone for your past failure." (Bahá'u'lláh: Gleanings, Page: 321)

Turn thy sight unto thyself, -We are commanded to know ourselves and this is a step in the knowledge of God.

"These sublime words were heard today from the rustling of the divine Lote-Tree which the Lord of Names hath, with the hand of celestial power, planted in the All-Highest Paradise: The first Taraz and the first effulgence which hath dawned from the horizon of the Mother Book is that man should know his own self and recognize that which leadeth unto loftiness or lowliness, glory or abasement, wealth or poverty." (Tablets of Bahá'u'lláh, pages 34-35)

that thou mayest find Me standing within thee, mighty, powerful and self-subsisting.- I have been to some of the very remote areas of the earth and have found man searching for his Creator from mountain tops to the deserts, in churches, mosques, temples, shrines and synagogues. Where we should be looking is within, not without. He said, "you will find me standing <u>within</u> thee, mighty, powerful and self subsisting."

"Whensoever the light of Manifestation of the King of Oneness settleth upon the throne of the heart and soul, His shining becometh visible in every limb and member." (Seven Valleys and Four Valleys, page 22)

We must be careful to understand that it is not God, the Unknowable Essence, that enters through the door of His love into the human heart, but it is the love of Bahá'u'lláh.

"For God is, in His Essence, holy above ascent and descent, entrance and exit; He hath through all eternity been free of the attributes of human creatures, and ever will remain so." (Bahá'u'lláh: Seven Valleys and Four Valleys, Pages: 22-23)

"Yea, these mentionings that have been made of the grades of knowledge relate to the knowledge of the Manifestations of that Sun of Reality, which casteth Its light upon the Mirrors." (Seven Valleys and Four Valleys, page 23)

"To every discerning and illuminated heart it is evident that God, the unknowable Essence, the Divine Being, is immensely exalted beyond every human attribute, such as corporeal existence, ascent and descent, egress and regress. Far be it from His glory that human tongue should adequately recount His praise, or that human heart comprehend His fathomless mystery. He is, and hath ever been, veiled in the ancient eternity of His Essence, and will remain in His Reality everlastingly hidden from the sight of men. "No vision taketh in Him, but He taketh in all vision; He is the Subtile, the All-Perceiving."...

The door of the knowledge of the Ancient of Days being thus closed in the face of all beings, the Source of infinite grace, according to His saying, "His grace hath transcended all things; My grace hath encompassed them all," hath caused those luminous Gems of Holiness to appear out of the realm of the spirit, in the noble form of the human temple, and be made manifest unto all men, that they may impart unto the world the mysteries of the unchangeable Being, and tell of the subtleties of His imperishable Essence.

These sanctified Mirrors, these Day Springs of ancient glory, are, one and all, the Exponents on earth of Him Who is the central Orb of the universe, its Essence and ultimate Purpose. From Him proceed their knowledge and power; from Him is derived their sovereignty. The beauty of their countenance is but a reflection of His image, and their revelation a sign of His deathless glory. They are the Treasuries of Divine knowledge, and the Repositories of celestial wisdom. Through them is transmitted a grace that is infinite, and by them is revealed the Light that can never fade.... These Tabernacles of Holiness, these Primal Mirrors which reflect the light of unfading glory, are but expressions of Him Who is the Invisible of the Invisibles." (Bahá'u'lláh: Gleanings, Pages: 46-48)

"But if I do, though ye believe not me, believe the works: that ye may know, and believe, that the Father is in me, and I in him." (Bible JOH 10:38)

"Muhammad is not the father of any of your men, but (he is) the Apostle of God, and the Seal of the Prophets: and God has full knowledge of all things." (Qur'án The Confederates 40 Al-Ahzab)

14. O SON OF MAN!
Thou art My dominion and My dominion perisheth not, wherefore fearest thou thy perishing? Thou art My light and My light shall never be extinguished, why dost thou dread extinction? Thou art My glory and My glory fadeth not; thou art My robe and My robe shall never be outworn. Abide then in thy love for Me, that thou mayest find Me in the realm of glory.

Thou art My dominion and My dominion perisheth not,- What is a dominion? From the previous Hidden Words it must be paradise, God's love, heavenly home and a safe and secure stronghold. Dominion also means a land that is ruled over by the King. In this case the land of the spirit is ruled over by God. This is another way of also saying that we belong to God.

"Dominion is God's, the Lord of the seen and the unseen, the Lord of creation". (The Kitab-i-Aqdas, page 23)

This Dominion of God is explained by Bahá'u'lláh in the following verse:

"Thus Jesus, Son of Mary, whilst seated one day and speaking in the strain of the Holy Spirit, uttered words such as these: "O people! My food is the grass of the field, wherewith I satisfy my hunger. My bed is the dust, my lamp in the night the light of the moon, and my steed my own feet. Behold, who on earth is richer than I?" By the righteousness of God! Thousands of treasures circle round this poverty, and a myriad kingdoms of glory yearn for such abasement! Shouldst thou attain to a drop of the ocean of the inner meaning of these words, thou wouldst surely forsake the world and all that is therein, and, as the Phoenix wouldst consume thyself in the flames of the undying Fire." (Bahá'u'lláh: The Kitab-i-Iqan, Pages: 130-131)

"Were ye to obey the Remembrance of God with absolute sincerity, We guarantee, by the leave of God, that on the Day of Resurrection, a vast dominion shall be yours in His eternal Paradise." (The Báb: Selections from the Báb, Page: 43)

The reason that we fear perishing is because we don't want to abandon our selfish desires for the desire of God.

"Abandon not the incorruptible benefits, and be not content with that which perisheth." (Gleanings, page 320)

"The essence of these words is this: they that tread the path of faith, they that thirst for the wine of certitude, must cleanse themselves of all that is earthly - their ears from idle talk, their minds from vain imaginings, their hearts from worldly affections, their eyes from that which perisheth. They should put their trust in God, and, holding fast unto Him, follow in His way." (The Kitab-i-Iqan, page 3)

Thou art My light and My light shall never be extinguished, why dost thou dread extinction?- Previously, Bahá'u'lláh said that we were His lamp and His light was within us. Then He stated that He placed within us the very essence of light. Now He assures us, if that lamp is lit and that light is kindled, it can never be put out.

"So much so that Pharaoh and his people finally arose and exerted their utmost endeavor to extinguish with the waters of falsehood and denial the fire of that sacred Tree, oblivious of the truth that no earthly water can quench the flame of divine wisdom, nor mortal blasts extinguish the lamp of everlasting dominion." (The Kitab-i-Iqan, page 11)

It is from the grace, love and mercy of God that we are saved from extinction.

"All praise to the unity of God, and all honor to Him, the sovereign Lord, the incomparable and all-glorious Ruler of the universe, Who, out of utter nothingness, hath created the reality of all things, Who, from naught, hath brought into being the most refined and subtle elements of His creation, and Who, rescuing His creatures from the abasement of remoteness and the perils of ultimate extinction, hath received them into His kingdom of incorruptible glory. Nothing short of His all-encompassing grace, His all-pervading mercy, could have possibly achieved it." (Gleanings, pages 64-65)

<u>**Thou art My glory and My glory fadeth not;**</u> - It is very difficult to try to comprehend how an insignificant creature such as man could be considered to be His dominion, light and glory. Does this only refer to the man who has studied, understood and applied the first thirteen Hidden Words to his life?

"Happy are ye, O ye the learned ones in Bahá. By the Lord! Ye are the billows of the Most Mighty Ocean, the stars of the firmament of Glory, the standards of triumph waving betwixt earth and heaven." (The Kitab-i-Aqdas, page 82)

"May the spirit and glory rest upon thee, and upon those who dwell upon the plain of holiness and who remain in the Cause of their Lord in manifest steadfastness!" (Bahá'í World Faith, page 207)

This glory that God has willed for us is a reflection of the glory of the Manifestation.

"From among all created things He hath singled out for His special favor the pure, the gem-like reality of man, and invested it with a unique capacity of knowing Him and of reflecting the greatness of His glory." (Gleanings, page 77)

"Every one of them is a mirror of God, reflecting naught else but His Self, His Beauty, His Might and Glory, if ye will understand. All else besides them are to be regarded as mirrors capable of reflecting the glory of these Manifestations Who are themselves the Primary Mirrors of the Divine Being, if ye be not devoid of understanding." (Gleanings, page 74)

"Upon the inmost reality of each and every created thing He hath shed the light of one of His names, and made it a recipient of the glory of one of His attributes. Upon the reality of man, however, He hath focused the radiance of all of His names and attributes, and made it a mirror of His own Self. Alone of all created things man hath been singled out for so great a favor, so enduring a bounty." (Bahá'u'lláh: Gleanings, Page: 65)

"O friends! Be not careless of the virtues with which ye have been endowed, neither be neglectful of your high destiny. Suffer not your labors to be wasted through the vain imaginations which certain hearts have devised. Ye are the stars of the heaven of understanding, the breeze that stirreth at the break of day, the soft-flowing waters upon which must depend the very life of all men, the letters inscribed upon His sacred scroll." (Bahá'u'lláh: Gleanings, Page: 196)

"Your behavior towards your neighbor should be such as to manifest clearly the signs of the one true God, for ye are the first among men to be re-created by His Spirit, the first to adore and bow the knee before Him, the first to circle round His throne of glory." (Bahá'u'lláh: Gleanings, Pages: 316-317)

thou art My robe and My robe shall never be outworn. -The robe is the covering or clothes and very near to the person. Bahá'u'lláh explains that His robe is the robe of virtue, the robe of sanctity.

"And when he determineth to leave his home, for the sake of the Cause of his Lord, let him put his whole trust in God, as the best provision for his journey, and array himself with the robe of virtue." (Gleanings, pages 334-335)

"A drop of the billowing ocean of His endless mercy hath adorned all creation with the ornament of existence, and a breath wafted from His peerless Paradise hath invested all beings with the robe of His sanctity and glory." (Gleanings, page 61)

Again Bahá'u'lláh gives us the definition of His robe when He tells us that it is to know Him and love Him. This robe is also eternal once we have put it on.

"All praise and glory be to God Who, through the power of His might, hath delivered His creation from the nakedness of non-existence, and clothed it with the mantle of life. From among all created things He hath singled out for His special favor the pure, the gem-like reality of man, and invested it with a unique capacity of knowing Him and of reflecting the greatness of His glory. This twofold distinction conferred upon him hath cleansed away from his heart the rust of every vain desire, and made him worthy of the vesture with which his

Creator hath deigned to clothe him. It hath served to rescue his soul from the wretchedness of ignorance.
This robe with which the body and soul of man hath been adorned is the very foundation of his well-being and development." (Gleanings, pages 77-78)

"I put on righteousness, and it clothed me: my judgment was as a robe and a diadem." (Bible JOB 29:14)

Say: "Verily my Lord doth cast the (mantle of) Truth (over His servants) - He that has full knowledge of (all) that is hidden." (Qur'án Sheba 48 Saba)

<u>*Abide then in thy love for Me, that thou mayest find Me in the realm of glory.*</u> - Once we reach this place, then He cautions us to stay there. This again denotes free will, meaning that I can still stray and perish if I want to. This means not to just say, "I believe," but to incorporate the divine teachings into one's life.

"For were men to abide by and observe the divine teachings, every trace of evil would be banished from the face of the earth." (Tablets of Bahá'u'lláh, page 176)

"Then shall the spirit of faith, through the grace of the Merciful, be breathed into thy being, and thou shalt be established and abide upon the seat of certitude." (Bahá'u'lláh: The Kitab-i-Iqan, Page: 236)

"Thus is it ordained by God, and God is All-Knowing, Most Forbearing. Those are limits set by God: those who obey God and His Apostle will be admitted to Gardens with rivers flowing beneath, to abide therein (for ever) and that will be the Supreme achievement." (Qur'án Women 13 An-Nisa)

"I am come a light into the world, that whosoever believeth on me should not abide in darkness." (Bible JOH 12:46)

15. O SON OF UTTERANCE!
Turn thy face unto Mine and renounce all save Me; for My sovereignty endureth and My dominion perisheth not. If thou seekest another than Me, yea, if thou searchest the universe for evermore, thy quest will be in vain.

As stated before, the son of utterance could mean the one who knows the teachings and is a teacher for Bahá'u'lláh.

"Whoso ariseth among you to teach the Cause of his Lord, let him, before all else, teach his own self, that his speech may attract the hearts of them that hear him." (Gleanings, page 277)

'Teach thou the Cause of God with an utterance which will cause the bushes to be enkindled, and the call `Verily, there is no God but Me, the Almighty, the Unconstrained' to be raised therefrom. Say: Human utterance is an essence which aspireth to exert its influence and needeth moderation." (Tablets of Bahá'u'lláh, page 143)

<u>Turn thy face unto Mine and renounce all save Me.</u> - Turn means for one to change direction; that is, instead of going in the direction away from God, to turn back in the direction towards God.

"Turn, then, thy face towards Him in such wise that the faces of all beings will turn in the direction of His shining and luminous Horizon, and say: Thou seest me, O my Lord, with my face turned towards the heaven of Thy bounty and the ocean of Thy favor, withdrawn from all else beside Thee." (Epistle to the Son of the Wolf, page 18)

The face that we must turn to is the face of Bahá'u'lláh. To see His face is to see the reflection of the face of God. We must always remember that God is Single, Alone and Unknowable.

"Turn yourselves towards Him Who hath turned towards you. He, verily, is the Face of God amongst you, and His Testimony and His Guide unto you." (Epistle to the Son of the Wolf, page 48)

Renounce is an interesting word. It seems to imply a total giving up of one's self.

"Who is there among you, O people, who will renounce the world, and draw nigh unto God, the Lord of all names? Where is he to be found who, through the power of My name that transcendeth all created things, will cast away the things that men possess, and cling, with all his might, to the things which God, the Knower of the unseen and of the seen, hath bidden him observe?" (Gleanings, page 34)

"The essence of true safety is to observe silence, to look at the end of things and to renounce the world." (Tablets of Bahá'u'lláh, page 156)

"Fair in the eyes of men is the love of things they covet: women and sons; heaped-up hoards of gold and silver; horses branded (for blood and excellence); and (wealth of) cattle and well-tilled land. Such are the possessions of this world's life; but in nearness to God is the best of the goals (to return to)." (Qur'án   The Family of Imran 14 Al-Imran)

"But have renounced the hidden things of dishonesty, not walking in craftiness, nor handling the word of God deceitfully; but by manifestation of the truth commending ourselves to every man's conscience in the sight of God." (Bible 2CO 4:2)

<u>for My sovereignty endureth and My Dominion perisheth not</u>.- This

sovereignty and dominion refers to the sovereignty and dominion of the Manifestation.

"He it is Who is transcendent in His sovereignty, Who is manifest through His signs, and is hidden through His mysteries." (Epistle to the Son of the Wolf, page 1)

"This sovereignty must needs be revealed and established either in the lifetime of every Manifestation of God or after His ascension unto His true habitation in the realms above...." (Gleanings, page 26)

"Therefore, these illuminated Souls, these beauteous Countenances have, each and every one of them, been endowed with all the attributes of God, such as sovereignty, dominion, and the like, even though to outward seeming they be shorn of all earthly majesty...." (Gleanings, pages 48-49)

"It will endure as long as the Kingdom of God, His sovereignty, His dominion and power will endure." (Gleanings, pages 155-156)

<u>**If thou seekest another than Me,**</u> This probably refers to the Manifestation. He is known as the tree at the end of the road or the tree beyond which there is no passing; this far and no further.

"......seek none other than me; and wouldst thou gaze upon my beauty, close thine eyes to the world and all that is therein; for my will and the will of another than I, even as fire and water, cannot dwell together in one heart." (Báb: The Dawn-Breakers, Page: 9)

"The "sacred Lote-Tree" is a reference to the Sadratu'l-Muntaha, the "Tree beyond which there is no passing". It is used here symbolically to designate Bahá'u'lláh." (Aqdas: Notes, page 236)

To enter the presence of Bahá'u'lláh is to enter the presence of God or as near as man can ever come to it.

"Enter thou My presence, that thou mayest behold what the eye of the universe hath never beheld, and hear that which the ear of the whole creation hath never heard, that haply thou mayest free thyself from the mire of vague fancies, and set thy face towards the Most Sublime Station, wherein this Wronged One calleth aloud: "The Kingdom is God's, the Almighty, the All-Praised!" (Bahá'u'lláh: Epistle to the Son of the Wolf, page 130)

"And since there can be no tie of direct intercourse to bind the one true God with His creation, and no resemblance whatever can exist between the transient and the Eternal, the contingent and the Absolute, He hath ordained that in every age and dispensation a pure and stainless Soul be made manifest in the kingdoms of earth and heaven." (Bahá'u'lláh: Gleanings, page 66)

"The door of the knowledge of the Ancient Being hath ever been, and will continue for ever to be, closed in the face of men. No man's understanding shall ever gain access unto His holy court. As a token of His mercy, however, and as a proof of His loving-kindness, He hath manifested unto men the Day Stars of His divine guidance, the Symbols of His divine unity, and hath ordained the knowledge of these sanctified Beings to be identical with the knowledge of His own Self. Whoso recognizeth them hath recognized God." (Bahá'u'lláh: Gleanings, pages 49-50)

"The purpose of God in creating man hath been, and will ever be, to enable him to know his Creator and to attain His Presence. To this most excellent aim, this supreme objective, all the heavenly Books and the divinely-revealed and weighty Scriptures unequivocally bear witness. Whoso hath recognized the Day Spring of Divine guidance and entered His holy court hath drawn nigh unto God and attained His Presence, a Presence which is the real Paradise, and of which the loftiest mansions of heaven are but a symbol. Such a man hath attained the knowledge of the station of Him Who is "at the distance of two bows," Who standeth beyond the Sadratu'l-Muntaha." (Bahá'u'lláh: Gleanings, Page: 70)

MECCA. - 62 Verses

"In the Name of God, the Compassionate, the Merciful
1. BY the STAR when it setteth
2. Your compatriot erreth not, nor is he led astray
3. Neither speaketh he from mere impulse
4. The Koran is no other than a revelation revealed to him
5. One terrible in power taught it him,
6. Endued with wisdom. With even balance stood he
7. In the highest part of the horizon:
8. Then came he nearer and approached,
9. And was at the distance of two bows, or even closer,
10. And he revealed to his servant what he revealed." (Qur'án The Star An-Najm)

"the Sadratu'l-Muntaha, Literally "the furthermost Lote-Tree", translated by Shoghi Effendi as "the Tree beyond which there is no passing". This is used as a symbol in Islam, for example in the accounts of Muhammad's Night Journey, to mark the point in the heavens beyond which neither men nor angels can pass in their approach to God, and thus to delimit the bounds of divine knowledge as revealed to mankind. Hence it is often used in the Bahá'í Writings to designate the Manifestation of God Himself." (Aqdas: Notes, Page: 220)

"Say, this of a certainty is the Garden of Repose, the loftiest Point of adoration, the Tree beyond which there is no passing, the blessed

Lote-Tree, the Most Mighty Sign, the most beauteous Countenance and the most comely Face.
FROM the beginning that hath no beginning all men have bowed in adoration before Him Whom God shall make manifest and will continue to do so until the end that hath no end." (Selections from the Báb , Page: 155)

thy *quest will be in vain.* According to the thirteenth Hidden Word, the only place one can find Bahá'u'lláh is standing within one's heart. Here, it informs us that the only one we should search for and find is Bahá'u'lláh. If one searches the universe forever more and looks for someone else his search will have no result but vain emptiness.

"Turn ye away from all that is on earth and seek none else but Me. I am the Sun of Wisdom and the Ocean of Knowledge. I cheer the faint and revive the dead. I am the guiding Light that illumineth the way. I am the royal Falcon on the arm of the Almighty." (Bahá'u'lláh: Tablets of Bahá'u'lláh, page 169)

"Turn thy sight unto thyself, that thou mayest find Me standing within thee, mighty, powerful and self-subsisting." (Bahá'u'lláh: Arabic Hidden Words, Page: 13)

"Having recognized thy powerlessness to attain to an adequate understanding of that Reality which abideth within thee, thou wilt readily admit the futility of such efforts as may be attempted by thee, or by any of the created things, to fathom the mystery of the Living God, the Day Star of unfading glory, the Ancient of everlasting days." (Bahá'u'lláh: Gleanings, Page: 165)

"Likewise, reflect upon the perfection of man's creation, and that all these planes and states are folded up and hidden away within him.

Dost thou reckon thyself only a puny form, When within thee the universe is folded?" (Seven Valleys and Four Valleys, Page: 34)

16. O SON OF LIGHT!
Forget all save Me and commune with My spirit. This is of the essence of My command, therefore turn unto it.

<u>*Forget all save Me*</u> -He says to forget all, but to save Him and if we save Him we in truth save everything. For all of His teachings are open doors to life and living.

> "All creatures that exist are dependent upon the Divine Bounty. Divine Mercy gives life itself. As the light of the sun shines on the whole world, so the Mercy of the infinite God is shed on all creatures. As the sun ripens the fruits of the earth, and gives life and warmth to all living beings, so shines the Sun of Truth on all souls, filling them with the fire of Divine love and understanding." ('Abdu'l-Bahá: Paris Talks*, page 25)

> "I now assure thee, O servant of God, that, if thy mind become empty and pure from every mention and thought and thy heart attracted wholly to the Kingdom of God, forget all else besides God and come in communion with the Spirit of God, then the Holy Spirit will assist thee with a power which will enable thee to penetrate all things, and a Dazzling Spark which enlightens all sides, a Brilliant Flame in the zenith of the heavens, will teach thee that which thou dost not know of the facts of the universe and of the divine doctrine." (`'Abdu'l-Bahá: Bahá'í World Faith*, page 369)

> "In the path of God one must forget himself entirely. He must not consider his own pleasure but seek the pleasure of others. He must not desire glory nor gifts of bounty for himself but seek these gifts and blessings for his brothers and sisters." ('Abdu'l-Bahá: Promulgation

of Universal Peace*, page 215)

"Draw nigh unto Him with a pure heart, cheerful face, gazing eye and a joyful spirit and plunge with thy whole being into the sea of the love of God and forget all else save Him, so that thou mayest be filled with such spiritual sentiments from the kingdom of God, which will take the reins of desire from thy hands and move thee with the power of thy Lord, just as the wind moveth a mote in the open air as it willeth." (Tablets of 'Abdu'l-Bahá Vol 1*, Page: 200)

"Brethren, I count not myself to have apprehended: but this one thing I do, forgetting those things which are behind, and reaching forth unto those things which are before, I press toward the mark for the prize of the high calling of God in Christ Jesus." (Bible PHI 3:13, 14)

<u>*and commune with My spirit.*</u>-To commune is a deeper level of communication than just to speak or talk. It carries with it the feeling of private and confidential exchanges. Who we are going to commune with? It is the spirit of Bahá'u'lláh.

"So the Spirit of God reaches us through the Souls of the Manifestations. We must learn to commune with Their Souls, and this is what the Martyrs seemed to have done, and what brought them such ecstacy of joy that life became nothing." (Shoghi Effendi: Unfolding Destiny, pages 406-407)

"Take thou the step of the spirit, so that, swift as the twinkling of an eye, thou mayest flash through the wilds of remoteness and bereavement, attain the Ridvan of everlasting reunion, and in one breath commune with the heavenly Spirits. For with human feet thou canst never hope to traverse these immeasurable distances, nor attain thy goal." (Bahá'u'lláh: The Kitab-i-Iqan, page 43)

"He that seeketh to commune with God, let him betake himself to the companionship of His loved ones; and he that desireth to hearken unto the word of God, let him give ear to the words of His chosen ones." (Bahá'u'lláh: Persian Hidden Words, page 56)
"I communed with mine own heart, saying, Lo, I am come to great estate, and have gotten more wisdom than all they that have been before me in Jerusalem: yea, my heart had great experience of wisdom and knowledge." (Bible ECC 1:16)

"They ask thee concerning the Spirit (of inspiration). Say: "The Spirit (cometh) by command of my Lord: of knowledge it is only a little that is communicated to you, (O men!)" (Qur'án Children of Israel 85 Al-Isra)

<u>**This is of the essence of My command, therefore turn unto it.**</u> – "<u>of</u> the essence" means that this is a part of the essence of His command. This would be that His command is more far reaching than just to forget our selves and to commune with His spirit. If it is "<u>of</u> the essence" it is then an important and obligatory command.

"Thine is the authority to command whatsoever Thou willest. I bear witness that Thou art to be praised in Thy doings, and to be obeyed in Thy behests, and to remain unconstrained in Thy bidding." (Bahá'u'lláh: Aqdas: Other Sections, page 94)

In order to turn unto this command one must turn to Bahá'u'lláh and obey Him.

"The Tongue" that "gives," as stated in those extracts, the "glad-tidings" is none other than the Voice of God referring to Bahá'u'lláh,..." (Shoghi Effendi: World Order of Bahá'u'lláh, page 137)

"Say: This is the Voice of God, if ye do but hearken. This is the Day Spring of the Revelation of God, did ye but know it. This is the Dawning-Place of the Cause of God, were ye to recognize it. This is the Source of the commandment of God, did ye but judge it fairly. This is the manifest and hidden Secret; would that ye might perceive it." (Bahá'u'lláh: Gleanings, page 33)

"Cause me, then, to turn wholly unto Thee, to put my whole trust in Thee, to seek Thee as my Refuge, and to flee unto Thy face." (Bahá'u'lláh: Prayers and Meditations, page 255)

"He who obeys the Apostle, obeys God." (Qur'án Women 80 An-Nisa)

17. O SON OF MAN!
Be thou content with Me and seek no other helper. For none but Me can ever suffice thee.

<u>Be thou content with Me and seek no other helper.</u>- There is only one God and so there can only be one helper. We should surely know that all God wants for us is that which is for our own good, and so we should not only be content, but also be thankful.

"But only as seeking the face of his Lord the Most High. And surely in the end he shall be well content." (Qur'án The Night 20-21 Al-Layl)

"BE thou content with the commandment of God, the True One, inasmuch as sovereignty, as recorded in the Mother Book by the hand of God, is surely invested in Him Who is His Remembrance..." (The Báb : Selections from the Báb, Page: 42)

"But godliness with contentment is great gain." (Bible 1TI 6:6)

"And if thou dwellest in the land of testimony, content thyself with that which He, Himself, hath revealed:" (Bahá'u'lláh: The Kitab-i-Iqan, Page: 91)

"I know not that which profiteth me or harmeth me; Thou art, verily, the All-Knowing, the All-Wise. Do Thou decree for me, O Lord, my God, and my Master, that which will make me feel content with Thine eternal decree and will prosper me in every world of Thine." (Bahá'u'lláh: Bahá'í Prayers (US), page 145)

"Be content, O people, with that which God hath desired for you and predestined unto you...." (Bahá'u'lláh: Gleanings, page 103)

"It behoveth thee to be content with the Will of God, and a true and loving and trusted friend to all the peoples of the earth, without any exceptions whatever." ('Abdu'l-Bahá: Selections ... 'Abdu'l-Bahá, page 26)
"Let Him be thy helper and enrich thyself with His treasures, for with Him are the treasuries of the heavens and of the earth." (Bahá'u'lláh: Gleanings, page 235)

".....and none wilt thou find as a refuge other than Him. And keep thy soul content with those who call on their Lord morning and evening, seeking his Face;" (Qur'án The Cave 28 Al-Kahf)

<u>for none but Me can ever suffice thee.</u> - Sufficient means enough, and He, of course, is all one needs. If we have Bahá'u'lláh we have everything and if we don't have Bahá'u'lláh we have nothing.

"In God, Who is the Lord of all created things, have I placed My whole trust. There is no God but Him, the Peerless, the Most Exalted. Unto Him have I resigned Myself and into His hands have I committed all My affairs. No God is there besides Him, the supreme Ruler, the resplendent Truth. Indeed all-sufficient is He for Me; independently of all things doth He suffice, while nothing in the heavens or in the earth but Him sufficeth." (The Báb: Selections from the Báb, page 18)

"Thou art, in truth, the All-Sufficing and behind Thee standeth the true God, He Who overshadoweth all things. Indeed sufficient unto Me is God, the Exalted, the Powerful, the Sustainer." (The Báb : Selections from the Báb , Page: 59)

"Not that we are sufficient of ourselves to think any thing as of ourselves; but our sufficiency is of God;" (Bible 2CO 3:5)

"All that is in Heaven and all that is in Earth is God's! God is a sufficient protector!" (Qur'án Women 131 An-Nisa)

"We had taught them to repeat certain verses which, every night, they chanted with extreme fervour. `God is sufficient unto me; He verily is the All-sufficing!' one row would intone, while the other would reply: `In Him let the trusting trust.'" (Nabil-i-Azam: The Dawn-Breakers, Page: 632)

"RID thou thyself of all attachments to aught except God, enrich thyself in God by dispensing with all else besides Him, and recite this prayer:

Say: God sufficeth all things above all things, and nothing in the heavens or in the earth or in whatever lieth between them but God, thy Lord, sufficeth. Verily, He is in Himself the Knower, the Sustainer, the Omnipotent. Regard not the all-sufficing power of God as an idle fancy."   (The Báb : Selections from the Báb , Page: 123)

18. O SON OF SPIRIT!
Ask not of Me that which We desire not for thee, then be content with

what We have ordained for thy sake, for this is that which profiteth thee, if therewith thou dost content thyself.

<u>*Ask not of Me that which We desire not for thee,*</u>- What God desires for us is revealed in His revelation. What He wants for us is for man to become a spiritual, life fulfilling, true human being.

"The first duty prescribed by God for His servants is the recognition of Him Who is the Dayspring of His Revelation and the Fountain of His laws, Who representeth the Godhead in both the Kingdom of His Cause and the world of creation. Whoso achieveth this duty hath attained unto all good; and whoso is deprived thereof hath gone astray, though he be the author of every righteous deed. It behoveth everyone who reacheth this most sublime station, this summit of transcendent glory, to observe every ordinance of Him Who is the Desire of the world. These twin duties are inseparable. Neither is acceptable without the other. Thus hath it been decreed by Him Who is the Source of Divine inspiration." (Bahá'u'lláh: The Kitab-i-Aqdas, page 19)

"Truly, We desire to behold you as manifestations of paradise on earth, that there may be diffused from you such fragrance as shall rejoice the hearts of the favoured of God." (Bahá'u'lláh: The Kitab-i-Aqdas, page 58)

"We, verily, desire for you naught save what shall profit you, and to this bear witness all created things, had ye but ears to hear." (Bahá'u'lláh: The Kitab-i-Aqdas, page 75)

"Whatsoever is revealed by Thee is the desire of my heart and the beloved of my soul." (Bahá'u'lláh: Aqdas: Other Sections, page 93)

"It is Our wish and desire that every one of you may become a source of all goodness unto men, and an example of uprightness to mankind." (Bahá'u'lláh: Gleanings, page 315)

"The statutes of the LORD are right, rejoicing the heart: the commandment of the LORD is pure, enlightening the eyes. The fear of the LORD is clean, enduring for ever: the judgments of the LORD are true and righteous altogether. More to be desired are they than gold, yea, than much fine gold: sweeter also than honey and the honeycomb." (Bible PSA 19:8-10

"Then verily, O man, who desirest to reach thy Lord, shalt thou meet him." (Qur'án Rending Asunder 6 Al-Inshiqaq)

<u>then be content with what We have ordained for thy sake,</u>- God has ordained all the good things of the earth for mankind's pleasure and enjoyment. We should be content with this and not want the things that will destroy us and the world.

"Should a man wish to adorn himself with the ornaments of the earth, to wear its apparels, or partake of the benefits it can bestow, no harm can befall him, if he alloweth nothing whatever to intervene between him and God, for God hath ordained every good thing, whether created in the heavens or in the earth, for such of His servants as truly believe in Him." (Bahá'u'lláh: Gleanings, page 276)

"Praise be unto Thee, O our God, that Thou hast sent down unto us that which draweth us nigh unto Thee, and supplieth us with every good thing sent down by Thee in Thy Books and Thy Scriptures." (Bahá'u'lláh : Aqdas: Other Sections, Pages: 97-98)

"Nothing save that which profiteth them can befall My loved ones. To this testifieth the Pen of God, the Most Powerful, the All-Glorious, the Best Beloved." "Let not the happenings of the world sadden you. I swear by God! The sea of joy yearneth to attain your presence, for every good thing hath been created for you, and will, according to the needs of the times, be revealed unto you." (Shoghi Effendi: The Advent of Divine Justice, Page: 82)

"We perceive in what numerous ways man has been able to bend the powers of nature to his will.
How grievous it is to see how man has used his God-given gift to frame instruments of war, for breaking the Commandment of God `Thou shalt not kill', and for defying Christ's injunction to `Love one another'.
God gave this power to man that it might be used for the advancement of civilization, for the good of humanity, to increase love and concord and peace. But man prefers to use this gift to destroy instead of to build, for injustice and oppression, for hatred and discord and devastation, for the destruction of his fellow-creatures, whom Christ has commanded that he should love as himself!" ('Abdu'l-Bahá: Paris Talks*, page 42)

for this is that which profiteth thee, if therewith thou dost content thyself. - It seems that if we are not content with what God has ordained for us, then even when what God has ordained happens to us, it would not be of any profit to us because we are not content with God's will.

"He enjoineth upon you that which shall profit you, though He Himself can well dispense with all creatures. Your evil doings can never harm Us, neither can your good works profit Us. We summon you wholly for the sake of God." (Bahá'u'lláh: Gleanings, page 140)

"For what shall it profit a man, if he shall gain the whole world, and lose his own soul?" (Bible MAR 8:36)

19. O SON OF THE WONDROUS VISION!

I have breathed within thee a breath of My own Spirit, that thou mayest be My lover. Why hast thou forsaken Me and sought a beloved other than Me?

O SON OF THE WONDROUS VISION! - This is a new title and if we have studied and even remotely understood the previous eighteen Hidden Words we should now, indeed, have a wondrous vision. According to numerology, 19 is a Vahid which means "complete." We have completed a set.

"This, indeed, is His Revelation which hath been manifested unto you in the person of this Youth. Glorified, then, be God for so effulgent, so precious, so wondrous a vision." (Bahá'u'lláh: Gleanings, page 257)

"In these days, the Holy Ones of the Realm of Glory, dwelling in the all-highest Paradise, yearn to return unto this world, and be of some service to the Cause of Bahá'u'lláh and prove their servitude to the Threshold of Abhá beauty."
What a wondrous vision these words unfold to our eyes! How great our privilege to labor in this Day in the Divine Vineyard!" (Shoghi Effendi: Bahá'í Administration, page 37)

". . . that Wondrous Vision which constitutes the brightest emanation of His Mind and the fairest fruit of the fairest civilization the world has yet seen." (Shoghi Effendi: World Order of Bahá'u'lláh, page 48)

"And, behold, the glory of the God of Israel was there, according to the vision that I saw in the plain." (Bible EZE 8:4)

"I saw in the night visions, and, behold, one like the Son of man came with the clouds of heaven, and came to the Ancient of days, and they brought him near before him. And there was given him dominion, and glory, and a kingdom, that all people, nations, and languages, should serve him: his dominion is an everlasting dominion, which shall not pass away, and his kingdom that which shall not be destroyed." (Bible DAN 7:13-14)

"This Book is without a doubt a Revelation sent down from the Lord of the Worlds." (Qur'án The Prostration 1 As-Sajdah)

I have breathed within thee a breath of My own Spirit, that thou mayest be My lover. - The very reason God has breathed within us a breath of spiritual life is so that we can love him and love, to be true love, must be freely given. This is the reason man has free will.

"For every one of you his paramount duty is to choose for himself that on which no other may infringe and none usurp from him. Such a thing - and to this the Almighty is My witness - is the love of God, could ye but perceive it." (Bahá'u'lláh: Gleanings, page 261)

"Through the movement of Our Pen of glory We have, at the bidding of the omnipotent Ordainer, breathed a new life into every human frame, and instilled into every word a fresh potency." (Bahá'u'lláh: Gleanings, pages 92-93)

"God Who breathed the breath of the Holy Spirit upon His servants will breathe it upon them now and hereafter." ('Abdu'l-Bahá: Promulgation of Universal Peace*, page 159)

"The element of free will is there and all we believers - and even the Manifestation of God Himself - can do is to offer the truth to mankind." (Shoghi Effendi: Unfolding Destiny, page 447)

When one breathes it involves both breathing in and breathing out, so in like manner, we must breathe in the teachings of God and in turn breathe them out to humanity. Bahá'u'lláh has breathed into us a breath of His own Spirit that we may become His lovers, and we in turn must breathe it out that others also may become His lovers.

"Say: Teach ye the Cause of God, O people of Bahá, for God hath prescribed unto every one the duty of proclaiming His Message, and regardeth it as the most meritorious of all deeds. Such a deed is acceptable only when he that teacheth the Cause is already a firm believer in God, the Supreme Protector, the Gracious, the Almighty." (Bahá'u'lláh: Gleanings, Page: 278)
"But teach (thy Message): for teaching benefits the Believers." (Qur'án The Winds 55 Adh-Dhariyat)

<u>*Why hast thou forsaken Me and sought a beloved other than Me?*</u> -This is a rhetorical question. God, being All-Knowing, knows why but asks the question so that we might come to know and understand ourselves.

"These sublime words were heard today from the rustling of the divine Lote-Tree which the Lord of Names hath, with the hand of celestial power, planted in the All-Highest Paradise:
     The first Taraz and the first effulgence which hath dawned from the horizon of the Mother Book is that man should know his own self and recognize that which leadeth unto loftiness or lowliness, glory or abasement, wealth or poverty." (Bahá'u'lláh: Tablets of Bahá'u'lláh, pages 34-35)

The way man forsakes God is to follow his corrupt inclinations and disobey the commands of God.

"Have ye cast away the precepts of God and His remembrance and have ye forsaken His laws and ordinances?" (Bahá'u'lláh: Tablets of Bahá'u'lláh, page 104)

"But the people of the world have forsaken the divine teachings and followed forms and imitations of the truth." ('Abdu'l-Bahá: Promulgation of Universal Peace*, page 106)

"Such is God, your Lord and Cherisher: to Him belongs (all) dominion. There is no god but He: then how are ye turned away (from your true Center)?" (Qur'án The Crowds 5 Az-Zumar)

"For our fathers have trespassed, and done that which was evil in the eyes of the LORD our God, and have forsaken him, and have turned away their faces from the habitation of the LORD, and turned their backs." (Bible 2CH 29:6)

20. O SON OF SPIRIT!

My claim on thee is great, it cannot be forgotten. My grace to thee is plenteous, it cannot be veiled. My love has made in thee its home, it cannot be concealed. My light is manifest to thee, it cannot be obscured.

<u>*My claim on thee is great, it cannot be forgotten.*</u> - God has every right to claim us as He created us and all things.

"Unto God, the Lord of Lords, belong the kingdoms of earth and heaven." (Bahá'u'lláh: Gleanings, page 16)

"All the world hath belonged and will always belong to God." (Bahá'u'lláh: Huququ'lláh, pages 497-498)

"Say: This is the Voice of God, if ye do but hearken. This is the Day Spring of the Revelation of God, did ye but know it. This is the Dawning-Place of the Cause of God, were ye to recognize it. This is the Source of the commandment of God, did ye but judge it fairly. This is the manifest and hidden Secret; would that ye might perceive it." (Bahá'u'lláh: Gleanings, page 33)

Knowing that this is the voice of God Himself, how could we possibly forget it?

<u>**My grace to thee is plenteous, it cannot be veiled.**</u>-Grace is something that is given freely and not earned. When we look at the gifts and bounties of God we can readily see that, in truth, everything God has given us is grace. Life and all the gifts of life are seen by all and can't be hidden or denied.

"Happy is the lover that hath inhaled the divine fragrance of his Best-Beloved from these words, laden with the perfume of a grace which no tongue can describe." (Bahá'u'lláh: The Kitab-i-Aqdas, pages 20-21)

"Everything Thou doest is pure justice, nay, the very essence of grace." (Bahá'u'lláh: Epistle to the Son of the Wolf, page 10)

"Nay, the manifold bounties of the Lord of all beings have, at all times, through the Manifestations of His Divine Essence, encompassed the earth and all that dwell therein. Not for a moment hath His grace been withheld, nor have the showers of His loving-kindness ceased to rain upon mankind." (Bahá'u'lláh: Gleanings, page 18)

"Every hidden thing hath been brought to light by virtue of the Will of the Supreme Ordainer, He Who hath ushered in the Last Hour, through Whom the Moon hath been cleft, and every irrevocable decree expounded." (Bahá'u'lláh: The Kitab-i-Aqdas, page 49)

<u>**My love has made in thee its home, it cannot be concealed.**</u> - Note that a home is not a house. A home is a place of love, warmth, security and also a place of comfort. When the love of Bahá'u'lláh is firmly set in the human heart one has that love, warmth, security and peace of mind and a

harmony of soul. This love is then impossible to conceal.

"For thus the Master of the house hath appeared within His home, and all the pillars of the dwelling are ashine with His light." (Bahá'u'lláh: Seven Valleys and Four Valleys, page 22)

"My home is the home of peace. My home is the home of joy and delight. My home is the home of laughter and exultation. Whosoever enters through the portals of this home, must go out with gladsome heart. This is the home of light; whosoever enters here must become illumined...." ('Abdu'l-Bahá: Family Life, page 397)

"Who has, out of His bounty, settled us in a Home that will last: no toil nor sense of weariness shall touch us therein." (Qur'án Originator / Creation35 Al-Fatir)

"Therefore we are always confident, knowing that, whilst we are at home in the body, we are absent from the Lord:" (Bible 2CO 5:6)

"And as the human heart, as fashioned by God, is one and undivided, it behoveth thee to take heed that its affections be, also, one and undivided. Cleave thou, therefore, with the whole affection of thine heart, unto His love, and withdraw it from the love of any one besides Him, that He may aid thee to immerse thyself in the ocean of His unity, and enable thee to become a true upholder of His oneness." (Bahá'u'lláh: Gleanings, pages 237-238)

<u>*My light is manifest to thee, it cannot be obscured.*</u> - As stated above by Bahá'u'lláh, when He takes up residence in the human heart all of the dwelling becomes aglow with His light. When the light of God is shining in the heart no earthly power can extinguish it or obscure it.

". . .oblivious of the truth that no earthly water can quench the flames of Divine wisdom, nor mortal blasts extinguish the lamp of everlasting dominion. Nay, rather, such water cannot but intensify the burning of the flame, and such blasts cannot but ensure the preservation of the lamp, . . ." (Bahá'u'lláh: Gleanings, page 19)

"Where is he to be found that hath the power to quench the fire which hath been kindled through the might of thy Lord, the All-Powerful, the All-Compelling, the Almighty?" (Bahá'u'lláh: Gleanings, page 341)

"O mankind! verily there hath come to you a convincing proof from your Lord: for We have sent unto you a light (that is) manifest." (Qur'án Women174 An-Nisa)

"And God said, Let there be light: and there was light." (Bible GEN 1:3)

21. O SON OF MAN!

Upon the tree of effulgent glory I have hung for thee the choicest fruits, wherefore hast thou turned away and contented thyself with that which is less good? Return then unto that which is better for thee in the realm on high.

<u>Upon the tree of effulgent glory I have hung for thee the choicest fruits,</u>-
If the tree of effulgent glory is Bahá'u'lláh, the choicest fruits would be His teachings, but "tree" is not capitalized. It must be that the tree of effulgent glory is the teachings, upon which Bahá'u'lláh has placed what is needed for our spiritual growth. This makes sense because, like the fruit coming out of the tree, the teachings are made manifest by Bahá'u'lláh; they are not placed upon Him. He then explains them to us. Upon the tree of His teachings He places what is needed for our spiritual sustenance. It would appear from the following quotes of the beloved Guardian that the choicest fruits are the writings and tablets. The tree of effulgent glory

might be the gift of knowledge and understanding given to man.

"With His arrival in Adrianople and the proclamation of His Mission the Orb of His Revelation climbed as it were to its zenith, and shone, as witnessed by the style and tone of His writings, in the plenitude of its summer glory. The period of His incarceration in Akka brought with it the ripening of a slowly maturing process, and was a period during which the choicest fruits of that mission were ultimately garnered." (Shoghi Effendi: God Passes By, page 205)

"These Tablets - mighty and final effusions of His indefatigable pen -must rank among the choicest fruits which His mind has yielded, and mark the consummation of His forty-year-long ministry." (Shoghi Effendi: God Passes By, page 216)

"Every tree hath been endowed with the choicest fruits, every ocean enriched with the most luminous gems. Man, himself, hath been invested with the gifts of understanding and knowledge. The whole creation hath been made the recipient of the revelation of the All-Merciful, and the earth the repository of things inscrutable to all except God, the Truth, the Knower of things unseen." (Shoghi Effendi: World Order of Bahá'u'lláh, page 169)

"There will every soul prove (the fruits of) the deeds it sent before: they will be brought back to God their rightful Lord," (Qur'án Jonah 30 Yunus)

". . .the All-Merciful shed upon the whole of creation the effulgent glory of His most excellent Names and His most exalted Attributes," (Bahá'u'lláh: The Kitab-i-Aqdas, page 59)

"Set your faces towards Him (Bahá'u'lláh), on this Day which God hath exalted above all other days, and whereon the All-Merciful hath shed the splendor of His effulgent glory upon all who are in heaven and all who are on earth". (Bahá'u'lláh: Epistle to the Son of the Wolf, page 47)

"The world is illumined with the effulgent glory of His countenance." (Bahá'u'lláh: Gleanings, page 12)

"They should put their trust in God, and, holding fast unto Him, follow in His way. Then will they be made worthy of the effulgent glories of the sun of divine knowledge and understanding, and become the recipients of a grace that is infinite and unseen,. . ." (Bahá'u'lláh: The Kitab-i-Iqan, page 3)

<u>**wherefore hast thou turned away and contented thyself with that which is less good?**</u> - Bahá'u'lláh asks a rhetorical question. Being All-Knowing and All-Wise, He knows the answer, but wants us to know and meditate on the reasons. Here again, we could refer to the analogy of God preparing a banquet for us on the top of the mountain, but we dig for roots at the base of the mountain.

"Woe to those who are contented with ignorance, whose hearts are gladdened by thoughtless imitation, who have fallen into the lowest depths of ignorance and foolishness, and who have wasted their lives!" ('Abdu'l-Bahá: Some Answered Questions, page 137)

"I earnestly exhort you: let not your hearts be fettered by the material things of this world; I charge you not to lie contentedly on the beds of negligence, prisoners of matter, but to arise and free yourselves from its chains!" ('Abdu'l-Bahá: Paris Talks*, page 37)

<u>**Return then unto that which is better for thee in the realm on high.**</u> --We are lovingly invited to return to God even though we may have strayed far away. In many places Bahá'u'lláh refers to this realm on high as His spiritual kingdom.

"Repentance is the return from disobedience to obedience." ('Abdu'l-Bahá: Some Answered Questions, page 91)

"Should anyone be afflicted by a sin, it behoveth him to repent thereof and return unto his Lord." (Bahá'u'lláh: The Kitab-i-Aqdas, page 37)

"We entreat God - exalted and glorified be He - to aid all men to be just and fair-minded, and to graciously assist them to repent and return unto Him. He, verily, heareth, and is ready to answer." (Bahá'u'lláh: Epistle to the Son of the Wolf, page 35)

"Wherefore, hearken ye unto My speech, and return ye to God and repent, that He, through His grace, may have mercy upon you, may wash away your sins, and forgive your trespasses. The greatness of His mercy surpasseth the fury of His wrath, and His grace encompasseth all who have been called into being and been clothed with the robe of life, be they of the past or of the future." (Bahá'u'lláh: Gleanings, page 130)

"God hath, through His tongue that uttereth the truth, testified in all His Tablets to these words: "I am He that liveth in the Abhá Realm of Glory." (Bahá'u'lláh: Gleanings, page 207)

"Except those who repent and make amends and openly declare (the truth), to them I turn; for I am Oft-Returning, Most Merciful." (Qur'án The Cow 160 Al-Baqarah)

"And saying, Repent ye: for the kingdom of heaven is at hand." (Bible MAT 3:2)

22. O SON OF SPIRIT!

Noble have I created thee, yet thou hast abased thyself. Rise then unto that for which thou wast created.

<u>*Noble have I created thee,*</u>--God created man to be a noble human being. The word noble is derived from people that were closely related to the King.

"The most noble being on the earth is man." ('Abdu'l-Bahá: Some Answered Questions, page 158)

"This is an evidence that man is the most noble of God's creatures." ('Abdu'l-Bahá: Promulgation of Universal Peace*, page 69)

"The attributes of his Divine nature are shown forth in love, mercy, kindness, truth and justice, one and all being expressions of his higher nature. Every good habit, every noble quality belongs to man's spiritual nature, whereas all his imperfections and sinful actions are born of his material nature." ('Abdu'l-Bahá: Paris Talks*, page 60)

"For thou art of a noble nature." (Qur'án The Pen 4 Al-Qalam)

"Yet I had planted thee a noble vine, wholly a right seed: how then art thou turned into the degenerate plant of a strange vine unto me?" (Bible JER 2:21)

<u>*yet thou hast abased thyself.*</u>-- Man does all the damage to himself. You will note that Bahá'u'lláh says "abased thyself." Abased seems to signify going as low as one can go.

"Such is the commandment of the Lord, aforetime and hereafter; beware lest ye choose instead the part of ignominy and abasement." (Bahá'u'lláh: The Kitab-i-Aqdas, page 69)

Bahá'u'lláh is very clear on how we bring about this abasement of ourselves.

"Say: Honesty, virtue, wisdom and a saintly character redound to the exaltation of man, while dishonesty, imposture, ignorance and hypocrisy lead to his abasement." (Bahá'u'lláh: Tablets of Bahá'u'lláh, page 57)

"The essence of abasement is to pass out from under the shadow of the Merciful and seek the shelter of the Evil One." (Bahá'u'lláh: Tablets of Bahá'u'lláh, page 156)

"What meanness is this, and what evident treason; that man should, for worldly advantages, personal profit, easy circumstances, or protection of life and property, cast himself into this great detriment and evident loss, and embark in a course of action which will conduce to the greatest abasement and involve the utmost infamy and disgrace both here and hereafter!" ('Abdu'l-Bahá: A Traveler's Narrative, page 50)

"And whosoever shall exalt himself shall be abased; and he that shall humble himself shall be exalted." (Bible MAT 23:12)

Rise then unto that for which thou wast created.-- Rise means to get up to a higher level. God is constantly urging us to bring ourselves up.

"Pass beyond the baser stages of doubt and rise to the exalted heights of certainty." (Bahá'u'lláh: Persian Hidden Words, page 9)

"May they rise from present material attainments to such a height that heavenly illumination may stream from this center to all the peoples of the world." ('Abdu'l-Bahá: Promulgation of Universal Peace*, page 20)

The purposes of our creation are three:
1. To know and love God
    a. Know and love the Manifestation of God
    b. Know and love God's creation
    c. Know and love our fellow man
2. To acquire divine virtues
3. To carry forward an ever advancing civilization.

1. "I bear witness, O my God, that Thou hast created me to know Thee and to worship Thee." (Bahá'u'lláh: Aqdas: Other Sections, page 100)

a. "Say: He it is Who is the Manifestation of Him Who is the Unknowable, the Invisible of the Invisibles, could ye but perceive it." (Bahá'u'lláh: Gleanings, page 30)

"That which beseemeth you is the love of God, and the love of Him Who is the Manifestation of His Essence, and the observance of whatsoever He chooseth to prescribe unto you, did ye but know it." (Bahá'u'lláh: Gleanings, pages 304-305)

"He Who is everlastingly hidden from the eyes of men can never be known except through His Manifestation, and His Manifestation can adduce no greater proof of the truth of His Mission than the proof of His own Person." (Bahá'u'lláh: Gleanings, page 49)
b. "I loved thy creation, hence I created thee." (Bahá'u'lláh: Arabic Hidden Words, page 4)

"And God saw every thing that he had made, and, behold, it was very good. And the evening and the morning were the sixth day." (Bible King James Version Genesis 1:31)

"In the creation of the heavens and the earth; in the alternation of the night and the day; in the sailing of the ships through the ocean for the profit of mankind; in the rain which God sends down from the skies, and the life which He gives therewith to an earth that is dead; in the beasts of all kinds that He scatters through the earth; in the change of the winds, and the clouds which they trail like their slaves between the sky and the earth; (here) indeed are signs for a people that are wise." (Qur'án The Cow (Al-Baqarah))

c. "For service in love for mankind is unity with God." ('Abdu'l-Bahá: Promulgation of Universal Peace*, page 186

"Ye were created to show love one to another and not perversity and rancour." (Bahá'u'lláh: Tablets of Bahá'u'lláh, page 138))

2. `What is the purpose of our lives?'
'Abdu'l-Bahá.- `"To acquire virtues." ('Abdu'l-Bahá: Paris Talks*, page 177)

"The first, the fundamental purpose underlying creation hath ever been, and will continue to be, none other than the appearance of trustworthiness and godliness, of sincerity and goodwill amongst mankind, for these qualities are the cause of peace, security and tranquillity. Blessed are those who possess such virtues." (Bahá'u'lláh: Trustworthiness, page 328)

"The purpose of the creation of man is the attainment of the supreme virtues of humanity through descent of the heavenly bestowals." ('Abdu'l-Bahá: Promulgation of Universal Peace*, page 4)

3. "All men have been created to carry forward an ever-advancing civilization." (Bahá'u'lláh: Gleanings, page 215)

23. O SON OF THE SUPREME!

To the eternal I call thee, yet thou dost seek that which perisheth. What hath made thee turn away from Our desire and seek thine own?

<u>To the eternal I call thee, yet thou dost seek that which perisheth</u>.-- The very purpose of God in sending His Manifestation was to bring man to his eternal home. Although He calls us and invites us to come, we must still make the effort to get there.

"Fair in the eyes of men is the love of things they covet: women and sons; heaped-up hoards of gold and silver; horses branded (for blood and excellence); and (wealth of) cattle and well-tilled land. Such are the possessions of this world's life; but in nearness to God is the best of the goals (to return to). Say: shall I give you glad tidings of things far better than those? For the righteous are gardens in nearness to their Lord, with rivers flowing beneath; therein is their eternal home; with companions pure (and holy), and the good pleasure of God. For in God's sight are (all) His servants." (Qur'án The Family of Imran 14-15 Al-Imran)

"Though the purpose of Him Who is the Eternal Truth hath been to confer everlasting life upon all men,. . ." (Bahá'u'lláh: Gleanings, page 116)

"There can be no doubt whatever that, in consequence of the efforts which every man may consciously exert and as a result of the exertion of his own spiritual faculties, this mirror can be so cleansed from the dross of earthly defilements and purged from satanic fancies as to be able to draw nigh unto the meads of eternal holiness and attain the courts of everlasting fellowship." (Bahá'u'lláh: Gleanings, page 262)

The things of this world that man expends his life on trying to get can never be of any lasting benefit to him. When we think of something perishable, we think of a rotting, stinking and worm covered thing. This is our alternative to the eternal. Bahá'u'lláh tells us that the things of the earth come from the bowels of the earth and we all know what is contained in the bowels.

"How puny and insignificant is the evanescent drop when compared with the waves and billows of God's limitless and everlasting Ocean, and how utterly contemptible must every contingent and perishable thing appear when brought face to face with the uncreated, the unspeakable glory of the Eternal!" (Bahá'u'lláh: Gleanings, pages 187-188)

"If true glory were to consist in the possession of such perishable things, then the earth on which ye walk must needs vaunt itself over you, because it supplieth you, and bestoweth upon you, these very things, by the decree of the Almighty. In its bowels are contained, according to what God hath ordained, all that ye possess." (Bahá'u'lláh: Gleanings, pages 252-253)

"For the wages of sin is death; but the gift of God is eternal life through Jesus Christ our Lord". (Bible ROM 6:23)

24. O SON OF MAN!
Transgress not thy limits, nor claim that which beseemeth thee not. Prostrate thyself before the countenance of thy God, the Lord of might and power.

Transgress not thy limits, --Mankind has been created in the station of servitude. He can never become anything higher. That is the high limit of man. Man was also not created in the station of the animal and to act like one is also a limit.

"But for every being there is a point which it cannot overpass - that is to say, he who is in the condition of servitude, however far he may progress in gaining limitless perfections, will never reach the condition of Deity." ('Abdu'l-Bahá: Some Answered Questions, page 230)

"The meditations of the profoundest thinker, the devotions of the holiest of saints, the highest expressions of praise from either human pen or tongue, are but a reflection of that which hath been created within themselves, through the revelation of the Lord, their God. Whoever pondereth this truth in his heart will readily admit that there are certain limits which no human being can possibly transgress." (Bahá'u'lláh: Gleanings, pages 317-318)

"To transgress the limits of one's own rank and station is, in no wise, permissible. The integrity of every rank and station must needs be preserved. By this is meant that every created thing should be viewed in the light of the station it hath been ordained to occupy." (Bahá'u'lláh: Gleanings, page 188)

nor claim that which beseemeth thee not. -- Beseemeth is doing or claiming something to one's own best interest. It is not to our own best interest to make false claims.

"Amongst the people is he who seateth himself amid the sandals by the door whilst coveting in his heart the seat of honour. Say: What manner of man art thou, O vain and heedless one, who wouldst appear as other than thou art? And among the people is he who layeth claim to inner knowledge, and still deeper knowledge concealed within this knowledge. Say: Thou speakest false! By God! What thou dost possess is naught but husks which We have left to thee as bones are left to dogs." (Bahá'u'lláh: The Kitab-i-Aqdas, page 31)

"This is a reference to people who claim access to esoteric knowledge and whose attachment to such knowledge veils them from the Revelation of the Manifestation of God. Elsewhere Bahá'u'lláh affirms: "They that are the worshippers of the idol which their imaginations have carved, and who call it Inner Reality, such men are in truth accounted among the heathen." (Bahá'u'lláh: Aqdas: Notes, pages 194-195)

"They should justify their claim to be Bahá'ís by deeds and not by name." ('Abdu'l-Bahá: Excellence in All Things, page 372)

<u>Prostrate thyself before the countenance of thy God, the Lord of might and power.</u>-- If one can see the face of Bahá'u'lláh in every face, then one must feel humbled before his fellow man. Man also can only behold the countenance of God in the face of the Manifestation of God.

"In every face, he seeketh the beauty of the Friend; in every country he looketh for the Beloved." (Bahá'u'lláh: Seven Valleys and Four Valleys, page 7)

"For whosoever exalteth himself shall be abased; and he that humbleth himself shall be exalted." (Bible LUK 14:11)

"This universal, this transcending love which the followers of the Bahá'í Faith feel for their fellow-men, of whatever race, creed, class or nation, is neither mysterious nor can it be said to have been artificially stimulated. It is both spontaneous and genuine. They whose hearts are warmed by the energizing influence of God's creative love cherish His creatures for His sake, and recognize in every human face a sign of His reflected glory." (Shoghi Effendi: World Order of Bahá'u'lláh, pages 197-198)

"He, verily, is the Face of God amongst you, and His Testimony and His Guide unto you." (Bahá'u'lláh: Epistle to the Son of the Wolf, page 48)

"By attaining, therefore, to the presence of these holy Luminaries, the "Presence of God" Himself is attained. From their knowledge, the knowledge of God is revealed, and from the light of their countenance, the splendour of the Face of God is made manifest." (Bahá'u'lláh: The Kitab-i-Iqan, page 142)

25. O SON OF SPIRIT!
Vaunt not thyself over the poor, for I lead him on his way and behold thee in thy evil plight and confound thee for evermore.

<u>*Vaunt not thyself over the poor,*</u>-- Some people are spiritually poor and some are materially poor and some of us are both. I think it is best if we do not vaunt ourselves over anyone. Vaunt is not only done by thinking of oneself as superior to someone else but by feeling that superiority; it may even be subconscious.

"You must love and be kind to everybody, care for the poor, protect the weak, heal the sick, teach and educate the ignorant." ('Abdu'l-Bahá: Promulgation of Universal Peace*, page 93)

"Blessed are the poor in spirit: for theirs is the kingdom of heaven." (Bible MAT 5:3)

"Beware that ye allow not wolves to become the shepherds of the fold, or pride and conceit to deter you from turning unto the poor and the desolate." (Bahá'u'lláh: Epistle to the Son of the Wolf, page 53)

"Thou art He, O God, Who hath proclaimed Himself as the Lord of Wealth, and characterized all that serve Him as poor and needy." (Bahá'u'lláh: Gleanings, page 134)

"Poverty as here referred to signifieth being poor in the things of the created world, rich in the things of God's world." (Bahá'u'lláh: Seven Valleys and Four Valleys, page 36)

"Therefore, you must be thankful to God that although in this world you are indigent, yet the treasures of God are within your reach; and although in the material realm you are poor, yet in the Kingdom of God you are precious." ('Abdu'l-Bahá: Promulgation of Universal Peace*, pages 32-33)

"Erelong shall your days pass away, as shall pass away the days of those who now, with flagrant pride, vaunt themselves over their neighbor. Soon shall ye be gathered together in the presence of God, and shall be asked of your doings, and shall be repaid for what your hands have wrought, and wretched the abode of the wicked doers!" (Bahá'u'lláh: Gleanings, page 226)

for I lead him on his way and behold thee in thy evil plight and confound thee for evermore.—I, for one, am already confounded enough and I surely don't want any more. God's love and bounty for the poor is a great gift. If God will lead me on my way, then I should ardently pray for that poverty which will assure me of His guidance.

"Blinded be the eye that gazeth on whatsoever may displease Thee, and confounded be the soul that seeketh the things that are contrary to Thy will." (Bahá'u'lláh: Prayers and Meditations, page 299)

"But the poor are especially beloved of God. Their lives are full of difficulties, their trials continual, their hopes are in God alone." ('Abdu'l-Bahá: Promulgation of Universal Peace*, page 216)

"Thus Jesus, Son of Mary, whilst seated one day and speaking in the strain of the Holy Spirit, uttered words such as these: "O people! My food is the grass of the field, wherewith I satisfy my hunger. My bed is the dust, my lamp in the night the light of the moon, and my steed my own feet. Behold, who on earth is richer than I?" By the righteousness of God! Thousands of treasures circle round this poverty, and a myriad kingdoms of glory yearn for such abasement!" (Bahá'u'lláh: The Kitab-i-Iqan, pages 130-131)

26. O SON OF BEING!

How couldst thou forget thine own faults and busy thyself with the faults of others? Whoso doeth this is accursed of Me.

<u>How couldst thou forget thine own faults and busy thyself with the faults of others?</u>--We all know that we have faults and what our faults are. It seems to be human nature to not want to look at our own problems, and it is much easier and more comfortable to look and think about the faults of others. We must overcome this type of human nature we have cultivated.

"Backbiting, slander and dwelling on the faults of others have been repeatedly condemned by Bahá'u'lláh." (Bahá'u'lláh: Aqdas: Notes, page 181)

"An hypocrite with his mouth destroyeth his neighbour: but through knowledge shall the just be delivered." (Bible Proverbs 11:9)

"Speak no evil, that thou mayest not hear it spoken unto thee, and magnify not the faults of others that thine own faults may not appear great; and wish not the abasement of anyone, that thine own abasement be not exposed." (Bahá'u'lláh: Persian Hidden Words, page 44)

"All religions teach that we should love one another; that we should seek out our own shortcomings before we presume to condemn the faults of others, that we must not consider ourselves superior to our neighbours!" ('Abdu'l-Bahá: Paris Talks*, page 147)

"Heedless souls are always seeking faults in others. What can the hypocrite know of others' faults when he is blind to his own?" ('Abdu'l-Bahá: Promulgation of Universal Peace*, page 244)

"As to backbiting, the House of Justice points out that learning not to concern oneself with the faults of others seems to be one of the most difficult lessons for people to master, and that failing in this is a fertile cause of disputes among Bahá'ís as it is among men and women in general." (Multiple Authors: Lights of Guidance, page 89)

"In `Star of the West', Volume 8, No. 10, on page 138, there is a record of a reply given by 'Abdu'l-Bahá in a private interview in Paris in 1913. He was asked `How shall I overcome seeing the faults of others - recognizing the wrong in others?', and He replied: `I will tell you. Whenever you recognize the fault of another, think of yourself! What are my imperfections? - and try to remove them. Do this whenever you are tried through the words or deeds of others. Thus you will grow, become more perfect. You will overcome self, you will not even have time to think of the faults of others...'" (Multiple Authors: Lights of Guidance, pages 89-90)

"It is obvious that if we listen to those who complain to us about the faults of others we are guilty of complicity in their backbiting. We should therefore, as tactfully as possible, but yet firmly, do our utmost to prevent others from making accusations or complaints against others in our presence." (Multiple Authors: Lights of Guidance, page 94)

Whoso doeth this is accursed of Me.--*Who* in the world would knowingly want God to put a curse on him?

(God) said: "Then get thee out from here; for thou art rejected, accursed." (Qur'án The Rocky Tract 34 Al-Hijr)

"A good man out of the good treasure of his heart bringeth forth that which is good; and an evil man out of the evil treasure of his heart bringeth forth that which is evil: for of the abundance of the heart his mouth speaketh." (Bible LUK 6:45)

27. O SON OF MAN!
Breathe not the sins of others so long as thou art thyself a sinner. Shouldst thou transgress this command, accursed wouldst thou be, and to this I bear witness.

<u>Breathe not the sins of others so long as thou art thyself a sinner.</u>--To breathe is a two way process. We breathe in and we breathe out, so this seems to imply that we should neither listen to nor take in other's sins, nor should we let them out. Sins are more serious than faults. Sins go against the laws of God. I could say breaking the laws of God but in reality one does not break the law. The law will be as strong and unbroken as ever. What gets broken is us - we break ourselves against the law.

"I am stirred by nothing else except the winds of Thy will, and breathe no word except the words which, by Thy leave and Thine inspiration, I am led to pronounce." (Bahá'u'lláh: Prayers and Meditations, page 108)

"Cleanse thou the rheum from out thine head And breathe the breath of God instead." (Bahá'u'lláh: Seven valleys and FourValleys, page 20)

"Every time the sin committed by any one amongst them was breathed in the Court of His Presence, the Ancient Beauty would be so filled with shame as to wish He could hide the glory of His countenance from the eyes of all men, for He hath, at all times, fixed His gaze on their fidelity, and observed its essential requisites." (Bahá'u'lláh: Gleanings, page 309)

"Obey ye My commandments, and follow not the ungodly, they who have been reckoned as sinners in God's Holy Tablet." (Bahá'u'lláh: The Kitab-i-Aqdas, page 43)

"THERE is no paradise, in the estimation of the believers in the Divine Unity, more exalted than to obey God's commandments, and there is no fire in the eyes of those who have known God and His signs, fiercer than to transgress His laws and to oppress another soul, even to the extent of a mustard seed." (The Báb: Selections from the Báb, page 79)

"There is no paradise more wondrous for any soul than to be exposed to God's Manifestation in His Day, to hear His verses and believe in them, to attain His presence, which is naught but the presence of God, to sail upon the sea of the heavenly kingdom of His good-pleasure, and to partake of the choice fruits of the paradise of His divine Oneness." (The Báb: Selections from the Báb, page 77)

<u>*Shouldst thou transgress this command, accursed wouldst thou be, and to this I bear witness.*</u>--This is similar in the punishment that comes from disobedience but is put in even stronger language. Transgress means going where we don't belong.

"Shouldst thou transgress this command ACCURSED ART THOU.' The condemnation of backbiting could hardly be couched in stronger language than in these passages, and it is obviously one of the foremost obligations for Bahá'ís to set their faces against this practice. Even if what is said against another person be true, the mentioning of his faults to others still comes under the category of backbiting, and is forbidden." (Lights of Guidance, page 88)

28. O SON OF SPIRIT!
Know thou of a truth: He that biddeth men be just and himself committeth iniquity is not of Me, even though he bear My name.

"Know verily that the essence of justice and the source thereof are both embodied in the ordinances prescribed by Him Who is the Manifestation of the Self of God amongst men, if ye be of them that recognize this truth." (Bahá'u'lláh: Gleanings, page 175)

"The essence of all that We have revealed for thee is Justice,. . ." (Bahá'u'lláh: Tablets of Bahá'u'lláh, page 157)

"That which harmeth Me is the conduct of those who, though they bear My name, yet commit that which maketh My heart and My pen to lament." (Bahá'u'lláh: Epistle to the Son of the Wolf, page 23)

29. O SON OF BEING!
Ascribe not to any soul that which thou wouldst not have ascribed to thee, and say not that which thou doest not. This is My command unto thee, do thou observe it.

<u>Ascribe not to any soul that which thou wouldst not have ascribed to thee,</u>--Ascribe primarily means to write, but in its larger meaning it means we must not write, say, think or do anything to another that we would not like to have written, said, thought about, or done to us.

<u>and say not that which thou doest not. This is My command unto thee, do thou observe it.</u>--What we say we will do we must do. This also implies that we should not be bragging about what we have or have not done. It comes through in a very positive manner that this is a command and we must do it.

"Methinks ye have clung to outward things, and forgotten the inner things, and say that which ye do not. Ye are lovers of names, and appear to have given yourselves up to them." (Bahá'u'lláh: Proclamation of Bahá'u'lláh, page 103)

"In all these journeys the traveler must stray not the breadth of a hair from the "Law," for this is indeed the secret of the "Path" and the fruit of the Tree of "Truth"; and in all these stages he must cling to the robe of obedience to the commandments, and hold fast to the cord of shunning all forbidden things, that he may be nourished from the cup of the Law and informed of the mysteries of Truth." (Bahá'u'lláh: Seven Valleys and Four Valleys, pages 39-40)

"You must endeavour always to live and act in direct obedience to the teachings and laws of Bahá'u'lláh, so that every individual may see in all the acts of your life that in word and in deed you are followers of the Blessed Perfection." ('Abdu'l-Bahá: Paris Talks*, page 167)

30. O SON OF MAN!
Deny not My servant should he ask anything from thee, for his face is My face; be then abashed before Me.

Deny not My servant should he ask anything from thee,--On the surface this would seem to imply giving whatever is needed to those who are serving His cause. For example if 'Abdu'l-Bahá asked you for something you would unhesitatingly give it to him. Then we have this statement of the Báb:

"Is there any Remover of difficulties save God? Say: Praised be God! He is God! All are His servants and all abide by His bidding!" (The Báb: Selections from the Báb, page 217)

If "all are His servants," then it seems that we must freely give to everyone. However, it does not say take away from My servant. For example, if I give to a beggar I am in fact taking away his nobility. If I give something to someone, but this 'giving' goes against the teachings of God, I am taking away from that person and not giving to them.

"It is unlawful to beg, and it is forbidden to give to him who beggeth.

In a Tablet 'Abdu'l-Bahá expounds the meaning of this verse. He states that "mendicancy is forbidden and that giving charity to people who take up begging as their profession is also prohibited". He further points out in that same Tablet: "The object is to uproot mendicancy altogether. However, if a person is incapable of earning a living, is stricken by dire poverty or becometh helpless, then it is incumbent on the wealthy or the Deputies to provide him with a monthly allowance for his subsistence... By `Deputies' is meant the representatives of the people, that is to say the members of the House of Justice."

"The prohibition against giving charity to people who beg does not preclude individuals and Spiritual Assemblies from extending financial assistance to the poor and needy or from providing them with opportunities to acquire such skills as would enable them to earn a livelihood" (Bahá'u'lláh: Aqdas: Notes, page 235)

<u>*for his face is My face; be then abashed before Me.*</u>--This clearly states that the face of Bahá'u'lláh is seen in every face and we should therefore be humble before our fellow man.

"And whensoever the portals of grace did open, and the clouds of divine bounty did rain upon mankind, and the light of the Unseen did shine above the horizon of celestial might, they all denied Him, and turned away from His face - the face of God Himself...." (Bahá'u'lláh: Gleanings, page 17)

"We are servants in Thy vineyard, spreaders of Thy religion, devoted worshipers of Thy countenance, humble towards Thy loved ones,..."
('Abdu'l-Bahá: Bahá'í Prayers (US edition), pages 139-140)

"... and arise to serve Thy Cause, and to be humble before Thy loved ones, and, in the presence of Thy favoured ones, to be nothingness itself." ('Abdu'l-Bahá: Selections ... 'Abdu'l-Bahá, pages 4-5)

31. O SON OF BEING!

Bring thyself to account each day ere thou art summoned to a reckoning; for death, unheralded, shall come upon thee and thou shalt be called to give account for thy deeds.

Thank God Bahá'u'lláh used the word "account." A good accounting not only considers the deficits, but also the gains; not only the negatives, but the positives. What mankind must do is make sure that on the balance sheet of his life he is in the black (positives) and not in the red (negatives). From birth to death we all are heading to one final place and that is the grave. No-one escapes and it will be the soul of man that will answer for what we have expended our lives on.

"God will not call you to account for thoughtlessness in your oaths, but for the intention in your hearts; and He is Oft-Forgiving, Most Forbearing." (Qur'án The Cow 225 (Al-Baqarah)

"Ye shall, of a truth, be asked of your doings, shall be called to account for your failure in duty with regard to the Cause of God, and for having disdainfully rejected His loved ones who, with manifest sincerity, have come unto you." Bahá'u'lláh: Gleanings, page 124)

"It follows, therefore, that every man hath been, and will continue to be, able of himself to appreciate the Beauty of God, the Glorified. Had he not been endowed with such a capacity, how could he be called to account for his failure?" (Bahá'u'lláh: Gleanings, page 143)

"Ye have, by reason of your failure, hindered the breath of God from being wafted over you, and have withheld from your souls the sweetness of its fragrance. Ye continue roving with delight in the valley of your corrupt desires. Ye, and all ye possess, shall pass away. Ye shall, most certainly, return to God, and shall be called to account for your doings in the presence of Him Who shall gather together the entire creation..." (Bahá'u'lláh: Gleanings, pages 246-247)

"For those who respond to their Lord, are (all) good things. But those who respond not to Him - even if they had all that is in the heavens and on earth, and as much more, (in vain) would they offer it for ransom. For them will the reckoning be terrible: their abode will be Hell - what a bed of misery!" (Qur'án The Thunder 18 (Ar-Rad))

"O our Lord! cover (us) with Thy Forgiveness - me, my parents, and (all) Believers, on the Day that the Reckoning will be established!" (Qur'án Abraham 41 (Ibrahim))

"Man is like to vanity: his days are as a shadow that passeth away." (Bible Psalms 144:4)

32. O SON OF THE SUPREME!

I have made death a messenger of joy to thee. Wherefore dost thou grieve? I made the light to shed on thee its splendor. Why dost thou veil thyself therefrom?

<u>I have made death a messenger of joy to thee.</u>--According to Bahá'u'lláh this earth is like a shadow of the next world and it is of little or no value. It has also been likened to the womb of the next world. We should look forward to going into the next world. We note that Bahá'u'lláh says "death is a messenger of <u>joy</u> to thee."

"... .that he will regard the world even as a shadow that vanisheth swifter than the twinkling of an eye." (Bahá'u'lláh: Prayers and Meditations, page 15)

"The light of the celestial world makes war against the world of shadow and illusion." ('Abdu'l-Bahá: Paris Talks*, page 85)

"Know thou that the Kingdom is the real world, and this nether place is only its shadow stretching out. A shadow hath no life of its own; its existence is only a fantasy, and nothing more; it is but images reflected in water, and seeming as pictures to the eye." ('Abdu'l-Bahá: Selections ... 'Abdu'l-Bahá, page 178)

"Rejoicest thou in that thou rulest a span of earth, when the whole world, in the estimation of the people of Bahá', is worth as much as the black in the eye of a dead ant?" (Bahá'u'lláh: Epistle to the Son of the Wolf, page 124)

"When the human soul soareth out of this transient heap of dust and riseth into the world of God, then veils will fall away, and verities will come to light, and all things unknown before will be made clear, and hidden truths be understood.
Consider how a being, in the world of the womb, was deaf of ear and blind of eye, and mute of tongue; how he was bereft of any perceptions at all. But once, out of that world of darkness, he passed into this world of light, then his eye saw, his ear heard, his tongue spoke. In the same way, once he hath hastened away from this mortal place into the Kingdom of God, then he will be born in the spirit; then the eye of his perception will open, the ear of his soul will hearken, and all the truths of which he was ignorant before will be made plain and clear." ('Abdu'l-Bahá: Selections ... 'Abdu'l-Bahá, page 177)

"For we are strangers before thee, and sojourners, as were all our fathers: our days on the earth are as a shadow, and there is none abiding." (Bible 1 Chronicles 29:15)

<u>*Wherefore dost thou grieve? I made the light to shed on thee its splendor.*</u>--The ones who should grieve are the ones left behind. It is natural to miss someone you love very much and to feel sad for the separation, even for a short time. The light of the next world will open for the departed soul. The true light, of course, is the light of the knowledge of God. From the knowledge of God comes all knowledge.

"The people that walked in darkness have seen a great light: they that dwell in the land of the shadow of death, upon them hath the light shined." (Bible Isaiah 9:2)

"Grieve thou not over the troubles and hardships of this nether world, nor be thou glad in times of ease and comfort, for both shall pass away. This present life is even as a swelling wave, or a mirage, or drifting shadows." ('Abdu'l-Bahá: Selections ... 'Abdu'l-Bahá, page 177)

"True knowledge, therefore, is the knowledge of God, and this is none other than the recognition of His Manifestation in each Dispensation." (The Báb: Selections from the Báb, page 89)

"Therefore, if man attains to the knowledge of the Manifestations of God, he will attain to the knowledge of God; and if he be neglectful of the knowledge of the Holy Manifestations, he will be bereft of the knowledge of God." ('Abdu'l-Bahá: Some Answered Questions, page 222)

"For the earth shall be filled with the knowledge of the glory of the LORD, as the waters cover the sea." (Bible Habakkuk 2:14)

"For God, who commanded the light to shine out of darkness, hath shined in our hearts, to give the light of the knowledge of the glory of God in the face of Jesus Christ." (Bible 2 Corinthians 4:6)

They said: "Glory to Thee, of knowledge we have none, save that Thou hast taught us: in truth it is Thou who art perfect in knowledge and wisdom." (Qur'án The Cow 32(Al-Baqarah))

"True knowledge, therefore, is the knowledge of God, and this is none other than the recognition of His Manifestation in each Dispensation." (The Báb: Selections from the Báb, page 89)

"From their knowledge, the knowledge of God is revealed, and from the light of their countenance, the splendour of the Face of God is made manifest." (Bahá'u'lláh: The Kitab-i-Iqan, page 142)

<u>Why dost thou veil thyself therefrom?</u>--We veil ourselves from the light of the knowledge of God. He is as open and manifest as the sun.

"Considering what God hath revealed, that "We are closer to man than his life-vein," the poet hath, in allusion to this verse, stated that, though the revelation of my Best-Beloved hath so permeated my being that He is closer to me than my life-vein, yet, notwithstanding my certitude of its reality and my recognition of my station, I am still so far removed from Him". (Bahá'u'lláh: Gleanings, page 185)

"It was We who created man and We know what dark suggestions his soul makes to him: for We are nearer to him than (his) jugular vein." (Qur'án Qaf 16)

33. O SON OF SPIRIT!
With the joyful tidings of light I hail thee: rejoice! To the court of holiness I summon thee; abide therein that thou mayest live in peace

for evermore.

With the joyful tidings of light I hail thee: rejoice!-- To receive joyful tidings of light from our Creator should cause our very souls to be consumed with joy. When we have received such a wonderful gift we should share it with everyone.

"**Arise thou to serve the Cause of thy Lord; then give the people the joyful tidings concerning this resplendent Light whose revelation hath been announced by God through His Prophets and Messengers.**" **(Bahá'u'lláh: Tablets of Bahá'u'lláh, page 242)**

"**With hearts set aglow by the fire of the love of God and spirits refreshed by the food of the heavenly spirit you must go forth as the disciples nineteen hundred years ago, quickening the hearts of men by the call of glad tidings, the light of God in your faces, severed from everything save God.**" **('Abdu'l-Bahá: Promulgation of Universal Peace* page 8)**

"**O ye beloved of the Lord! Strive to become the manifestations of the love of God, the lamps of divine guidance shining amongst the kindreds of the earth with the light of love and concord. All hail to the revealers of this glorious light!**" **('Abdu'l-Bahá: Selections ... 'Abdu'l-Bahá, page 28)**

To hail someone is to call out to them with a loud and clear voice that all can hear. The message of Bahá'u'lláh would be of great importance to the one being hailed.

"**Joy be to thee, O thou that hast drained the Cup of His love!**" **and the Tongue of Grandeur will hail thee, "Great is the blessedness that awaiteth thee, O My servant, for thou hast attained unto that which none hath attained, except such as have detached themselves from all that is in the heavens and all that is on the earth, and who are the** emblems of true detachment." (Bahá'u'lláh: Gleanings, page 149)

"The statutes of the LORD are right, rejoicing the heart: the commandment of the LORD is pure, enlightening the eyes." (Bible Psalms 19:8)

<u>*To the court of holiness I summon thee;*</u>--Bahá'u'lláh is extending to us a loving invitation, in the form of a summons, to enter into His Court. For one to enter into such a court would require compliance with the first Hidden Word; that is, to "posses a pure kindly and radiant heart." This is followed by strict obedience to what His pen has revealed.

"Blind thine eyes, that is, to all save My beauty; stop thine ears to all save My word; empty thyself of all learning save the knowledge of Me; that with a clear vision, a pure heart and an attentive ear thou mayest enter the court of My holiness." (Bahá'u'lláh: Persian Hidden Words, page 11)

"The purpose of the one true God in manifesting Himself is to summon all mankind to truthfulness and sincerity, to piety and trustworthiness, to resignation and submissiveness to the Will of God, to forbearance and kindliness, to uprightness and wisdom. His object is to array every man with the mantle of a saintly character, and to adorn him with the ornament of holy and goodly deeds." (Bahá'u'lláh: Gleanings, page 299)

"Thy Lord hath never raised up a prophet in the past who failed to summon the people to His Lord, and today is truly similar to the times of old, were ye to ponder over the verses revealed by God." (The Báb: Selections from the Báb, page 161)

<u>*abide therein that thou mayest live in peace for evermore.*</u>--Once we enter His Holy Court it seems that since we still have free will, we can go

out again if we want, as Bahá'u'lláh cautions us to stay there. If we do stay we will live in peace forever.

"At the gate of the garden some stand and look within, but do not care to enter. Others step inside, behold its beauty, but do not penetrate far. Still others encircle this garden, inhaling the fragrance of the flowers, having enjoyed its full beauty, pass out again, the same gate. But there are always some who enter and, becoming intoxicated with the splendour of what they behold, remain for life to tend the garden." ('Abdu'l-Bahá Source not known)

"In all these journeys the traveler must stray not the breadth of a hair from the "Law," for this is indeed the secret of the "Path" and the fruit of the Tree of "Truth"; and in all these stages he must cling to the robe of obedience to the commandments, and hold fast to the cord of shunning all forbidden things, that he may be nourished from the cup of the Law and informed of the mysteries of Truth." (Bahá'u'lláh: Seven Valleys and Four Valleys, pages 39-40)

"But give glad tidings to those who believe and work righteousness, that their portion is Gardens, beneath which rivers flow. Every time they are fed with fruits therefrom, they say: "Why, this is what we were fed with before," for they are given things in similitude; and they have therein companions (pure and holy); and they abide therein (for ever)." (Qur'án 25 The Cow (Al-Baqarah))

"I have surely built thee an house to dwell in, a settled place for thee to abide in for ever." (Bible 1 Kings 8:13)

34. O SON OF SPIRIT!
The spirit of holiness beareth unto thee the joyful tidings of reunion; wherefore dost thou grieve? The spirit of power confirmeth thee in His cause; why dost thou veil thyself? The light of His countenance

doth lead thee; how canst thou go astray?

<u>The spirit of holiness beareth unto thee the joyful tidings of reunion; wherefore dost thou grieve?</u>--It is by the grace and the bounty of God that we are to be reunited with His Spirit of holiness.

"Sanctified art Thou, O my God! I beseech Thee by Thy generosity, whereby the portals of Thy bounty and grace were opened wide, whereby the Temple of Thy Holiness was established upon the throne of eternity; and by Thy mercy whereby Thou didst invite all created things unto the table of Thy bounties and bestowals; and by Thy grace whereby Thou didst respond, in Thine own Self with Thy word "Yea!" (Bahá'u'lláh: Bahá'í Prayers (US), pages 97-98)

As to the question, why do we grieve? Probably the answer to this is because we don't know, understand or fully realize the true purposes of why we were created. When we do know this, we often don't spend our days trying to achieve this purpose.

"The people of God should not be grieved. By the righteousness of God, that which is destined for them is far beyond the power of reckoners to reckon." (Bahá'u'lláh: Huququ'llah, page 501)

"How much more grievous would it be, were aught else to be mentioned in that Presence, were man's heart, his tongue, his mind, or his soul, to be busied with anyone but the Well-Beloved, were his eyes to behold any countenance other than His beauty, were his ear to be inclined to any melody but His voice, and were his feet to tread any way but His way." (Bahá'u'lláh: The Kitab-i-Iqan, page 180)

"We said: "Get ye down all from here; and if, as is sure, there comes to you guidance from Me," whosoever follows My guidance on them shall be no fear, nor shall they grieve." (Qur'án The Cow 38

(Al-Baqarah)

"And grieve not the holy Spirit of God, whereby ye are sealed unto the day of redemption." (Bible Ephesians 4:30)

The spirit of power confirmeth thee in His cause; why dost thou veil thyself?--Over and over again Bahá'u'lláh assures us of His love and support and this support is backed up by the power and might of the spirit of God. Again He questions us with another rhetorical question. God, being All-Knowing and All-Wise, surely knows the answer. The question is put to us so that we might meditate, reflect and realize why indeed we do veil ourselves from the Glory of God. It seems to me that one reason is that we were brought up in an environment alien and opposite to the teachings of Bahá'u'lláh.

"**Shoghi Effendi, in a letter written on his behalf, states: We cannot segregate the human heart from the environment outside us and say that once one of these is reformed everything will be improved. Man is organic with the world. His inner life moulds the environment and is itself also deeply affected by it. The one acts upon the other and every abiding change in the life of man is the result of these mutual reactions." (The Compilations: Volume 1, page 84)**

It would appear that if we are to remove the veils that come in between ourselves and our Creator, we must start making these changes in our own lives.

"**Not by the force of numbers, not by the mere exposition of a set of new and noble principles, not by an organized campaign of teaching - no matter how worldwide and elaborate in its character - not even by the staunchness of our faith or the exaltation of our enthusiasm, can we ultimately hope to vindicate in the eyes of a critical and sceptical** age the supreme claim of the Abhá Revelation. One thing and only one thing will unfailingly and alone secure the undoubted triumph of this sacred Cause, namely, the extent to which our own inner life and private character mirror forth in their manifold aspects the splendor of those eternal principles proclaimed by Bahá'u'lláh." (Shoghi Effendi: Bahá'í Administration, page 66)

What this evidently signifies is that society won't change it, God won't change it, and the veils will remain in place until we, of our own volition, decide to change ourselves in conformity with Bahá'u'lláh's teachings.

"Confirming the souls of the disciples, and exhorting them to continue in the faith, and that we must through much tribulation enter into the kingdom of God." (Bible Acts 14:22)

The light of His countenance doth lead thee; how canst thou go astray?--The face of Bahá'u'lláh is lit by the light and spirit of God Himself.

"All on the earth shall pass away; and this is the face of your Lord, the Almighty, the Well-Beloved." (Bahá'u'lláh: The Kitab-i-Aqdas, page 57)

"He, verily, is the Face of God amongst you, and His Testimony and His Guide unto you." (Bahá'u'lláh: Epistle to the Son of the Wolf, page 48)

"The eyes of all beings have been opened to behold the beauty of Thy radiant countenance, yet none hath succeeded in gazing on the brightness of the light of Thy face." (Bahá'u'lláh: Prayers and Meditations, pages 87-88)

"Verily I say, this is the Day in which mankind can behold the Face, and hear the Voice, of the Promised One. The Call of God hath been

raised, and the light of His countenance hath been lifted up upon men. It behoveth every man to blot out the trace of every idle word from the tablet of his heart, and to gaze, with an open and unbiased mind, on the signs of His Revelation, the proofs of His Mission, and the tokens of His glory." (Bahá'u'lláh: Gleanings, pages 10-11)

From the above passage one could possibly understand that the light of His Countenance signifies His Revelation. Therefore, it would follow that throughout the ages it will be the light of the Revelation of Bahá'u'lláh that will lead us. If we truly follow that light it would be impossible to go astray.

"There be many that say, Who will shew us any good? LORD, lift thou up the light of thy countenance upon us." (Bible Psalms 4:6)

"O mankind! verily there hath come to you a convincing proof from your Lord: for We have sent unto you a light (that is) manifest. Then those who believe in God, and hold fast to Him, soon will He admit them to Mercy and Grace from Him, and guide them to Himself by a straight Way." (Qur'án Women 174-175 (An-Nisa)

35. O SON OF MAN!
Sorrow not save that thou art far from Us. Rejoice not save that thou art drawing near and returning unto Us.

<u>*Sorrow not save that thou art far from Us.*</u>--The only cause for being sorrowful is for man to be far removed from God. God does not remove Himself from man. Man by his own acts removes himself from God.

"It is the waywardness of the heart that removeth it far from God, and condemneth it to remoteness from Him." (Bahá'u'lláh: Gleanings, page 186)

"At all times I am near unto thee, but thou art ever far from Me." (Bahá'u'lláh: Persian Hidden Words, page 21)

"Wonder not, if my Best-Beloved be closer to me than mine own self; wonder at this, that I, despite such nearness, should still be so far from Him."... Considering what God hath revealed, that "We are closer to man than his life-vein," the poet hath, in allusion to this verse, stated that, though the revelation of my Best-Beloved hath so permeated my being that He is closer to me than my life-vein, yet, notwithstanding my certitude of its reality and my recognition of my station, I am still so far removed from Him. By this he meaneth that his heart, which is the seat of the All-Merciful and the throne wherein abideth the splendor of His revelation, is forgetful of its Creator, hath strayed from His path, hath shut out itself from His glory, and is stained with the defilement of earthly desires." (Bahá'u'lláh: Gleanings, page 185)

"That they should seek the Lord, if haply they might feel after him, and find him, though he be not far from every one of us:" (Bible Acts 17:27)

"It was We who created man and We know what dark suggestions his soul makes to him: for We are nearer to him than (his) jugular vein." (Qur'án Qaf 16 (Qaf)

Rejoice not save that thou art drawing near and returning unto Us.-- True happiness can only be obtained in this life by striving with heart and soul to come closer to Bahá'u'lláh. The magnet that will draw us nearer to Him is prayer, meditation and to strive with heart and soul to follow His teachings to the very best of our ability.

"Do thou therefore strive with all thy heart and soul that thou mayest abide in this nest and thrive till eternity." ('Abdu'l-Bahá: Japan Will

Turn Ablaze*, page 40)

"Return, then, unto God, your Maker, and be not of the heedless..." (Bahá'u'lláh: Proclamation of Bahá'u'lláh, page 8)

"And shalt return unto the LORD thy God, and shalt obey his voice according to all that I command thee this day, thou and thy children, with all thine heart, and with all thy soul;" (Bible Deuteronomy 30:2)

"O ye who believe! do your duty to God, seek the means of approach unto Him, and strive with might and main in His cause: that ye may prosper." (Qur'án The Table Spread 38 (Al-Maidah)

36. O SON OF MAN!
Rejoice in the gladness of thine heart, that thou mayest be worthy to meet Me and to mirror forth My beauty.

From the previous three Hidden Words Bahá'u'lláh is hailing us with tidings of light, summoning us to the court of holiness, inviting us to eternal peace, sending us tidings of reunion with our Creator, confirming us in His cause, and leading us by the light of His countenance, and all this in order that we can once more enter the garden of Eden with our maker with joy and ecstatic happiness. If we are obedient and have absorbed these ideas into our lives we would then be radiantly happy and prepared to meet Bahá'u'lláh and to reflect His beauty.

"Upon the reality of man, however, He hath focused the radiance of all of His names and attributes, and made it a mirror of His own Self. Alone of all created things man hath been singled out for so great a favor, so enduring a bounty. These energies with which the Day Star of Divine bounty and Source of heavenly guidance hath endowed the reality of man lie, however, latent within him, even as the flame is hidden within the candle and the rays of light are potentially present

in the lamp. The radiance of these energies may be obscured by worldly desires even as the light of the sun can be concealed beneath the dust and dross which cover the mirror. Neither the candle nor the lamp can be lighted through their own unaided efforts, nor can it ever be possible for the mirror to free itself from its dross. It is clear and evident that until a fire is kindled the lamp will never be ignited, and unless the dross is blotted out from the face of the mirror it can never represent the image of the sun nor reflect its light and glory. And since there can be no tie of direct intercourse to bind the one true God with His creation, and no resemblance whatever can exist between the transient and the Eternal, the contingent and the Absolute, He hath ordained that in every age and dispensation a pure and stainless Soul be made manifest in the kingdoms of earth and heaven." (Bahá'u'lláh: Gleanings, pages 65-66)

We need help and that help comes only through the Manifestation in the day in which we live. Once we have found that help then we must put forth every effort to follow the instructions to the very best of our ability.

"The greater the effort exerted for the refinement of this sublime and noble mirror, the more faithfully will it be made to reflect the glory of the names and attributes of God, and reveal the wonders of His signs and knowledge." (Bahá'u'lláh: Gleanings, page 262)

"Strive therefore, with heart and soul, to follow the precepts of the Blessed Perfection, and rest assured that if ye succeed in living the life he marks out for you, Eternal Life and everlasting joy in the Heavenly Kingdom will be yours, and celestial sustenance will be sent to strengthen you all your days." ('Abdu'l-Bahá: Paris Talks*, page 114)

"The first thing to do is to acquire a thirst for Spirituality, then Live the Life! Live the Life! Live the Life! The way to acquire this thirst is to meditate upon the future life. Study the Holy Words, read your Bible, read the Holy Books, especially study the Holy Utterances of Bahá'u'lláh; Prayer and Meditation, take much time for these two." ('Abdu'l-Bahá: The Importance of Deepening, page 204)

"Be glad in the LORD, and rejoice, ye righteous: and shout for joy, all ye that are upright in heart." (Bible Psalms 32:11)

"There can be no doubt whatever that, in consequence of the efforts which every man may consciously exert and as a result of the exertion of his own spiritual faculties, this mirror can be so cleansed from the dross of earthly defilements and purged from satanic fancies as to be able to draw nigh unto the meads of eternal holiness and attain the courts of everlasting fellowship." (Bahá'u'lláh: Gleanings, page 262)

37. O SON OF MAN!

Divest not thyself of My beauteous robe, and forfeit not thy portion from My wondrous fountain, lest thou shouldst thirst for evermore.

<u>*Divest not thyself of My beauteous robe,*</u>-- In many places, Bahá'u'lláh talks about His robe. Now if we are not to take off this robe and discard it, then we should try to understand the true spiritual meaning of the robe. We have one of the definitions in the fourteenth Hidden Word, in which He states that we are His robe.

"thou art My robe and My robe shall never be outworn." (Bahá'u'lláh: Arabic Hidden Words, page 14)

.... "donned the robe of discipleship". (Bahá'u'lláh: Aqdas: Notes, page 243)

"The robe of sanctity. . ." (Bahá'u'lláh: Bahá'í Prayers (US), page 219)

"... and conferred upon Him the robe of Prophethood" (Bahá'u'lláh: Gleanings, page 23)

"Its robe is the Revelation vouchsafed unto it by God." (Bahá'u'lláh: Gleanings, page 81)

"Suffer not yourselves to be deprived of the robe of forbearance and justice, that the sweet savors of holiness may be wafted from your hearts upon all created things." (Bahá'u'lláh: Gleanings, page 305)

"... and array himself with the robe of virtue." (Bahá'u'lláh: Gleanings, pages 334-335)

"... have been arrayed with the new robe of divine Unity," (Bahá'u'lláh: The Kitab-i-Iqan, pages 112-113)

"... arrayed them with the beauteous robe of faith," (Bahá'u'lláh: The Kitab-i-Iqan, page 117)

"In this day the world is redolent with the fragrances of the robe of the Revelation of the Ancient King ..." (Bahá'u'lláh: Proclamation of Bahá'u'lláh, page 104)

"In all these journeys the traveler must stray not the breadth of a hair from the "Law," for this is indeed the secret of the "Path" and the fruit of the Tree of "Truth"; and in all these stages he must cling to the robe of obedience to the commandments, and hold fast to the cord of shunning all forbidden things, that he may be nourished from the cup of the Law and informed of the mysteries of Truth." (Bahá'u'lláh: Seven Valleys and Four Valleys, pages 39-40)

This robe, or obedience to the commandments of God, seems to sum up the true meaning of not to divest oneself from His beauteous robe.

"But this thing commanded I them, saying, Obey my voice, and I will be your God, and ye shall be my people: and walk ye in all the ways that I have commanded you, that it may be well unto you." (Bible Jeremiah 7:23)

"I will greatly rejoice in the LORD, my soul shall be joyful in my God; for he hath clothed me with the garments of salvation, he hath covered me with the robe of righteousness, as a bridegroom decketh himself with ornaments, and as a bride adorneth herself with her jewels." (Bible Isaiah 61:10)

"And He it is Who makes the Night as a Robe for you;" (Qur'án The Criterion 47 Al-Furqan)

<u>and forfeit not thy portion from My wondrous fountain,</u>--Like the robe, the fountain would be the gushing and never ending fountain of the living waters of revelation.

"The first duty prescribed by God for His servants is the recognition of Him Who is the Dayspring of His Revelation and the Fountain of His laws, Who representeth the Godhead in both the Kingdom of His Cause and the world of creation. Whoso achieveth this duty hath attained unto all good; and whoso is deprived thereof hath gone astray, though he be the author of every righteous deed. It behoveth everyone who reacheth this most sublime station, this summit of transcendent glory, to observe every ordinance of Him Who is the Desire of the world. These twin duties are inseparable. Neither is acceptable without the other. Thus hath it been decreed by Him Who is the Source of Divine inspiration." (Bahá'u'lláh: The Kitab-i-Aqdas, page 19)

"Thereupon I arose before all Thy creatures, strengthened by Thy help and Thy power, and summoned all the multitudes unto Thee, and announced unto all Thy servants Thy favors and Thy gifts, and invited them to turn towards this Ocean, every drop of the waters of which crieth out, proclaiming unto all that are in heaven and on earth that He is, in truth, the Fountain of all life, and the Quickener of the entire creation, and the Object of the adoration of all worlds, and the Best-Beloved of every understanding heart, and the Desire of all them that are nigh unto Thee." (Bahá'u'lláh: Prayers and Meditations, page 104)

"For with thee is the fountain of life: in thy light shall we see light." (Bible Psalms 36:9)

"And he said unto me, It is done. I am Alpha and Omega, the beginning and the end. I will give unto him that is athirst of the fountain of the water of life freely." (Bible Revelations 21:6)

"Round will be passed to them a Cup from a clear-flowing fountain," (Qur'án Those who set ranks 45 As-Saffat)

<u>*lest thou shouldst thirst for evermore.*</u>--Evidently there is no other water than this water from the fountain of God's revelation.

"...they that thirst for understanding partake of the Salsabíl of divine wisdom." (Bahá'u'lláh: The Kitab-i-Iqan, page 63)

"Is there any man of insight, O my God, that can behold Thee with Thine own eye, and where is the thirsty one who can direct his face towards the living waters of Thy love?" (Bahá'u'lláh: Prayers and Meditations, page 8)

"This new Revelation has in reality been the water of life unto the thirsty, a sea of knowledge unto the searcher, a message of condolence to the weary and a new spirit and life to the whole world." (Shoghi Effendi: Bahiyyih Khanum, page 188)

"But whosoever drinketh of the water that I shall give him shall never thirst; but the water that I shall give him shall be in him a well of water springing up into everlasting life." (Bible John 4:14)

"Their thirst will be slaked with Pure Wine sealed:" (Qur'án Dealing in Fraud 25 Al-Mutaffifin)

38. O SON OF BEING!
Walk in My statutes for love of Me and deny thyself that which thou desirest if thou seekest My pleasure.

<u>*Walk in My statutes for love of Me*</u>--A very important message is in this statement. We obey the teachings of Bahá'u'lláh because we love Him and not because we have to or we fear His punishment. We should not even follow the commands of God for the rewards of heaven, but only because we love Him.

"In the highest prayer, men pray only for the love of God, not because they fear Him or hell, or hope for bounty or heaven...." ('Abdu'l-Bahá: Prayer, Meditation, ..., page 236)

"The importance of love for God as the motive of obedience to His Laws" (Bahá'u'lláh: Aqdas: Other Sections, page 163)

"Observe ye the statutes and precepts of your Lord, and walk ye in this Way which hath been laid out before you in righteousness and truth." (Bahá'u'lláh: The Kitab-i-Aqdas, page 45)

"But those of faith are overflowing in their love for God." (Qur'án

The Cow 165 Al-Baqarah)

"But whoso keepeth his word, in him verily is the love of God perfected: hereby know we that we are in him." (Bible 1JO 2:5)

<u>deny thyself that which thou desirest if thou seekest My pleasure.</u>--As long as man's pleasures are in accordance with God's laws and commandments no denial is necessary. It is when man's desires are not in line with God's that we must deny ourselves.

"Be not forgetful of the law of God in whatever thou desirest to achieve, now or in the days to come." (Bahá'u'lláh: Gleanings, page 240)

"If anyone desires a reward in this life, in God's (gift) is the reward (both) of this life and of the Hereafter: for God is He that heareth and seeth (all things)." (Qur'án Women 134 An-Nisa)

"Aid me to do what Thou desirest, and to fulfill what Thou pleasest." (Bahá'u'lláh: Prayers and Meditations, page 22)

Kaf or Gaf (K or G) referreth to Kuffi ("free"), that is, "Free thyself from that which thy passion desireth; then advance unto thy Lord." (Bahá'u'lláh: Seven Valleys and Four Valleys, pages 42-43)

"For verily I say unto you, That many prophets and righteous men have desired to see those things which ye see, and have not seen them; and to hear those things which ye hear, and have not heard them." (Bible MAT 13:17)

39. O SON OF MAN!
Neglect not My commandments if thou lovest My beauty, and forget

not My counsels if thou wouldst attain My good pleasure.

Neglect not My commandments if thou lovest My beauty,--If a man is a true lover of beauty then to find that beauty is to find it in obedience to His commandments.

"Know assuredly that My commandments are the lamps of My loving providence among My servants, and the keys of My mercy for My creatures. Thus hath it been sent down from the heaven of the Will of your Lord, the Lord of Revelation." (Bahá'u'lláh: The Kitab-i-Aqdas, page 20)

The commandments of God, when followed by the individuals and by the governments, can only lead to a happy individual and a truly free and happy society.

"Say: True liberty consisteth in man's submission unto My commandments, little as ye know it. Were men to observe that which We have sent down unto them from the Heaven of Revelation, they would, of a certainty, attain unto perfect liberty. Happy is the man that hath apprehended the Purpose of God in whatever He hath revealed from the Heaven of His Will that pervadeth all created things. Say: The liberty that profiteth you is to be found nowhere except in complete servitude unto God, the Eternal Truth." (Bahá'u'lláh: The Kitab-i-Aqdas, pages 63-64)

If we want the love of God, and we want in turn to love Him, the only path is through obedience to His commandments.

"These sublime words have, in this day, been heard from the Lote-Tree beyond which there is no passing: `I belong to him that loveth Me, that holdeth fast My commandments, and casteth away the things forbidden him in My Book.'" (Bahá'u'lláh: Epistle to the Son

of the Wolf, page 25)

"Know therefore that the LORD thy God, he is God, the faithful God, which keepeth covenant and mercy with them that love him and keep his commandments to a thousand generations;" (Bible Deuteronomy 7:9)

"Shall we adore that which thou commandest us?" (Qur'án The Criterion 60 (Al-Furqan))

forget not My counsels if thou wouldst attain My good pleasure. --A counsel is professional advice and with Bahá'u'lláh we have the most perfect professional giving us His counsel. The word counsel also implies free will, meaning I can follow it if I want.

"This is the Counsel of God; would that thou mightest heed it! This is the Bounty of God; would that thou mightest receive it! This is the Utterance of God; if only thou wouldst apprehend it! This is the Treasure of God; if only thou couldst understand!" (Bahá'u'lláh: The Kitab-i-Aqdas, page 87)

"Hearken now unto my voice, I will give thee counsel, and God shall be with thee. . ." (Bible Exodus 18:19)

"And they returned with Grace and Bounty from God: no harm ever touched them; for they followed the good pleasure of God: and God is the Lord of bounties unbounded." (Qur'án The Family of Imran 174 (Al-Imran))

"I know also, my God, that thou triest the heart, and hast pleasure in uprightness." (Bible 1 Chronicles 29:17)

40. O SON OF MAN!

Wert thou to speed through the immensity of space and traverse the expanse of heaven, yet thou wouldst find no rest save in submission to Our command and humbleness before Our Face.

This Hidden Word tells us that even if man were able to speed throughout the vast reaches of space, and in the spiritual kingdom examine all the spiritual paths, he could find no safety nor refuge except in Bahá'u'lláh. This also confirms the idea that we must not only find the manifestation of God but also follow all of His commands.

"O ye lovers of the One true God! Strive, that ye may truly recognize and know Him, and observe befittingly His precepts." (Bahá'u'lláh: Gleanings, page 5)

"The first and foremost testimony establishing His truth is His own Self. Next to this testimony is His Revelation." (Bahá'u'lláh: Gleanings, page 105)

"A twofold obligation resteth upon him who hath recognized the Day Spring of the Unity of God, and acknowledged the truth of Him Who is the Manifestation of His oneness. The first is steadfastness in His love, such steadfastness that neither the clamor of the enemy nor the claims of the idle pretender can deter him from cleaving unto Him Who is the Eternal Truth, a steadfastness that taketh no account of them whatever. The second is strict observance of the laws He hath prescribed - laws which He hath always ordained, and will continue to ordain, unto men, and through which the truth may be distinguished and separated from falsehood." (Bahá'u'lláh: Gleanings, pages 289-290)

"Humble yourselves in the sight of the Lord, and he shall lift you up." (Bible James 4:10)

"Return unto God, humble, submissive and lowly; verily, He will put away from thee thy sins, for thy Lord, of a certainty, is the Forgiving, the Mighty, the All-Merciful." (Bahá'u'lláh: The Kitab-i-Aqdas, Page: 87)

"If anyone desires a religion other than Islam (submission to God),never will it be accepted of him; and in the Hereafter he will be in the ranks of those who have lost (all spiritual good)." (Qur'án The Family of Imran 85 (Al-Imran)

It seems to me that one of the ways we can humble ourselves before the face of God is to be humble before the face of others.

"In every face, he seeketh the beauty of the Friend; in every country he looketh for the Beloved." (Bahá'u'lláh: Seven Valleys and Four Valleys, Page: 7)

"Deny not My servant should he ask anything from thee, for his face is My face; be then abashed before Me." (Bahá'u'lláh: Arabic Hidden Words, Page: 30)

"We are servants in Thy vineyard, spreaders of Thy religion, devoted worshipers of Thy countenance, humble towards Thy loved ones," ('Abdu'l-Bahá: Bahá'í Prayers (US edition), Page: 139)

".......have engraved on thee Mine image and revealed to thee My beauty" (Bahá'u'lláh: Arabic Hidden Words, Page: 3)

"If my people, which are called by my name, shall humble themselves, and pray, and seek my face, and turn from their wicked ways; then will I hear from heaven, and will forgive their sin, and will heal their land." (Bible 2CH 7:14)

"And whosoever shall exalt himself shall be abased; and he that shall humble himself shall be exalted." (Bible MAT 23:12)

"(All) faces shall be humbled before (Him) - the Living, the Self-Subsisting," (Qur'án Ta Ha 111 Ta-Ha)

41. O SON OF MAN!
Magnify My cause that I may reveal unto thee the mysteries of My greatness and shine upon thee with the light of eternity.

To magnify something is to make it larger. When we think about magnifying Bahá'u'lláh we soon come to understand that this is not possible for He is far above all mention and praise. His teachings are also far beyond our ability to fully understand the profound implications of them.

"How can I make mention of Thee, assured as I am that no tongue, however deep its wisdom, can befittingly magnify Thy name, nor can the bird of the human heart, however great its longing, ever hope to ascend into the heaven of Thy majesty and knowledge." (Bahá'u'lláh: Gleanings, page 3)

"He hath everlastingly existed and will everlastingly continue to exist. He hath been and will ever remain inscrutable unto all men, inasmuch as all else besides Him have been and shall ever be created through the potency of His command. He is exalted above every mention or praise and is sanctified beyond every word of commendation or every comparison. No created thing comprehendeth Him, while He in truth comprehendeth all things. Even when it is said `no created thing comprehendeth Him', this refers to the Mirror of His Revelation, that is Him Whom God shall make manifest. Indeed too high and exalted is He for anyone to allude unto Him." (The Báb: Selections from the Báb, page 113)

"How can feeble reason encompass the Qur'án, Or the spider snare a phoenix in his web?" (Bahá'u'lláh: Seven Valleys and Four Valleys, Page: 33)

In striving with heart and soul to teach the Cause to the best of our ability, even though we don't fully understand it, this will open the door for the light of God to shine upon us not only in this world, but also in the world of eternity.

"Blessed are they that remember the one true God, that magnify His Name, and seek diligently to serve His Cause." (Bahá'u'lláh: Gleanings, page 110)

"Arise and deliver thy warning! And thy Lord do thou magnify!" (Qur'án The Cloaked One 2 & 3 (Al-Mudathir))

"O magnify the LORD with me, and let us exalt his name together." (Bible Psalms 34:3)

Bahá'u'lláh states in many places, "reveal the mysteries," and this would imply that which was before a mystery has in this most great revelation been revealed.

"Thus We instruct thee in the interpretation of the traditions, and reveal unto thee the mysteries of divine wisdom, that haply thou mayest comprehend the meaning thereof, and be of them that have quaffed the cup of divine knowledge and understanding." (Bahá'u'lláh: The Kitab-i-Iqan, Pages: 32-33)

"Thus We reveal unto thee the mysteries of the Cause of God, and bestow upon thee the gems of divine wisdom, that haply thou mayest soar on the wings of renunciation to those heights that are veiled from the eyes of men." (Bahá'u'lláh: The Kitab-i-Iqan, Page: 97)

"Shouldst thou make firm thy feet in the love of God and hold steadfast to the Great Cause, God will reveal unto thee mysteries unheard by the ears and incomprehensible by the intellects." ('Abdu'l-Bahá: Tablets of 'Abdu'l-Bahá Vol 3*, Page: 519)

"Behold, I will bring it health and cure, and I will cure them, and will reveal unto them the abundance of peace and truth." (Bible JER 33:6)

"This Book is without a doubt a Revelation sent down from the Lord of the Worlds." (Qur'án The Prostration Sura 32:30:1 As-Sajdah)

42. O SON OF MAN!
Humble thyself before Me, that I may graciously visit thee. Arise for the triumph of My cause, that while yet on earth thou mayest obtain the victory.

This tells us, if and when we can arise for the triumph of His cause, that we should not be proud in our achievement but truly humble knowing that it is God's bounty. Whose teachings are they? Bahá'u'lláh's. Whose inspiration is it? Bahá'u'lláh's. Whose cause is it? Bahá'u'lláh's.
Whose angels are they that stand rank upon rank and file upon file that will rush to our assistance? Bahá'u'lláh's.

"We behold you from Our realm of glory, and shall aid whosoever will arise for the triumph of Our Cause with the hosts of the Concourse on high and a company of Our favored angels." (Bahá'u'lláh: Gleanings, Page: 139)

"Do they not look at God's creation, (even) among (inanimate) things -how their (very) shadows turn round, from the right and the left, prostrating themselves to God, and that in the humblest manner? And to God doth obeisance all that is in the heavens and on earth, whether moving (living) creatures or the angels: for none are arrogant (before their Lord)." (Qur'án The Bees 48 & 49 (An-Nahl))

"Humility exalteth man to the heaven of glory and power, whilst pride abaseth him to the depths of wretchedness and degradation." (Bahá'u'lláh: Epistle to the Son of the Wolf, page 30)

"Beseech ye the one true God to grant that ye may taste the savor of such deeds as are performed in His path, and partake of the sweetness of such humility and submissiveness as are shown for His sake. Forget your own selves, and turn your eyes towards your neighbor. Bend your energies to whatever may foster the education of men." (Bahá'u'lláh: Gleanings, page 9)

"Humble yourselves in the sight of the Lord, and he shall lift you up." (Bible James 4:10)
"Whosoever therefore shall humble himself as this little child, the same is greatest in the kingdom of heaven." (Bible Mathew 18:4)

The victory it would seem is the victory over one's self. According to this Hidden Word there are two steps. The first step is to be truly humble and not just present a superficial act of humility. The second step is to serve the Cause of Bahá'u'lláh.

"Arise, O people, and, by the power of God's might, resolve to gain the victory over your own selves, that haply the whole earth may be freed and sanctified from its servitude to the gods of its idle fancies - gods that have inflicted such loss upon, and are responsible for the misery of, their wretched worshipers." (Bahá'u'lláh: Gleanings, page 93)

"O God! Confer victory upon us. O God! Enable us to conquer self and overcome desire." ('Abdu'l-Bahá: Promulgation of Universal

Peace*, page 458)

"For whatsoever is born of God overcometh the world: and this is the victory that overcometh the world, even our faith." (Bible 1John 5:4)

"It is such as obey God and His Apostle, and fear God and do right, that will win (in the end)." (Qur'án The Light 52 An-Nur)

43. O SON OF BEING!
Make mention of Me on My earth, that in My heaven I may remember thee, thus shall Mine eyes and thine be solaced.

To make mention of the name of Bahá'u'lláh while living upon His earth opens the door for an endless accumulation of bounties. Then we are assured of continuing bounties in the here-after.

Whoso openeth his lips in this Day and maketh mention of the name of his Lord, the hosts of Divine inspiration shall descend upon him from the heaven of My name, the All-Knowing, the All-Wise. On him shall also descend the Concourse on high, each bearing aloft a chalice of pure light." (Bahá'u'lláh: Gleanings, page 280)
"Make my prayer, O my Lord, a fountain of living waters whereby I may live as long as Thy sovereignty endureth, and may make mention of Thee in every world of Thy worlds." (Bahá'u'lláh: Prayers and Meditations, page 318)

"If any do desire a reward in this life, We shall give it to him; and if any do desire a reward in the hereafter, We shall give it to him. And swiftly shall We reward those that (serve Us with)gratitude." (Qur'án The Family of Imran 145 (Al-Imran))

"I will go in the strength of the Lord GOD: I will make mention of thy righteousness, even of thine only." (Bible Psalms 71:16)

44. O SON OF THE THRONE!

Thy hearing is My hearing, hear thou therewith. Thy sight is My sight, do thou see therewith, that in thine inmost soul thou mayest testify unto My exalted sanctity, and I within Myself may bear witness unto an exalted station for thee.

"Turn thy sight unto thyself, that thou mayest find Me standing within thee, mighty, powerful and self-subsisting." (Bahá'u'lláh: Arabic Hidden Words, Page: 13)

It would seem that the whole earth is the foot-stool of God and His throne is where Bahá'u'lláh is seated and established.

"This is the Day whereon the unseen world crieth out: "Great is thy blessedness, O earth, for thou hast been made the foot-stool of thy God, and been chosen as the seat of His mighty throne." (Bahá'u'lláh: Gleanings, page 30)

Bahá'u'lláh, in "The Tablet of Carmel" establishes His throne on that blessed mountain and the seat of our Universal House of Justice is now seated upon this throne as stated below.

"Rejoice, for God hath in this Day established upon thee His throne, hath made thee the dawning-place of His signs and the day spring of the evidences of His Revelation." (Bahá'u'lláh: Gleanings, page 15)

"He, verily, loveth the spot which hath been made the seat of His throne, which His footsteps have trodden, which hath been honored by His presence, from which He raised His call, and upon which He shed His tears." (Bahá'u'lláh: Gleanings, pages 15-16)

Thy hearing is My hearing, hear thou therewith. Thy sight is My sight,

do thou see therewith,--Might this not mean that man should become so in tune with the Manifestation of God, and in following His teachings, and in living the Bahá'í life to such an extent that he would then hear and see for himself as Bahá'u'lláh would hear and see?

"With the ear of God he heareth, with the eye of God he beholdeth the mysteries of divine creation. He steppeth into the sanctuary of the Friend, and shareth as an intimate the pavilion of the Loved One." (Bahá'u'lláh: Seven Valleys and Four Valleys, Pages: 17-18)

"They whose sight is keen, whose ears are retentive, whose hearts are enlightened, and whose breasts are dilated, recognize both truth and falsehood, and distinguish the one from the other." (Bahá'u'lláh: Epistle to the Son of the Wolf, page 9)

"Beseech God to grant unto men hearing ears, and sharp sight, and dilated breasts, and receptive hearts, that haply His servants may attain unto their hearts' Desire, and set their faces towards their Beloved." (Bahá'u'lláh: Epistle to the Son of the Wolf, pages 44-45)

"He seeth in himself neither name nor fame nor rank, but findeth his own praise in praising God. He beholdeth in his own name the name of God; to him, "all songs are from the King," and every melody from Him. He sitteth on the throne of "Say, all is from God," and taketh his rest on the carpet of "There is no power or might but in God." (Bahá'u'lláh: Seven Valleys and Four Valleys, Page: 18)

"In the eyes of the All-Merciful a true man appeareth even as a firmament; its sun and moon are his sight and hearing, and his shining and resplendent character its stars." (Bahá'u'lláh: Tablets of Bahá'u'lláh, page 220)

"It is He Who brought you forth from the wombs of your mothers

when ye knew nothing; and He gave you hearing and sight and intelligence and affections: that ye may give thanks (to God)." (Qur'án The Bees 78 (An-Nahl))

"But blessed are your eyes, for they see: and your ears, for they hear." (Bible Matthew 13:16)

that in thine inmost soul thou mayest testify unto My exalted sanctity, and I within Myself may bear witness unto an exalted station for thee.-- It would seem that if we would see with the eye of Bahá'u'lláh and hear with the ear of Bahá'u'lláh we would be a living testimony for Him, not in a superficial way but in a deep and meaningful way.

"My tongue, my pen, my whole being, testify to Thy power, Thy might, Thy grace and Thy bounty, that Thou art God and there is none other God but Thee, the Powerful, the Mighty." (Bahá'u'lláh: Bahá'í Prayers (US), pages 144-145)

"Our Lord! we believe in what thou hast revealed, and we follow the Apostle; then write us down among those who bear witness." (Qur'án The Family of Imran 53(Al-Imran)

"The essence of religion is to testify unto that which the Lord hath revealed, and follow that which He hath ordained in His mighty Book." (Bahá'u'lláh: Tablets of Bahá'u'lláh, page 155)

The only way to obtain that exalted station is to do what God tells us to do, and not do what He tells us not to do. There are no short cuts.

"If ye follow in His way, His incalculable and imperishable blessings will be showered upon you." (Bahá'u'lláh: Gleanings, page 9)

"My sheep hear my voice, and I know them, and they follow me: And

I give unto them eternal life; and they shall never perish," (Bible John 10:27-28)

45. O SON OF BEING!

Seek a martyr's death in My path, content with My pleasure and thankful for that which I ordain, that thou mayest repose with Me beneath the canopy of majesty behind the tabernacle of glory.

Seek a martyr's death in My path,--What does it mean in this day to be a martyr?

"The martyr's field is the place of detachment from self, that the anthems of eternity may be upraised." ('Abdu'l-Bahá: Selections ... 'Abdu'l-Bahá, page 76)

If one is on the path of Bahá'u'lláh, that would mean following the road signs and obeying them. To be a martyr in this day would be to give your life to Bahá'u'lláh in living sacrifice.

"The community of the organized promoters of the Faith of Bahá'u'lláh in the American continent - the spiritual descendants of the dawn-breakers of an heroic Age, who by their death proclaimed the birth of that Faith -must, in turn, usher in, not by their death but through living sacrifice, that promised World Order, the shell ordained to enshrine that priceless jewel, the world civilization, of which the Faith itself is the sole begetter." (Shoghi Effendi: The Advent of Divine Justice, page 7)

"The death of self is needed here, not rhetoric:" (Bahá'u'lláh: Seven Valleys and Four Valleys, page 52)

"According to my earnest expectation and my hope, that in nothing I shall be ashamed, but that with all boldness, as always, so now also

Christ shall be magnified in my body, whether it be by life, or by death. For to me to live is Christ, and to die is gain." (Bible Philippians 1:20-21)

There is a passage in the Tablet of Ahmad that states if one chants the tablet, his reward will be that of a hundred martyrs. Now does this mean that in the spiritual kingdom of God man will gain such a reward? Does it mean that the man who chants it can go through the agony, pain and sacrifice of a hundred martyrs during one's lifetime? With the idea of living martyrdoms it no doubt means both.

"For verily, God hath ordained for the one who chants it, the reward of a hundred martyrs and a service in both worlds." (Bahá'u'lláh: Bahá'í Prayers (US), page 213)

<u>content with My pleasure and thankful for that which I ordain,</u>--As pointed out in the twelfth Hidden Word, God made us perfectly but we mess it up. His pleasures, and all of His teachings, have only one purpose and that is for the exaltation and benefit of man. Of course, we should be eternally grateful. If all the atoms of the earth could be turned into radiant suns of thanksgiving it could still not express the gratitude we should have for God. He brought us into existence, and sent us the teachings and guidance for a happy and productive life.

"Happy is the man that hath apprehended the Purpose of God in whatever He hath revealed from the Heaven of His Will that pervadeth all created things." (Bahá'u'lláh: The Kitab-i-Aqdas, page 64)

"The purpose of these Educators, in all they said and taught, was to preserve man's exalted station." (Bahá'u'lláh: Aqdas: Questions and Answers, page 139)

"These words have streamed from the pen of this Wronged One in one of His Tablets: "The purpose of the one true God, exalted be His glory, hath been to bring forth the Mystic Gems out of the mine of man .." .(Bahá'u'lláh: Epistle to the Son of the Wolf, page 13)

<u>that thou mayest repose with Me beneath the canopy of majesty behind the tabernacle of glory.</u> --Repose is to comfortably rest. A canopy is a protective covering over our heads. The tabernacle is the holy of holies or the tent in which the Ark of the Covenant of God was conveyed from place to place. This indicates that man can find that repose with Bahá'u'lláh; protected under His majesty, and safe if he is standing firmly behind His covenant. The Báb, referring to Bahá'u'lláh said:

"Say, this of a certainty is the Garden of Repose, the loftiest Point of adoration, the Tree beyond which there is no passing, the blessed Lote-Tree, the Most Mighty Sign, the most beauteous Countenance and the most comely Face." (The Báb: Selections from the Báb, page 155)

"Behold, thou art called a Jew, and restest in the law, and makest thy boast of God," (Bible Romans 2:17)

". . .and those who work righteousness will spread their couch (of repose) for themselves (in heaven):" (Qur'án The Romans 44 (Ar-Rum))

"Blessed the wayfarer who directeth his steps towards the Tabernacle of My glory and majesty. Blessed the distressed one who seeketh refuge beneath the shadow of My canopy." (Bahá'u'lláh: Tablets of Bahá'u'lláh, page 16)
"Who has made the earth your couch, and the heaven your canopy; and sent down rain from the heavens; and brought forth therewith

fruits for your sustenance; then set not up rivals unto God when ye know (the truth)." (Qur'án The Cow 22 Al-Baqarah))

"LORD, who shall abide in thy tabernacle? who shall dwell in thy holy hill? He that walketh uprightly, and worketh righteousness, and speaketh the truth in his heart." (Bible Psalms 15:1-2)

"Remember We made the house a place of assembly for men and a place of safety; and take ye the station of Abraham as a place of prayer; and We covenanted with Abraham and Isma'il, that they should sanctify My House for those who compass it round, or use it as a retreat, or bow, or prostrate themselves (therein in prayer)." (Qur'án The Cow 125 Al-Baqarah)

46. O SON OF MAN!
Ponder and reflect. Is it thy wish to die upon thy bed, or to shed thy life-blood on the dust, a martyr in My path, and so become the manifestation of My command and the revealer of My light in the highest paradise? Judge thou aright, O servant!

Ponder and reflect.--To ponder something is to turn it over and over in one's mind to try to understand it. Reflect is to look back at what you were pondering before. We had this word "ponder" in the second Hidden Word in which Bahá'u'lláh tells us not only to ponder with our minds, but to do it with our hearts; in other words, think so deeply about it that it is felt. Then action is required. Too often man might think deeply about things of the spirit but does nothing about what he has come to understand.

"Live thou in accord with the teachings of Bahá'u'lláh. Do not only read them. There is a vast difference between the soul who merely reads the words of Bahá'u'lláh and the one who tries to live them. Read thou "The Hidden Words". Ponder over their meanings and embody the behests into thy life...." ("Star of the West" Vol. 7, No. 18,

p. 178)

"Do they not ponder over the Word (of God)," (Qur'án The Believers 68 Al-Muminun)

"Ponder the path of thy feet, and let all thy ways be established." (Bible Proverbs 4:26)

"This subject needs deep thought. Then the cause of these changes will be evident and apparent. Blessed are those who reflect!" ('Abdu'l-Bahá: Some Answered Questions, page 96)

"This book of the law shall not depart out of thy mouth; but thou shalt meditate therein day and night, that thou mayest observe to do according to all that is written therein: for then thou shalt make thy way prosperous, and then thou shalt have good success." (Bible Joshua 1:8)

<u>Is it thy wish to die upon thy bed, or to shed thy life-blood on the dust, a martyr in My path,</u>--We all live, and as surely as we live we will all die. God created us all and gave us the wonderful gift of life and breathed within us an eternal breath of His own spirit. Here we are being invited to offer up that life to Him in service.

"Now, if ever, is the time to emulate the example of these heroes, saints and martyrs. Now is the time to pour out one's substance as copiously and as readily, as the Dawn-breakers of the Heroic Age of the Faith have shed their life-blood in the path of this most precious Cause. No more befitting tribute can be paid to the memory of these luminous souls, by those who carry the torch of Divine Guidance after them, than by a corresponding manifestation of solidarity, self-abnegation, zeal and devotion, Which will impel them to forsake their homes, sacrifice their treasure, brave every danger, endure every hardship, expend every ounce of energy, that the Plan which they have spontaneously and unitedly sponsored may, through its triumphant termination, carry them a stage further along the broad highway of their destiny." (Shoghi Effendi: Dawn of a New Day, pages 134-135)

It seems appropriate to point out that the life-blood of the Cause of Bahá'u'lláh in this day is the fund.

"The supply of funds, in support of the National Treasury, constitutes, at the present time, the life-blood of these nascent institutions you are laboring to erect. Its importance cannot, surely, be overestimated. Untold blessings shall no doubt crown every effort directed to that end." (Shoghi Effendi: Directives of the Guardian, page 31)

and so become the manifestation of My command and the revealer of My light in the highest paradise?--By giving one's life to the Cause of God in living sacrifice, by contributing one's wealth or by actual martyrdom, Bahá'u'lláh is assuring us of undreamt of spiritual bounties. To be the manifestation of His command and the revealer of His light would be to reach the station of living the Bahá'í life in all of its implications.

"strengthen us that we may arise to help Thy Cause and offer ourselves as a living sacrifice in the pathway of guidance." ('Abdu'l-Bahá: Selections ... 'Abdu'l-Bahá, page 315)

47. O SON OF MAN!
By My beauty! To tinge thy hair with thy blood is greater in My sight than the creation of the universe and the light of both worlds. Strive then to attain this, O servant!

"Think not of those who are slain in God's way as dead. Nay, they live, finding their sustenance in the presence of their Lord." (Qur'án

The Family of Imran 169 (Al-Imran))

"For the LORD loves justice, And does not forsake His saints; They are preserved forever," (Bible Psalms 37:28)

"This is a Revelation, under which, if a man shed for its sake one drop of blood, myriads of oceans will be his recompense." (Bahá'u'lláh: Gleanings, pages 5-6)

We have seen how the killing of the Bahá'is in Iran in the late 1980's and early 90's made such an impact that the proclamation of Bahá'u'lláh was made throughout the whole world.

"Every drop of blood shed by the valiant martyrs, every sigh heaved by the silent victims of oppression, every supplication for divine assistance offered by the faithful, has released, and will continue mysteriously to release, forces over which no antagonist of the Faith has any control, and which, as marshaled by an All-Watchful Providence, have served to noise abroad the name and fame of the Faith to the masses of humanity in all continents, millions of whom had previously been totally ignorant of the existence of the Faith or had but a superficial, and oft-times erroneous, understanding of its teachings and history." (The Compilations: Volume 1, page 167)

48. O SON OF MAN!
For everything there is a sign. The sign of love is fortitude under My decree and patience under My trials.

"Verily in this there are Signs for such as are firmly patient and constant - grateful and appreciative." (Qur'án Abraham 5 (Ibrahim))

We can see that all the trials are God sent trials and if one truly loves God one would soon discover this reality. Even the problems, tests and trials brought about by man's disobedience are heaven sent to set mankind on the proper path.

"Were it not for calamity, how would the sun of Thy patience shine, O Light of the worlds?" (Bahá'u'lláh: Bahá'í Prayers (US), page 220)

"He, verily, shall increase the reward of them that endure with patience.
Know ye that trials and tribulations have, from time immemorial, been the lot of the chosen Ones of God and His beloved, and such of His servants as are detached from all else but Him, they whom neither merchandise nor traffic beguile from the remembrance of the Almighty, they that speak not till He hath spoken, and act according to His commandment." (Bahá'u'lláh: Gleanings, page 129)

A decree of God is an order from the King of Kings that must be obeyed. Obeying the order requires fortitude and patience. For us to be impatient with ourselves in following the orders seems to be a good thing.

"Everything that is hath come to be through His irresistible decree. Whenever My laws appear like the sun in the heaven of Mine utterance, they must be faithfully obeyed by all, though My decree be such as to cause the heaven of every religion to be cleft asunder." (Bahá'u'lláh: The Kitab-i-Aqdas, page 21)

"Say: Nothing will happen to us except what God has decreed for us: He is our protector: and on God let the believers put their trust." (Qur'án Repentance 51 At-Taubah)

"Arise in His name, put your trust wholly in Him, and be assured of ultimate victory." (Nabil-i-Azam: The Dawn-Breakers, Page: 94)

49. O SON OF MAN!

The true lover yearneth for tribulation even as doth the rebel for forgiveness and the sinful for mercy.

"How numerous the tribulations which have rained, and will soon rain, upon Me! I advance with My face set towards Him Who is the Almighty, the All-Bounteous, whilst behind Me glideth the serpent. Mine eyes have rained down tears until My bed is drenched. I sorrow not for Myself, however. By God! Mine head yearneth for the spear out of love for its Lord." (Bahá'u'lláh: Proclamation of Bahá'u'lláh, pages 59-60)

This shows us that the Manifestation of God also yearned for tribulation in the path of God which is a good example for us to follow.

"LORD, all my desire is before You; And my sighing is not hidden from You." (Bible Psalms 38:9)

In many places, Bahá'u'lláh points out that tribulation and troubles are in fact a bounty and blessing.

"Verily I say: Whatever befalleth in the path of God is the beloved of the soul and the desire of the heart. Deadly poison in His path is pure honey, and every tribulation a draught of crystal water." (Bahá'u'lláh: Epistle to the Son of the Wolf, page 17)

"Say: Tribulation is a horizon unto My Revelation." (Bahá'u'lláh : Gleanings, page 42)

There is a divine wisdom in suffering and tribulation.

"The mind and spirit of man advance when he is tried by suffering. The more the ground is ploughed the better the seed will grow, the better the harvest will be. Just as the plough furrows the earth deeply, purifying it of weeds and thistles, so suffering and tribulation free man from the petty affairs of this worldly life until he arrives at a state of complete detachment." ('Abdu'l-Bahá : Paris Talks, page 178)

"And he who does not take his cross and follow after Me is not worthy of Me." (Bible Matthew 10:38)

"Should calamity exist in the greatest degree, rejoice, for these things are the gifts and favors of God." (To Live The Life 'Abdu'l-Bahá)

50. O SON OF MAN!
If adversity befall thee not in My path, how canst thou walk in the ways of them that are content with My pleasure? If trials afflict thee not in thy longing to meet Me, how wilt thou attain the light in thy love for My beauty?

This follows the previous Hidden Word and seems to further explain why man must suffer on this plane of existence.

"Verily, I have heard Thy Call, O All-Glorious Beloved; and now is the face of Bahá flaming with the heat of tribulation and with the fire of Thy shining word, and He hath risen up in faithfulness at the place of sacrifice, looking toward Thy pleasure, O Ordainer of the worlds." (Bahá'u'lláh: Bahá'í Prayers (US), Page: 221)

51. O SON OF MAN!
My calamity is My providence, outwardly it is fire and vengeance, but inwardly it is light and mercy. Hasten thereunto that thou mayest become an eternal light and an immortal spirit. This is My command unto thee, do thou observe it.

"Whose trial is the healer of the sicknesses of them who have embraced Thy Cause, Whose calamity is the highest aspiration of such as are rid of all attachment to any one but Thyself!" (Bahá'u'lláh : Prayers and Meditations, Page: 132)

"calamity, however afflictive, is but bounty pouring down upon me, like copious rain." ('Abdu'l-Bahá : Selections ... 'Abdu'l-Bahá , Page: 222)

"Indeed this fresh ordeal that has, in pursuance of the mysterious dispensations of Providence, afflicted the Faith, at this unexpected hour, far from dealing a fatal blow to its institutions or existence, should be regarded as a blessing in disguise, not a "calamity" but a "providence" of God, not a devastating flood but a "gentle rain" on a "green pasture," a "wick" and "oil" unto the "lamp" of His Faith, a "nurture" for His Cause, "water for that which has been planted in the hearts of men," a "crown set on the head" of His Messenger for this Day." (Shoghi Effendi: Citadel of Faith, Page: 139)

"They confronted me in the day of my calamity, but the LORD was my support." (Bible 2 Samuel 22:19)

"No kind of calamity can occur, except by the leave of God: and if anyone believes in God, (God) guides his heart (aright): for God knows all things." (Qur'án The Loss and Gain 11 At-Taghabun)

"Be sure We shall test you with something of fear and hunger, some loss in goods or lives or the fruits (of your toil), but give glad tidings to those who patiently persevere. Who say, when afflicted with calamity: " To God we belong, and to Him is our return." (Qur'án The Cow 155- 156 Al-Baqarah)

52. O SON OF MAN!
Should prosperity befall thee, rejoice not, and should abasement come

upon thee, grieve not, for both shall pass away and be no more.
"Be generous in prosperity, and thankful in adversity." (Bahá'u'lláh : Epistle to the Son of the Wolf, Page: 93)

"Then We changed their suffering into prosperity" (Qur'án The Heights 95 Al-Araf)

"But we see Jesus, who was made a little lower than the angels, for the suffering of death crowned with glory and honor, that He, by the grace of God, might taste death for everyone." (Bible Hebrews 2:9)

"Be unrestrained as the wind, while carrying the Message of Him Who hath caused the Dawn of Divine Guidance to break. Consider, how the wind, faithful to that which God hath ordained, bloweth upon all the regions of the earth, be they inhabited or desolate. Neither the sight of desolation, nor the evidences of prosperity, can either pain or please it. It bloweth in every direction, as bidden by its Creator." (Bahá'u'lláh: Gleanings, Page: 339)

"No doubt is there whatever that these tribulations will be followed by the outpourings of a supreme mercy, and these dire adversities be succeeded by an overflowing prosperity." (Bahá'u'lláh: Proclamation of Bahá'u'lláh, Page: 59)

These Hidden Words seem to give us a deeper understanding of the trials and tribulations of life. Trials help us to develop the divine attribute of patience, and give us a better insight into why these Holy Manifestations of God allowed themselves to suffer on this plain of existence. Bahá'u'lláh most eloquently explains this in His Fire Tablet.

"Were it not for the cold, how would the heat of Thy words prevail, O Expounder of the worlds?
Were it not for calamity, how would the sun of Thy patience shine, O

Light of the worlds?

Lament not because of the wicked. Thou wert created to bear and endure, O Patience of the worlds.

How sweet was Thy dawning on the horizon of the Covenant among the stirrers of sedition, and Thy yearning after God, O Love of the worlds.

By Thee the banner of independence was planted on the highest peaks, and the sea of bounty surged, O Rapture of the worlds.

By Thine aloneness the Sun of Oneness shone, and by Thy banishment the land of Unity was adorned. Be patient, O Thou Exile of the worlds.

We have made abasement the garment of glory, and affliction the adornment of Thy temple, O Pride of the worlds.

Thou seest the hearts are filled with hate, and to overlook is Thine, O Thou Concealer of the sins of the worlds." (Bahá'u'lláh: Bahá'í Prayers (US), Page: 220)

"For you know the grace of our Lord Jesus Christ, that though He was rich, yet for your sakes He became poor, that you through His poverty might become rich." (Bible 2 Corinthians 8:9)

"My brethren, take the prophets, who spoke in the name of the Lord, as an example of suffering and patience." (Bible James 5:10)

"Or do ye think that ye shall enter the Garden (of Bliss) without such (trials)?" (Qur'án The Cow 214 Al-Baqarah)

"No one should expect, upon becoming a Bahá'í, that his faith will not be tested, and to our finite understanding of such matters these tests may occasionally seem unbearable." (Multiple Authors: Lights of Guidance, Page: 342)

Think men that when they say, "We believe," they shall be let alone and not be put to proof? (Qur'án The Spider 1 Al-Ankabut)

53. O SON OF BEING!

If poverty overtake thee, be not sad; for in time the Lord of wealth shall visit thee. Fear not abasement, for glory shall one day rest on thee.

"The generous soul will be made rich, and he who waters will also be watered himself." (Bible Proverbs 11:25)

"And if ye fear poverty, soon will God enrich you, if He wills, out of his bounty, for God is All-Knowing, All-Wise." (Qur'án Repentance 28 At-Taubah)

"It bestoweth wealth without gold, and conferreth immortality without death." (Bahá'u'lláh: Gleanings, Page: 269)

"This is a Revelation that infuseth strength into the feeble, and crowneth with wealth the destitute." (Bahá'u'lláh: Gleanings, Page: 184)

This wealth Bahá'u'lláh talks about must be that wealth of spirituality. As we know, most of the people born into extreme poverty, no matter how hard they work, they and their families end their lives in extreme poverty.

"I ask Thee, by the eternal billows of Thy loving-kindness and the shining lights of Thy tender care and favor, to grant that which shall draw me nigh unto Thee and make me rich in Thy wealth." (Bahá'u'lláh: Bahá'í Prayers (US), Page: 144)

"It bestoweth wealth without gold, and conferreth immortality without death." (Bahá'u'lláh : Gleanings, Page: 269)

"The essence of wealth is love for Me; whoso loveth Me is the possessor of all things, and he that loveth Me not is indeed of the poor and needy." (Bahá'u'lláh: Tablets of Bahá'u'lláh, Page: 156)

Another view is that when a person knows himself, then wealth is needed and this, of course, is the wealth of both worlds.

"**The first Taraz and the first effulgence which hath dawned from the horizon of the Mother Book is that man should know his own self and recognize that which leadeth unto loftiness or lowliness, glory or abasement, wealth or poverty. Having attained the stage of fulfilment and reached his maturity, man standeth in need of wealth, and such wealth as he acquireth through crafts or professions is commendable and praiseworthy in the estimation of men of wisdom, and especially in the eyes of servants who dedicate themselves to the education of the world and to the edification of its peoples.**" (Bahá'u'lláh: Tablets of Bahá'u'lláh, Pages: 34-35)

"**Thus it is incumbent on every one to engage in crafts and professions, for therein lies the secret of wealth, O men of understanding!**" (Bahá'u'lláh: Persian Hidden Words, Page: 80)

Not only is work a means to acquire wealth but Bahá'u'lláh has elevated such work to the station of prayer and worship of God.

"**The most despised of men in the sight of God are those who sit idly and beg. Hold ye fast unto the cord of material means, placing your whole trust in God, the Provider of all means. When anyone occupieth himself in a craft or trade, such occupation itself is regarded in the estimation of God as an act of worship; and this is naught but a token of His infinite and all-pervasive bounty.**" (Bahá'u'lláh: Tablets of Bahá'u'lláh, Page: 26)

"For the LORD your God has blessed you in all the work of your hand." (Bible Deuteronomy 2:7

54. O SON OF BEING!
If thine heart be set upon this eternal, imperishable dominion, and this ancient, everlasting life, forsake this mortal and fleeting sovereignty.

"Know ye in truth that wealth is a mighty barrier between the seeker and his desire, the lover and his beloved. The rich, but for a few, shall in no wise attain the court of His presence nor enter the city of content and resignation. Well is it then with him, who, being rich, is not hindered by his riches from the eternal kingdom, nor deprived by them of imperishable dominion. By the Most Great Name! The splendor of such a wealthy man shall illuminate the dwellers of heaven even as the sun enlightens the people of the earth!" (Bahá'u'lláh: Persian Hidden Words, Page: 53)

"The (material) things which ye are given are but the conveniences of this life and the glitter thereof; but that which is with God is better and more enduring: will ye not then be wise?" (Qur'án The Narrations 60 Al-Qasas)

"And again I say to you, it is easier for a camel to go through the eye of a needle than for a rich man to enter the kingdom of God." (Bible Matthew 19:24)

"If, however, the wealth of this world, and worldly glory and repute, do not block his entry therein, that rich man will be favoured at the Holy Threshold and accepted by the Lord of the Kingdom." ('Abdu'l-Bahá: Selections ...'Abdu'l-Bahá, Page: 195)

We have a dichotomy between the need for wealth for the progress of the

Cause and the need to give it all up. The Guardian even called money the life blood of the Cause.

"FUND (The Life-blood of these Nascent Institutions)" (Shoghi Effendi: Directives of the Guardian, Page: 31)

All the good things of the earth God has put here for mankind's use and enjoyment, but these things are not to be worshiped. This following quote explains the seeming dichotomy.

"Whatsoever deterreth you, in this Day, from loving God is nothing but the world. Flee it, that ye may be numbered with the blest. Should a man wish to adorn himself with the ornaments of the earth, to wear its apparels, or partake of the benefits it can bestow, no harm can befall him, if he alloweth nothing whatever to intervene between him and God, for God hath ordained every good thing, whether created in the heavens or in the earth, for such of His servants as truly believe in Him. Eat ye, O people, of the good things which God hath allowed you, and deprive not yourselves from His wondrous bounties. Render thanks and praise unto Him, and be of them that are truly thankful." (Bahá'u'lláh: Gleanings, Page: 276)

55. O SON OF BEING!
Busy not thyself with this world, for with fire We test the gold, and with gold We test Our servants.

This Hidden Word would indicate that to have a golden heart would require the tests of fire, and wealth can be a test for those that posses it.

"Thou wouldst test him with the benefits of this world and of the next that he might become preoccupied therewith and forget Thy remembrance." (The Báb: Selections from the Báb , Page: 192)

"Verily God hath made adversity as a morning dew upon His green pasture, and a wick for His lamp which lighteth earth and heaven." (Bahá'u'lláh : Epistle to the Son of the Wolf, Page: 17)

The way that gold is tested for purity is by having it assayed. Bahá'u'lláh is the divine assayer for testing the purity of hearts.

"Ye are like clear but bitter water, which to outward seeming is crystal pure but of which, when tested by the Divine Assayer, not a drop is accepted." (Bahá'u'lláh: Epistle to the Son of the Wolf, Page: 16)

"By this divinely-appointed touchstone, the claims and pretensions of all men must needs be assayed, so that the truthful may be known and distinguished from the imposter." (Bahá'u'lláh: Kitab-i-Iqan, Page: 227)

56. O SON OF MAN!

Thou dost wish for gold and I desire thy freedom from it. Thou thinkest thyself rich in its possession, and I recognize thy wealth in thy sanctity therefrom. By My life! This is My knowledge, and that is thy fancy; how can My way accord with thine?

"So He said to him, "Why do you call Me good? No one is good but One, that is, God. But if you want to enter into life, keep the commandments."
He said to Him, "Which ones?" Jesus said, " 'You shall not murder,' 'You shall not commit adultery,' 'You shall not steal,' 'You shall not bear false witness,' 'Honor your father and your mother,' and, 'You shall love your neighbor as yourself.' "
The young man said to Him, "All these things I have kept from my youth. What do I still lack?"
Jesus said to him, "If you want to be perfect, go, sell what you have

and give to the poor, and you will have treasure in heaven; and come, follow Me."

But when the young man heard that saying, he went away sorrowful, for he had great possessions.

Then Jesus said to His disciples, "Assuredly, I say to you that it is hard for a rich man to enter the kingdom of heaven.

"And again I say to you, it is easier for a camel to go through the eye of a needle than for a rich man to enter the kingdom of God." (Bible Matthew 19 17 to 24)

The followers of Jesus when they heard this observed that no one would be able to get to heaven as it was not possible for a camel to go through the eye of a needle.

"When His disciples heard it, they were exceedingly amazed, saying, "Who then can be saved?"

But Jesus looked at them and said to them, "With men this is impossible, but with God all things are possible." (Bible Matthew 19-25 and 26)

One time when I was teaching in the Middle East, the Bahá'í I was with said that he would meet me later at the eye of the needle. When I questioned him he explained that it was a small archway going into the center of town. I arrived there early and I realized that this archway was built to keep the camels out of the town square so they could not mess it up. I realized that a camel could indeed get through the eye of the needle, but <u>only if</u> it took the load off of its back and got down on its knees to pass through.

Along this line that we can only get to heaven with the aid and help of the Manifestation of God, is the Bridge of Sirat. It is said that this is the bridge between earth and heaven and is finer than a hair and sharper than a sword. One side is the earth, the other side is heaven and below is the nethermost fire.

"One owned a house and wished to sell it; the other was to be the purchaser. They had agreed that this transaction should be effected and the contract be written with the knowledge of Ali. He, the exponent of the law of God, addressing the scribe, said: "Write thou: `A dead man hath bought from another dead man a house. That house is bounded by four limits. One extendeth toward the tomb, the other to the vault of the grave, the third to the Sirat, the fourth to either Paradise or hell.'" Reflect, had these two souls been quickened by the trumpet-call of Ali, had they risen from the grave of error by the power of his love, the judgment of death would certainly not have been pronounced against them." (Bahá'u'lláh: The Kitab-i-Iqan, Pages: 119-120)

"If one will ponder but for a while this utterance of Ali in his heart, one will surely discover all mysteries hidden in the terms "grave," "tomb," "sirat," "paradise" and "hell." But oh! how strange and pitiful! Behold, all the people are imprisoned within the tomb of self, and lie buried beneath the nethermost depths of worldly desire! Wert thou to attain to but a dewdrop of the crystal waters of divine knowledge, thou wouldst readily realize that true life is not the life of the flesh but the life of the spirit." (Bahá'u'lláh: The Kitab-i-Iqan, Page: 120)

"Still others must have recalled with throbbing hearts the Islamic tradition foreshadowing the appearance of Fatimih herself unveiled while crossing the Bridge (Sirat) on the promised Day of Judgment." (Shoghi Effendi: God Passes By, Page: 32)

This world and all its riches has as much value in the sight of God as the black of an eye of a dead ant. When we strive with heart and soul for its wealth we are expending our life for nothing.

"Rejoicest thou in that thou rulest a span of earth, when the whole world, in the estimation of the people of Bahá, is worth as much as the black in the eye of a dead ant?" (Bahá'u'lláh : Epistle to the Son of the Wolf, Page: 56)

"If true glory were to consist in the possession of such perishable things, then the earth on which ye walk must needs vaunt itself over you, because it supplieth you, and bestoweth upon you, these very things, by the decree of the Almighty. In its bowels are contained, according to what God hath ordained, all that ye possess. From it, as a sign of His mercy, ye derive your riches. Behold then your state, the thing in which ye glory! Would that ye could perceive it!"
"Nay! By Him Who holdeth in His grasp the kingdom of the entire creation! Nowhere doth your true and abiding glory reside except in your firm adherence unto the precepts of God, your wholehearted observance of His laws, your resolution to see that they do not remain unenforced, and to pursue steadfastly the right course." (Bahá'u'lláh : Gleanings, Pages: 252-253)

"Behold then your state, the thing in which ye glory!" We all know what is in our bowels so it surely requires us to seriously perceive it and realize the waste of our lives in the pursuance of wealth and material possessions.

"O my people! This life of the present is nothing but (temporary) convenience: it is the Hereafter that is the Home that will last." (Qur'án The Forgiver 39 Ghafir)

57. O SON OF MAN!
Bestow My wealth upon My poor, that in heaven thou mayest draw from stores of unfading splendor and treasures of imperishable glory. But by My life! To offer up thy soul is a more glorious thing couldst

thou but see with Mine eye.

We note here that what Bahá'u'lláh is asking us to do is to bestow His wealth upon His poor. It is neither our wealth nor our poor. This is another confirmation of the name of God "the All possessing." The only real and lasting wealth is the knowledge of God and His laws.

"The small shall be made great, and the powerless shall be given strength; they that are of tender age shall become the children of the Kingdom, and those that have gone astray shall be guided to their heavenly home." (From a Tablet - translated from the Persian) ('Abdu'l-Bahá: Crisis and Victory, Page: 155)

"Lo, the All-Possessing is come. Earth and heaven, glory and dominion are God's, the Lord of all men, and the Possessor of the Throne on high and of earth below!" (Bahá'u'lláh : Aqdas: Other Sections, Page: 99)

"Is it not lawful for me to do what I wish with my own things?" (Bible Matthew 20:15)

"When you possess these divine susceptibilities, you will be able to awaken and develop them in others. We cannot give of our wealth to the poor unless we possess it. How can the poor give to the poor? How can the soul that is deprived of the heavenly bounties develop in other souls capacity to receive those bounties?" ('Abdu'l-Bahá: Promulgation of Universal Peace, Page: 7)

"I am poor, O my Lord, and Thou art the Rich." (Bahá'u'lláh: Prayers and Meditations, Page: 215)

In the light of these quotes, although the material poor must be cared for, the reality of poverty is a wholly spiritual condition. This substantiates the statement that the greatest gift we can give to another is the gift of teaching His Cause.

"You have given him the greatest gift in the world: the Faith." (Shoghi Effendi: Unfolding Destiny, Page: 441)

"Regarding your question concerning helping the poor: The Bahá'í should not go so far as to refrain from extending charity to the needy, if they are able and willing to do so. However, in this, as in many other things, they should exert moderation. The greatest gift that we can give to the poor and the down-trodden is to aid to build up the divine institutions inaugurated in this day by Bahá'u'lláh as these institutions, and this World Order when established, will eliminate the causes of poverty and the injustices which afflict the poor. We should, therefore, do both, support our Bahá'í Fund, and also be kind and generous to the needy." (Multiple Authors: Lights of Guidance, Pages: 124-125)

"The small shall be made great, and the powerless shall be given strength; they that are of tender age shall become the children of the Kingdom, and those that have gone astray shall be guided to their heavenly home." (From a Tablet - translated from the Persian) ('Abdu'l-Bahá: Crisis and Victory, Page: 155)

58. O SON OF MAN!
The temple of being is My throne; cleanse it of all things, that there I may be established and there I may abide.

What is the temple referring to here? Is it my being? Is it my heart? Is it the Houses of Worship? Is it the Holy shrines of the Báb and Bahá'u'lláh?

"And the pilgrimage to the temple, is a service due to God from those who are able to journey thither." (Qur'án The Family of Imran 91 Al-

Imran)

"He only should visit the temples of God who believeth in God and the last day, and observeth prayer, and payeth the legal alms, and dreadeth none but God. These haply will be among the rightly guided." (Qur'án Repentance 18 At-Taubah)

"The LORD is in His holy temple, The Lord's throne is in heaven; His eyes behold, His eyelids test the sons of men." (Bible Psalms 11:4)

"I beseech Thee by Thy generosity, whereby the portals of Thy bounty and grace were opened wide, whereby the Temple of Thy Holiness was established upon the throne of eternity;" (Bahá'u'lláh: Bahá'í Prayers (US), Pages: 97-98)

"Trustworthiness is as a stronghold to the city of humanity, and as eyes to the human temple. Whosoever remaineth deprived thereof shall, before His Throne, be reckoned as one bereft of vision." (Bahá'u'lláh: Trustworthiness, Page: 330)

"As this physical frame is the throne of the inner temple, whatever occurs to the former is felt by the latter." (Multiple Authors: Lights of Guidance, Page: 201)

59. O SON OF BEING!
Thy heart is My home; sanctify it for My descent. Thy spirit is My place of revelation; cleanse it for My manifestation.

This heart must be the home of the Manifestation of God for that unknowable Essence does not enter or exit and is beyond ascending or descending. "Finding Me standing within thee" must refer to Bahá'u'lláh.

"To every discerning and illuminated heart it is evident that God, the unknowable Essence, the Divine Being, is immensely exalted beyond every human attribute, such as corporeal existence, ascent and descent, egress and regress. Far be it from His glory that human tongue should adequately recount His praise, or that human heart comprehend His fathomless mystery. He is, and hath ever been, veiled in the ancient eternity of His Essence, and will remain in His Reality everlastingly hidden from the sight of men. "No vision taketh in Him, but He taketh in all vision; He is the Subtile, the All-Perceiving."...

"The door of the knowledge of the Ancient of Days being thus closed in the face of all beings, the Source of infinite grace, according to His saying, "His grace hath transcended all things; My grace hath encompassed them all," hath caused those luminous Gems of Holiness to appear out of the realm of the spirit, in the noble form of the human temple, and be made manifest unto all men, that they may impart unto the world the mysteries of the unchangeable Being, and tell of the subtleties of His imperishable Essence."

"These sanctified Mirrors, these Day Springs of ancient glory, are, one and all, the Exponents on earth of Him Who is the central Orb of the universe, its Essence and ultimate Purpose. From Him proceed their knowledge and power; from Him is derived their sovereignty. The beauty of their countenance is but a reflection of His image, and their revelation a sign of His deathless glory. They are the Treasuries of Divine knowledge, and the Repositories of celestial wisdom. Through them is transmitted a grace that is infinite, and by them is revealed the Light that can never fade.... These Tabernacles of Holiness, these Primal Mirrors which reflect the light of unfading glory, are but expressions of Him Who is the Invisible of the Invisibles. By the revelation of these Gems of Divine virtue all the names and attributes of God, such as knowledge and power, sovereignty and dominion, mercy and wisdom, glory, bounty, and grace, are made manifest." (Bahá'u'lláh: Gleanings, Pages: 46-48)

"......that you may know and believe that the Father is in Me, and I in Him." (Bible John 10:38)

"He who obeys the Apostle, obeys God" (Qur'án Women 80 An-Nisa)

Once the Manifestation of God is established in His home, the human heart, then and only then can its spirit begin to reflect to others. This reflection is also conditional upon humanity striving with heart and soul to acquire the divine attributes as one of the conditions of why they were created.

`What is the purpose of our lives?'
'Abdu'l-Bahá. - `To acquire virtues. ('Abdu'l-Bahá: Paris Talks, Page: 177)

"He has brought forth everything necessary for the life of this world, but man is a creation intended for the reflection of divine virtues." ('Abdu'l-Bahá: Promulgation of Universal Peace, Pages: 302-303)
"This indicates that man is of the image and likeness of God - that is to say, the perfections of God, the divine virtues, are reflected or revealed in the human reality." ('Abdu'l-Bahá: Promulgation of Universal Peace, Page: 69)

"Turn thy sight unto thyself, that thou mayest find Me standing within thee, mighty, powerful and self-subsisting." (Bahá'u'lláh: Arabic Hidden Words, Page: 13)

"I bear witness, O my God, that Thou hast created me to know Thee and to worship Thee." (Bahá'u'lláh: Aqdas: Other Sections, Page: 100)

60. O SON OF MAN!

Put thy hand into My bosom, that I may rise above thee, radiant and resplendent.

This is a difficult concept as Bahá'u'lláh is asking us to put our hand into His bosom. It may be that the bosom and heart are one and the same. Yet in the writings there seems to be a difference.

"**Illumine his heart, gladden his bosom, kindle his light, that he may serve Thy Cause and Thy servants.**" ('Abdu'l-Bahá: Selections ... 'Abdu'l-Bahá, Page: 320)

"**Thou hast ordained for me that which shall bring solace to mine eyes, gladden my bosom and rejoice my heart,**" (Bahá'u'lláh: Tablets of Bahá'u'lláh, Page: 113)

Could it be that the bosom is the receptacle that contains the heart? The bosom also seems to refer to the soul. As we know, it is the spirit of faith that inspires the soul of man.

"**..... thus causing the freshest and loveliest blossoms, and the mightiest and loftiest trees to spring forth from the illumined bosom of man.**" (Bahá'u'lláh: The Kitab-i-Iqan, Page: 48)

The statement below, about a telegraph station, should give us additional food for thought as the bosom then becomes a place of connection to the Supreme Concourse.

"**Each bosom must be a telegraph station - one terminus of the wire attached to the soul, the other fixed in the Supreme Concourse.....**" ('Abdu'l-Bahá: Promulgation of Universal Peace*, Page: 183)

Once we can get into the telegraph station of Bahá'u'lláh and make the connection from my soul to His Supreme Concourse, then He will rise above us radiant and resplendent.

61. O SON OF MAN!
Ascend unto My heaven, that thou mayest obtain the joy of reunion, and from the chalice of imperishable glory quaff the peerless wine.

"Thy Paradise is My love; thy heavenly home, reunion with Me." (Bahá'u'lláh: Arabic Hidden Words, Page: 6)

"…..inasmuch as he will inherit the heavenly home, through the revelation of Thy favours, and will partake of the goodly gifts Thou hast provided therein; for the things which are with Thee are inexhaustible. This indeed is Thy blessing which according to the good-pleasure of Thy Will Thou dost bestow on those who tread the path of Thy love." (The Báb: Selections from the Báb, Page: 189)

"Those who faithfully observe their trust and their covenants; And who (strictly) guard their prayers -. Those will be the heirs,. Who will inherit Paradise: they will dwell therein (forever)." (Qur'án The Believers 8-11 Al-Muminun)

In order to ascend one must go up, and that requires an effort on our part. Peerless signifies something that has no equal and imperishable mean it will last forever.

62. O SON OF MAN!
Many a day hath passed over thee whilst thou hast busied thyself with thy fancies and idle imaginings. How long art thou to slumber on thy bed? Lift up thy head from slumber, for the Sun hath risen to the zenith, haply it may shine upon thee with the light of beauty.

"Night hath succeeded day, and day hath succeeded night, and the hours and moments of your lives have come and gone, and yet none of you hath, for one instant, consented to detach himself from that which perisheth. Bestir yourselves, that the brief moments that are still yours may not be dissipated and lost. Even as the swiftness of lightning your days shall pass, and your bodies shall be laid to rest beneath a canopy of dust. What can ye then achieve? How can ye atone for your past failure?" (Bahá'u'lláh: Gleanings, Page: 321)

"In the morning the breeze of My grace passed by thee, and found thee sleeping on the bed of heedlessness, and wept over thy condition, and turned back." ('Abdu'l-Bahá : A Traveler's Narrative, Page: 69)

"They have hearts wherewith they understand not, eyes wherewith they see not, and ears wherewith they hear not. They are like cattle, nay more misguided: for they are heedless (of warning)." (Qur'án The Heights 179 Al-Araf)

The sun of the revelation of Bahá'u'lláh has come up and is shining in all of its mid-summer glory. When the sun comes up, turn off the lamp.

"By the righteousness of God! The Dawn hath truly brightened and the light hath shone forth and the night hath receded. Happy are they that comprehend. Happy are they that have attained thereunto." (Bahá'u'lláh: Tablets of Bahá'u'lláh , Page: 41)

"At this hour the morn of knowledge hath arisen and the lamps of wayfaring and wandering are quenched." (Bahá'u'lláh: Seven Valleys and Four Valleys, Page: 16)

"But take diligent heed to do the commandment and the law which Moses the servant of the LORD commanded you, to love the LORD your God, to walk in all His ways, to keep His commandments, to hold fast to Him, and to serve Him with all your heart and with all your soul." (Bible Joshua 22:5)

"Therefore take heed that the light which is in you is not darkness. If then your whole body is full of light, having no part dark, the whole body will be full of light, as when the bright shining of a lamp gives you light." (Bible Luke 11:35-36)

63. O SON OF MAN!

The light hath shone on thee from the horizon of the sacred Mount and the spirit of enlightenment hath breathed in the Sinai of thy heart. Wherefore, free thyself from the veils of idle fancies and enter into My court, that thou mayest be fit for everlasting life and worthy to meet Me. Thus may death not come upon thee, neither weariness nor trouble.

Sinai refers to the mountain where Moses encountered the burning bush and heard the voice of God. Here, Bahá'u'lláh seems to indicate that this mountain is in the human heart and thus the burning bush would be a heart that was on fire with the love of God.

"This is a traditional Jewish and Islamic title of Moses. Bahá'u'lláh states that with the coming of His Revelation "human ears have been privileged to hear what He Who conversed with God heard upon Sinai". Sinai, The mountain where the Law was revealed by God to Moses. The Spirit of God, This is one of the titles used in the Islamic and Bahá'í Writings to designate Jesus Christ." (Bahá'u'lláh: Aqdas: Notes, Page: 215)

"on the Sinai of Divine knowledge" (Bahá'u'lláh Epistle to the Son of the Wolf, Page: 41)

"the Sinai of Utterance," (Bahá'u'lláh : Epistle to the Son of the Wolf, Page: 43)

"the Sinai of Wisdom." (Bahá'u'lláh : Epistle to the Son of the Wolf, Page: 86) "the Sinai of light" (Bahá'u'lláh Gleanings, Page: 19)

"the Sinai of Holiness" (Bahá'u'lláh: Gleanings, Page: 61)

"the Sinai of assurance." (Bahá'u'lláh: Tablets of Bahá'u'lláh, Page: 103)

"Verily, I say, so fierce is the blaze of the Bush of love, burning in the Sinai of the heart, that the streaming waters of holy utterance can never quench its flame. Oceans can never allay this Leviathan's burning thirst, and this Phoenix of the undying fire can abide nowhere save in the glow of the countenance of the Well-Beloved." (Bahá'u'lláh: The Kitab-i-Iqan, Page: 61)

"Kindle the fire that burns in me in the Sinai of Thy Singleness, and awaken the eternal life that is latent in me, through Thy bounty and grace." ('Abdu'l-Bahá: Bahá'í Prayers (UK edition), Page: 83)

"Tur" and "Sinai" should not be taken literally; the first is an allusion to Mt. Sinai, which in this case means the Manifestation of God; the second, "Sinai", represents the human heart." (Shoghi Effendi: Light of Divine Guidance Vol.2, Pages: 66-67)

"And remember We took your covenant and We raised above you (the towering height) of Mount (Sinai) (saying): Hold firmly to what We have given you and bring (ever) to remembrance what is therein, perchance ye may fear God." (Qur'án The Cow 63 Al-Baqarah)

The spirit of enlightenment that breathed in the human heart signifies that not only do we take into our hearts the knowledge of God but we must be also breathing it out to others, and in this way it is a loving invitation to teach. We don't just breathe in; we must also breathe out. The veils of idle fancies can mean spending all your time and effort in trying to prove something in the dim and distant past that can't be proven anyway.

"Rend thou asunder the veils of idle fancies and vain imaginings, that thou mayest behold the Day-Star of knowledge shining from this resplendent Horizon." (Bahá'u'lláh: Epistle to the Son of the Wolf, Page: 80)

"Cease idly repeating the traditions of the past, for the day of service, of steadfast action, is come. Now is the time to show forth the true signs of God, to rend asunder the veils of idle fancy, to promote the Word of God, and to sacrifice ourselves in His path. Let deeds, not words, be our adorning!" ('Abdu'l-Bahá Memorials of the Faithful, Page: 201)

"Rend thou asunder the veils of idle fancies and vain imaginings, that thou mayest behold the Day-Star of knowledge shining from this resplendent Horizon." (Bahá'u'lláh: Epistle to the Son of the Wolf, Page: 80)

"Arise, O people, and, by the power of God's might, resolve to gain the victory over your own selves, that haply the whole earth may be freed and sanctified from its servitude to the gods of its idle fancies - gods that have inflicted such loss upon, and are responsible for the misery of, their wretched worshipers." (Bahá'u'lláh: Gleanings, Page: 93)

Only with the power of God's might can we ever hope to free ourselves from the veils of idle fancies and vain imaginings and enter into His court. Once freed from self we would then be fit for eternity. We must pray for help.

64. O SON OF MAN!
My eternity is My creation, I have created it for thee. Make it the

garment of thy temple. My unity is My handiwork; I have wrought it for thee; clothe thyself therewith, that thou mayest be to all eternity the revelation of My everlasting being.

This statement of God creating eternity confounds the mind of man. The very definition of eternity is that it has always existed and will always exist. Perhaps this means the eternity of the Manifestation of God when He Manifests Himself.

"Consider the hour at which the supreme Manifestation of God revealeth Himself unto men. Ere that hour cometh, the Ancient Being, Who is still unknown of men and hath not as yet given utterance to the Word of God, is Himself the All-Knower in a world devoid of any man that hath known Him." (Bahá'í Gleanings, Page: 151)

"Nay, all else besides these Manifestations, live by the operation of Their Will, and move and have their being through the outpourings of Their grace." (Bahá'u'lláh Gleanings, Page: 179)

"He shone forth from the Sinai of light upon the world. He summoned all the peoples and kindreds of the earth to the kingdom of eternity, and invited them to partake of the fruit of the tree of faithfulness." (Bahá'u'lláh: The Kitab-i-Iqan, Page: 11)

"Make eternity the garment of thy temple" would indicate that if the temple of man is his spiritual nature, then the garment of eternity would be putting on the robe of divine virtues; that is, living the Bahá'í life or strict obedience to His commands.

"A single breeze of His affluence doth suffice to adorn all mankind with the robe of wealth; and one drop out of the ocean of His bountiful grace is enough to confer upon all beings the glory of everlasting life." (Bahá'u'lláh: The Kitab-i-Iqan, Page: 53)

Bahá'u'lláh's unity has been made for man. Not only must we put on this robe of unity with man and all creation, but more importantly would be our unity with Him.

"From eternity Thou hast, in Thy transcendent oneness, been immeasurably exalted above Thy servants' conception of Thy unity, and wilt to eternity remain, in Thine unapproachable singleness, far above the praise of Thy creatures." (Bahá'u'lláh: Prayers and Meditations, Page: 130)

"I, therefore, the prisoner of the Lord, beseech you to have a walk worthy of the calling with which you were called, with all lowliness and gentleness, with longsuffering, bearing with one another in love, endeavoring to keep the unity of the Spirit in the bond of peace. There is one body and one Spirit, just as you were called in one hope of your calling; one Lord, one faith, one baptism; one God and Father of all, who is above all, and through all, and in you all." (Bible Ephesians 4:1-4:6)

"Verily, this Brotherhood of yours is a single Brotherhood, and I am your Lord and Cherisher: therefore serve Me (and no other)." (Qur'án The Prophets 92 Al-Anbiya)

65. O SON OF MAN!
My majesty is My gift to thee, and My grandeur the token of My mercy unto thee. That which beseemeth Me none shall understand, nor can anyone recount. Verily, I have preserved it in My hidden storehouses and in the treasuries of My command, as a sign of My loving-kindness unto My servants and My mercy unto My people.

'Abdu'l-Bahá was the exemplar and the essence of service and humility and as a result we can readily see that divine majesty. To attain that majesty would surely be a wondrous gift. The same is true of His grandeur.

"These are the melodies, sung by Jesus, Son of Mary, in accents of majestic power in the Ridvan of the Gospel, revealing those signs that must needs herald the advent of the Manifestation after Him." (Bahá'u'lláh: The Kitab-i-Iqan, Page: 24)

"Because He bore injustice, justice hath appeared on earth, and because He accepted abasement, the majesty of God hath shone forth amidst mankind." (Bahá'u'lláh: The Kitab-i-Aqdas, Page: 76)

"Thou seest, O my Lord, this stranger hastening to his most exalted home beneath the canopy of Thy majesty and within the precincts of Thy mercy; and this transgressor seeking the ocean of Thy forgiveness; and this lowly one the court of Thy glory; and this poor creature the orient of Thy wealth." (Bahá'u'lláh: Aqdas: Other Sections, Page: 94)

" Isaiah saith: "The Lord alone shall be exalted in that Day." Concerning the greatness of the Revelation He saith: "Enter into the rock, and hide thee in the dust, for fear of the Lord, and for the glory of His majesty." (Bahá'u'lláh: Epistle to the Son of the Wolf, Page: 146)

"Far, far from Thy glory be what mortal man can affirm of Thee, or attribute unto Thee, or the praise with which he can glorify Thee! Whatever duty Thou hast prescribed unto Thy servants of extolling to the utmost Thy majesty and glory is but a token of Thy grace unto them, that they may be enabled to ascend unto the station conferred upon their own inmost being, the station of the knowledge of their own selves." (Bahá'u'lláh: Gleanings, Pages: 4-5)

That which no one will ever understand is the Manifestation Himself and the Unknowable Essence.

"The conceptions of the devoutest of mystics, the attainments of the most accomplished amongst men, the highest praise which human tongue or pen can render are all the product of man's finite mind and are conditioned by its limitations. Ten thousand Prophets, each a Moses, are thunderstruck upon the Sinai of their search at His forbidding voice, "Thou shalt never behold Me!"; whilst a myriad Messengers, each as great as Jesus, stand dismayed upon their heavenly thrones by the interdiction, "Mine Essence thou shalt never apprehend!" From time immemorial He hath been veiled in the ineffable sanctity of His exalted Self, and will everlastingly continue to be wrapt in the impenetrable mystery of His unknowable Essence. Every attempt to attain to an understanding of His inaccessible Reality hath ended in complete bewilderment, and every effort to approach His exalted Self and envisage His Essence hath resulted in hopelessness and failure." (Bahá'u'lláh: Gleanings, Pages: 62-63)

These hidden storehouses and the treasures of His command are hidden in the way the Manifestation reveals them. That is, as man evolves into a more spiritual being, the sign of His mercy and loving kindness will bring to light those jewels of understanding which the present generation has no idea about and cannot comprehend.

"It hath been decreed by Us that the Word of God and all the potentialities thereof shall be manifested unto men in strict conformity with such conditions as have been foreordained by Him Who is the All-Knowing, the All-Wise. We have, moreover, ordained that its veil of concealment be none other except its own Self. Such indeed is Our Power to achieve Our Purpose. Should the Word be allowed to release suddenly all the energies latent within it, no man

could sustain the weight of so mighty a Revelation." (Bahá'u'lláh: Gleanings, Pages: 76-77)

"However, when He, the Spirit of truth, has come, He will guide you into all truth; for He will not speak on His own authority, but whatever He hears He will speak; and He will tell you things to come." (Bible John 16:13)

66. O CHILDREN OF THE DIVINE AND INVISIBLE ESSENCE!
Ye shall be hindered from loving Me and souls shall be perturbed as they make mention of Me. For minds cannot grasp Me nor hearts contain Me.

Here we have a new title that seems to refer to those who accept and recognize the Manifestation in the day in which we live. Through Him they make contact with that Creator of all that is.

" I ask Thee, O Lord of all being and King of the seen and unseen, by Thy power, Thy majesty and Thy sovereignty, to grant that my name may be recorded by Thy pen of glory among Thy devoted ones, them whom the scrolls of the sinful hindered not from turning to the light of Thy countenance, O prayer-hearing, prayer-answering God!" (Bahá'u'lláh: Bahá'í Prayers (US), Page: 164)

Referring to the above quote about the Unknowable Essence, one can never love or relate to an invisible and unknowable thing. In His infinite love and wisdom He sends that wonderful Manifestation and even that creation is still beyond our understanding and comprehension.

"Know thou of a certainty that the Unseen can in no wise incarnate His Essence and reveal it unto men. He is, and hath ever been, immensely exalted beyond all that can either be recounted or perceived. From His retreat of glory His voice is ever proclaiming:

"Verily, I am God; there is none other God besides Me, the All-Knowing, the All-Wise. I have manifested Myself unto men, and have sent down Him Who is the Day Spring of the signs of My Revelation. Through Him I have caused all creation to testify that there is none other God except Him, the Incomparable, the All-Informed, the All-Wise." He Who is everlastingly hidden from the eyes of men can never be known except through His Manifestation, and His Manifestation can adduce no greater proof of the truth of His Mission than the proof of His own Person." (Bahá'u'lláh: Gleanings, Page: 49)

"Praised be Thou, O Lord my God! Every time I attempt to make mention of Thee, I am hindered by the sublimity of Thy station and the overpowering greatness of Thy might. For were I to praise Thee throughout the length of Thy dominion and the duration of Thy sovereignty, I would find that my praise of Thee can befit only such as are like unto me, who are themselves Thy creatures, and who have been generated through the power of Thy decree and been fashioned through the potency of Thy will. And at whatever time my pen ascribeth glory to any one of Thy names, methinks I can hear the voice of its lamentation in its remoteness from Thee, and can recognize its cry because of its separation from Thy Self. I testify that everything other than Thee is but Thy creation and is held in the hollow of Thy hand. To have accepted any act or praise from Thy creatures is but an evidence of the wonders of Thy grace and bountiful favors, and a manifestation of Thy generosity and providence." (Bahá'u'lláh: Prayers and Meditations, Page: 125)

Should every atom of this vast and limitless creation be turned into a sun of thanks for the favor of this revelation and this Manifestation it would be inadequate to express it.

67. O SON OF BEAUTY!

By My spirit and by My favor! By My mercy and by My beauty! All that I have revealed unto thee with the tongue of power, and have written for thee with the pen of might, hath been in accordance with thy capacity and understanding, not with My state and the melody of My voice.

"But the falcon of the mystic heaven hath many a wondrous carol of the spirit in His breast, and the Persian bird keepeth in His soul many a sweet Arab melody; yet these are hidden, and hidden shall remain." (Bahá'u'lláh: Seven Valleys and Four Valleys, Page: 29)

"In these planes, the nightingale of the heart hath other songs and secrets, which make the heart to stir and the soul to clamor, but this mystery of inner meaning may be whispered only from heart to heart, confided only from breast to breast." (Bahá'u'lláh: Seven Valleys and Four Valleys, Page: 30)

Bahá'u'lláh's example of the sun and the mirror helps us to understand this idea that the teachings of God are revealed to us in accordance with our capacities to receive it. Some of these mirrors of the human heart are large and some are small.

"He - glorified be His mention - resembleth the sun. Were unnumbered mirrors to be placed before it, each would, according to its capacity, reflect the splendor of that sun, and were none to be placed before it, it would still continue to rise and set, and the mirrors alone would be veiled from its light." (Bahá'u'lláh: Epistle to the Son of the Wolf, Page: 156)

"Consider that which hath been sent down unto Muhammad, the Apostle of God. The measure of the Revelation of which He was the bearer had been clearly foreordained by Him Who is the Almighty, the All-Powerful. They that heard Him, however, could apprehend

His purpose only to the extent of their station and spiritual capacity. He, in like manner, uncovered the Face of Wisdom in proportion to their ability to sustain the burden of His Message." (Bahá'u'lláh: Gleanings, Page: 77)

"Know of a certainty that in every Dispensation the light of Divine Revelation hath been vouchsafed unto men in direct proportion to their spiritual capacity. Consider the sun. How feeble its rays the moment it appeareth above the horizon. How gradually its warmth and potency increase as it approacheth its zenith, enabling meanwhile all created things to adapt themselves to the growing intensity of its light. How steadily it declineth until it reacheth its setting point. Were it, all of a sudden, to manifest the energies latent within it, it would, no doubt, cause injury to all created things.... In like manner, if the Sun of Truth were suddenly to reveal, at the earliest stages of its manifestation, the full measure of the potencies which the providence of the Almighty hath bestowed upon it, the earth of human understanding would waste away and be consumed; for men's hearts would neither sustain the intensity of its revelation, nor be able to mirror forth the radiance of its light. Dismayed and overpowered, they would cease to exist." (Bahá'u'lláh: Gleanings, Pages: 87-88)

"The whole duty of man in this Day is to attain that share of the flood of grace which God poureth forth for him. Let none, therefore, consider the largeness or smallness of the receptacle. The portion of some might lie in the palm of a man's hand, the portion of others might fill a cup, and of others even a gallon-measure." (Bahá'u'lláh: Gleanings, Page: 8)

"We will not task a soul beyond its ability." (Qur'án The Cattle 153 Al-Anam)

68. O CHILDREN OF MEN!

Know ye not why We created you all from the same dust? That no one should exalt himself over the other. Ponder at all times in your hearts how ye were created. Since We have created you all from one same substance it is incumbent on you to be even as one soul, to walk with the same feet, eat with the same mouth and dwell in the same land, that from your inmost being, by your deeds and actions, the signs of oneness and the essence of detachment may be made manifest. Such is My counsel to you, O concourse of light! Heed ye this counsel that ye may obtain the fruit of holiness from the tree of wondrous glory.

"The incomparable Creator hath created all men from one same substance, and hath exalted their reality above the rest of His creatures. Success or failure, gain or loss, must, therefore, depend upon man's own exertions. The more he striveth, the greater will be his progress." (Bahá'u'lláh : Gleanings, Pages: 81-82)

"Among His Signs is this, that He created you from dust; and then, Behold, ye are men scattered (far and wide)!" (Qur'án The Romans 20 Ar-Rum)

"Let no one imagine that by Our assertion that all created things are the signs of the revelation of God is meant that - God forbid - all men, be they good or evil, pious or infidel, are equal in the sight of God. Nor doth it imply that the Divine Being - magnified be His name and exalted be His glory - is, under any circumstances, comparable unto men, or can, in any way, be associated with His creatures. Such an error hath been committed by certain foolish ones who, after having ascended into the heavens of their idle fancies, have interpreted Divine Unity to mean that all created things are the signs of God, and that, consequently, there is no distinction whatsoever between them." (Bahá'u'lláh: Gleanings, Page: 187)

It is important for us to understand that God alone is the judge and only He can do this. Our position should be, "That no one should exalt himself over the other."

"Be servants of each other, and know that we are less than anyone else. Be as one soul in many bodies; for the more we love each other, the nearer we shall be to God; but know our love, our unity, our obedience must not be by confession, but reality." (To Live The Life 'Abdu'l-Bahá)

"These things I command you, that you love one another." (Bible John 15:17)

"Have we not created you of a sorry germ," (Qur'án The Emissaries 20 Al-Mursalat)

This oneness, love and unity is not only individual but collective. There is no longer we and they or us and them. It is all of us, that is humanity.

"Consort with the followers of all religions in a spirit of friendliness and fellowship." Whatsoever hath led the children of men to shun one another, and hath caused dissensions and divisions amongst them, hath, through the revelation of these words, been nullified and abolished." (Bahá'u'lláh: Gleanings, Page: 95)

This teaching of 'loving thy neighbor,' which exists in all other religions, is one of the most important in the Old and New Testaments.

"'You shall not take vengeance, nor bear any grudge against the children of your people, but you shall love your neighbor as yourself: I am the LORD." (Bible LEV 19:18)

"In that day,' says the LORD of hosts, 'Everyone will invite his

neighbor under his vine and under his fig tree.' " (Bible ZEC 3:10)

"We did send apostles before thee amongst the religious sects of old:" (Qur'án The Rocky Tract 10 Al-Hijr)

69. O YE SONS OF SPIRIT!

Ye are My treasury, for in you I have treasured the pearls of My mysteries and the gems of My knowledge. Guard them from the strangers amidst My servants and from the ungodly amongst My people.

"Say: God hath made My hidden love the key to the Treasure; would that ye might perceive it! But for the key, the Treasure would to all eternity have remained concealed; would that ye might believe it! Say: This is the Source of Revelation, the Dawning-place of Splendour, Whose brightness hath illumined the horizons of the world. Would that ye might understand! This is, verily, that fixed Decree through which every irrevocable decree hath been established." (Bahá'u'lláh : The Kitab-i-Aqdas, Page: 24)

"Through the bestowals of the Lord, however, and His infinite favour, thou hast attained unto the hidden secret and the well-guarded treasure. Preserve then, in the name of God, this lofty station and conceal it from the eyes of betrayers." (Bahá'u'lláh: Women, Page: 359)

"Just now the soil of human hearts seems like black earth, but in the innermost substance of this dark soil there are thousands of fragrant flowers latent. We must endeavor to cultivate and awaken these potentialities, discover the secret treasure in this very mine and depository of God, bring forth these resplendent powers long hidden in human hearts. Then will the glories of both worlds be blended and increased and the quintessence of human existence be made manifest." ('Abdu'l-Bahá : Promulgation of Universal Peace*, Page: 294)

"Now therefore, if you will indeed obey My voice and keep My covenant, then you shall be a special treasure to Me above all people; for all the earth is Mine." (Bible EXO 19:5)

"For where your treasure is, there your heart will be also." (Bible MAT 6:21)

"With Him are the keys of the Unseen, the treasures that none knoweth but He. He knoweth whatever there is on the earth and in the sea." (Qur'án The Cattle 59 Al-Anam)

"The Great Being saith: The Word is the master key for the whole world, inasmuch as through its potency the doors of the hearts of men, which in reality are the doors of heaven, are unlocked. No sooner had but a glimmer of its effulgent splendour shone forth upon the mirror of love than the blessed word `I am the Best-Beloved' was reflected therein. It is an ocean inexhaustible in riches, comprehending all things. Every thing which can be perceived is but an emanation therefrom. High, immeasurably high is this sublime station, in whose shadow moveth the essence of loftiness and splendour, wrapt in praise and adoration." (Tablets of Bahá'u'lláh Page: 173)

"The `Master Key' to self-mastery is self-forgetting. The road to the palace of life is through the path of renunciation." (Multiple Authors: Lights of Guidance, Page: 115)

"And I will give you the keys of the kingdom of heaven, and whatever you bind on earth will be bound in heaven, and whatever you loose on earth will be loosed in heaven." (Bible MAT 16:19)

"To Him belong the keys of the heavens and the earth: He enlarges and restricts the Sustenance to whom He will: for He knows full well all things." (Qur'án The Consultation 12 Ash-Shura)

"Thus have the billows of the Ocean of Utterance surged, casting forth the pearls of the laws decreed by the Lord of all mankind." (Bahá'u'lláh : The Kitab-i-Aqdas, Page: 28)

"Cast away, in My name that transcendeth all other names, the things ye possess, and immerse yourselves in this Ocean in whose depths lay hidden the pearls of wisdom and of utterance, an ocean that surgeth in My name, the All-Merciful." (Bahá'u'lláh : Gleanings, Page: 33)

"Glory be unto Thee, O Lord of the world and Desire of the nations, O Thou Who hast become manifest in the Greatest Name whereby the pearls of wisdom and utterance have appeared from the shells of the great sea of Thy knowledge, and the heavens of divine revelation have been adorned with the light of the appearance of the Sun of Thy countenance." (Tablets of Bahá'u'lláh , Pages: 33-34)

"Again, the kingdom of heaven is like a merchant seeking beautiful pearls, who, when he had found one pearl of great price, went and sold all that he had and bought it." (Bible. MAT 13:45 & 46)

"Magnify Thou, O Lord my God, Him Who is the Primal Point, the Divine Mystery, the Unseen Essence, the Day-Spring of Divinity, and the Manifestation of Thy Lordship, through Whom all the knowledge of the past and all the knowledge of the future were made plain, through Whom the pearls of Thy hidden wisdom were uncovered, and the mystery of Thy treasured name disclosed," (Bahá'u'lláh: Prayers and Meditations, Pages: 84-85)

"By My life! Couldst thou but know the things sent down by My Pen, and discover the treasures of My Cause, and the pearls of My mysteries which lie hid in the seas of My names and in the goblets of My words, thou wouldst for longing after His glorious and sublime Kingdom, lay down thy life in the path of God." (Bahá'u'lláh : Epistle to the Son of the Wolf, Pages: 58-59)

"Behold, how many are the mysteries that lie as yet unravelled within the tabernacle of the knowledge of God, and how numerous the gems of His wisdom that are still concealed in His inviolable treasuries!"
(Bahá'u'lláh: The Kitab-i-Iqan, Page: 167)

"O my brother! A divine Mine only can yield the gems of divine knowledge, and the fragrance of the mystic Flower can be inhaled only in the ideal Garden, and the lilies of ancient wisdom can blossom nowhere except in the city of a stainless heart." (Bahá'u'lláh : The Kitab-i-Iqan, Page: 191)

Guard them from the strangers amidst My servants and from the ungodly amongst My people. This statement appears to hold a warning for that treasure ("ye are my treasure"), to not only protect His lovers from outside attacks, but also from attacks from within His Cause.

"My imprisonment doeth Me no harm, neither the tribulations I suffer, nor the things that have befallen Me at the hands of My oppressors. That which harmeth Me is the conduct of those who, though they bear My name, yet commit that which maketh My heart and My pen to lament." (Bahá'u'lláh : Epistle to the Son of the Wolf, Page: 23)

"The voice of the Divine Herald, proceeding out of the throne of God, declareth: O ye My loved ones! Suffer not the hem of My sacred vesture to be smirched and mired with the things of this world, and follow not the promptings of your evil and corrupt desires."

(Bahá'u'lláh: Gleanings, Page: 200)

"The living waters of My mercy, O Ali, are fast pouring down, and Mine heart is melting with the heat of My tenderness and love. At no time have I been able to reconcile Myself to the afflictions befalling My loved ones, or to any trouble that could becloud the joy of their hearts. Every time My name "the All-Merciful" was told that one of My lovers had breathed a word that runneth counter to My wish, it repaired, grief-stricken and disconsolate to its abode; and whenever My name "the Concealer" discovered that one of My followers had inflicted any shame or humiliation on his neighbor, it, likewise, turned back chagrined and sorrowful to its retreats of glory, and there wept and mourned with a sore lamentation." (Bahá'u'lláh : Gleanings, Pages: 308-309)

It was from one of Christ's disciples from the very center of the core group that this heinous betrayal of Jesus took place.

"Then He answered and said, 'He who dipped his hand with Me in the dish will betray Me.' The Son of Man goes as it is written of Him, but woe to that man by whom the Son of Man is betrayed! It would have been good for that man if he had not been born." (Bible Mat 26:23-24)

"Then Judas, His betrayer, seeing that He had been condemned, was remorseful and brought back the thirty pieces of silver to the chief priests and elders, saying, 'I have sinned by betraying innocent blood.' And they said, 'What is that to us? You see to it.' Then he threw down the pieces of silver in the temple and departed, and went and hanged himself." (Bible MAT 27:3-6

70. O SON OF HIM THAT STOOD BY HIS OWN ENTITY IN THE KINGDOM OF HIS SELF!

Know thou, that I have wafted unto thee all the fragrances of holiness, have fully revealed to thee My word, have perfected through thee My bounty and have desired for thee that which I have desired for My Self. Be then content with My pleasure and thankful unto Me.

This title may be referring to the Manifestation of God as He alone stands by His own entity in the Kingdom of His self. This could also refer to the Word of God that flows through the Manifestation. This Hidden Word sums up the out-pouring of God's grace and love that was manifested in the Arabic Hidden Words.

"Know thou, moreover, that the Word of God - exalted be His glory - is higher and far superior to that which the senses can perceive, for it is sanctified from any property or substance. It transcendeth the limitations of known elements and is exalted above all the essential and recognized substances. It became manifest without any syllable or sound and is none but the Command of God which pervadeth all created things. It hath never been withheld from the world of being. It is God's all-pervasive grace, from which all grace doth emanate. It is an entity far removed above all that hath been and shall be." (Tablets of Bahá'u'lláh, Pages: 140-141)

"The Essence of the Divine Entity and the Unseen of the unseen is holy above imagination and is beyond thought. Consciousness doth not reach It. Within the capacity of comprehension of a produced (or created) reality that Ancient Reality cannot be contained. It is a different world; from it there is no information; arrival thereat is impossible; attainment thereto is prohibited and inaccessible. This much is known: It exists and Its existence is certain and proven - but the condition is unknown." ('Abdu'l-Bahá :   Japan Will Turn Ablaze*, Page: 23)

"And Moses alone shall come near the LORD, but they shall not come near; nor shall the people go up with him." (Bible EXO 24:2)

"For I have given to them the words which You have given Me; and they have received them, and have known surely that I came forth from You; and they have believed that You sent Me." (Bible John 17:8)

"Knowest thou not that to God (alone) belongeth the dominion of the heavens and the earth? He punisheth whom He pleaseth, and He forgiveth whom He pleaseth: and God hath power over all things." (Qur'án The Table Spread 43 Al-Maidah)

"I bear witness, O friends! that the favor is complete, the argument fulfilled, the proof manifest and the evidence established." (Bahá'u'lláh : Persian Hidden Words, Page: 82)

"I have, moreover, with the hand of divine power, unsealed the choice wine of My Revelation, and have wafted its holy, its hidden, and musk-laden fragrance upon all created things." (Bahá'u'lláh : Gleanings, Page: 328)

"All glory be to this Day, the Day in which the fragrances of mercy have been wafted over all created things, a Day so blest that past ages and centuries can never hope to rival it, a Day in which the countenance of the Ancient of Days hath turned towards His holy seat." (Bahá'u'lláh: Tablets of Bahá'u'lláh, Page: 3)

"This," He furthermore declares, "is the king of days," the "Day of God Himself," the "Day which shall never be followed by night," the "Springtime which autumn will never overtake," "the eye to past ages and centuries," for which "the soul of every Prophet of God, of every Divine Messenger, hath thirsted," for which "all the divers kindreds of the earth have yearned," through which "God hath proved the hearts of the entire company of His Messengers and Prophets, and beyond them those that stand guard over His sacred and inviolable Sanctuary, the inmates of the Celestial Pavilion and dwellers of the Tabernacle of Glory." "In this most mighty Revelation," He moreover, states, "all the Dispensations of the past have attained their highest, their final consummation." (Shoghi Effendi: God Passes By, Page: 99)

"O ye who believe! turn to God with sincere repentance: in the hope that your Lord will remove from you your ills and admit you to Gardens beneath which Rivers flow - the Day that God will not permit to be humiliated the Prophet and those who believe with him. Their Light will run forward before them and by their right hands, while they say, "Our Lord! perfect our Light for us, and grant us Forgiveness; for Thou has power over all things." (Qur'án forbidden 8 At-Tahrim)

"And if thine eyes be turned towards justice, choose thou for thy neighbor that which thou choosest for thyself." (Bahá'u'lláh : Epistle to the Son of the Wolf, Page: 30)

"Thou shalt love thy neighbour as thyself." (Bible MAT 19:19)

71. O SON OF MAN!
Write all that We have revealed unto thee with the ink of light upon the tablet of thy spirit. Should this not be in thy power, then make thine ink of the essence of thy heart. If this thou canst not do, then write with that crimson ink that hath been shed in My path. Sweeter indeed is this to Me than all else, that its light may endure for ever.

"All that I have revealed unto thee with the tongue of power, and have written for thee with the pen of might, hath been in accordance with thy capacity and understanding, not with My state and the melody of My voice." (Bahá'u'lláh : Arabic Hidden Words, Page: 67)

"It is incumbent upon every man of insight and understanding to strive to translate that which hath been written into reality and action." (Tablets of Bahá'u'lláh , Page: 166)

"What profit is there in agreeing that universal friendship is good, and talking of the solidarity of the human race as a grand ideal? Unless these thoughts are translated into the world of action, they are useless." ('Abdu'l-Bahá: Paris Talks*, Page: 16)

"Let it now be seen what your endeavors in the path of detachment will reveal. In this wise hath the divine favor been fully vouchsafed unto you and unto them that are in heaven and on earth. All praise to God, the Lord of all Worlds." (Bahá'u'lláh: Persian Hidden Words, Page: 82)

"Thou hast helped me to attain this manifest grace; that Thou hast reddened the dust with my blood, spilled out upon Thy path, so that it puts forth crimson flowers." ('Abdu'l-Bahá: Memorials of the Faithful, Page: 177)

"O thou Remnant of God! I have sacrificed myself wholly for Thee; I have accepted curses for Thy sake; and have yearned for naught but martyrdom in the path of Thy love. Sufficient Witness unto me is God, the Exalted, the Protector, the Ancient of Days!" (Bahá'u'lláh: The Kitab-i-Iqan, Page: 231)

"Every day has certain needs. In those early days the Cause needed Martyrs, and people who would stand all sorts of torture and persecution in expressing their faith and spreading the message sent by God. Those days are, however, gone. The Cause at present does not need martyrs who would die for the faith, but servants who desire to teach and establish the Cause throughout the world. To live to teach in the present day is like being martyred in those early days. It is the spirit that moves us that counts, not the act through which that spirit expresses itself; and that spirit is to serve the Cause of God with our heart and soul." (Shoghi Effendi: Living the Life, Page: 5)

"FRIENDS, the time is coming when I shall be no longer with you. I have done all that could be done. I have served the Cause of Bahá'u'lláh to the utmost of my ability. I have labored night and day all the years of my life. 0 how I long to see the believers shouldering the responsibilities of the Cause! This is the time of the proclamation of the Kingdom of Abhá ! This is the hour of Union and Accord! This is the day of the spiritual harmony of the friends of God! All the resources of my physical strength are exhausted and the spirit of my life is the news of the Unity of the people of Bahá. I am straining my ears toward the East and toward the West, toward the North and toward the South, perchance I might hear the songs of love and good fellowship raised from the meetings of the believers. My days are numbered, and save this there is no joy left for me. 0 how I yearn to see the friends united like unto a strand of shining pearls like the brilliant Pleiades, like the rays of the sun and the gazelles of one meadow! The nightingale of significance is singing for them; will they not listen? The bird of paradise is warbling; will they not heed? The Angel of the Kingdom of Abhá is calling to them; will they not hearken? The Messenger of the Covenant is pleading; will they not obey? Ah me! I am waiting, waiting to hear the glad news that the believers are the embodiment of sincerity and loyally, that they are the 'incarnation of love and amity and the visible symbols of unity and concord! Will they not rejoice my heart? Will they not satisfy my cravings? Will they not comply with my request? Will they not fulfill my anticipations? Will they not answer my call?

I am waiting. I am patiently l waiting!" ('Abdu'l-Bahá Abbas) (Star of The West Vol. 5,p. 104)

"And in closing, dearly-beloved friends, what more appropriate thought with which to conclude my fervent plea than these pregnant words fallen from the lips of Bahá'u'lláh: 'O My friends! I bear witness that the Divine Bounty has been vouchsafed unto you, His Argument has been made manifest, His Proof has been revealed, and His Guidance has shone forth upon you. Let it now be seen what your endeavors in the path of renunciation can reveal.' Your true brother, SHOGHI. Haifa, Palestine, December 6, 1928. To the beloved of the Lord" (Shoghi Effendi: Bahá'í Administration, Pages: 155-156)

IN THE HEART OF WORDS II

BY
Jenabe E. Caldwell

From the Hidden Words of Bahá'u'lláh in Persian
Introduction

It is our prayer and hope that those that have gone through the Arabic Hidden Words and read the comments and quotes have been stimulated to study, meditate and ponder them, looking for the "spiritual" meaning.

"Immerse yourselves in the ocean of My words, that ye may unravel its secrets, and discover all the pearls of wisdom that lie hid in its depths."   (Bahá'u'lláh: The Kitab-i-Aqdas, Page: 85)

"It is my hope that you may put forth your most earnest endeavor to accomplish this end, that you may investigate and study the Holy Scriptures word by word so that you may attain knowledge of the mysteries hidden therein. Be not satisfied with words, but seek to understand the spiritual meanings hidden in the heart of the words." ('Abdu'l-Bahá: Promulgation of Universal Peace*, Page: 459)

For this section we will use only quotes and no further comments. As you study together you will be able to unravel the mysteries hidden therein.

"They have even failed to realize, all this time, that, in every age, the reading of the scriptures and holy books is for no other purpose except to enable the reader to apprehend their meaning and unravel their innermost mysteries. Otherwise reading, without understanding, is of no abiding profit unto man." (Bahá'u'lláh: The Kitab-i-Iqan, Page: 172)

"Observe My commandments, for the love of My beauty. Happy is the lover that hath inhaled the divine fragrance of his Best-Beloved from these words, laden with the perfume of a grace which no tongue can describe." (Bahá'u'lláh: The Kitab-i-Aqdas, Pages: 20-21)

"We have announced unto everyone that one single word from Thee excelleth all that hath been sent down in the Bayan." (Bahá'u'lláh: The Kitab-i-Aqdas, Page: 65)

"The Hidden Words is a treasury of divine mysteries. When thou ponderest its contents, the doors of the mysteries will open." (The Importance of Deepening, Page: 197)

THE HIDDEN WORDS OF BAHÁ'U'LLÁH part II–from the Persian

In the Name of the Lord of Utterance, The Mighty.

"The seas of Divine wisdom and Divine utterance have risen under the breath of the breeze of the All-Merciful. Hasten to drink your fill, O men of understanding!" (Bahá'u'lláh: The Kitab-i-Aqdas, Page: 20)

"This is the Utterance of the All-Merciful, would that ye had ears to hear! Say: This is the essence of knowledge, did ye but understand." (Bahá'u'lláh: The Kitab-i-Aqdas, Page: 69)

"And when thou enterest into the place of resurrection, and God asketh thee by what proof thou hast believed in this Revelation, draw forth the Tablet and say: 'By this Book, the holy, the mighty, the incomparable.'" (Bahá'u'lláh: Epistle to the Son of the Wolf, Page: 103)

1. O YE PEOPLE THAT HAVE MINDS TO KNOW AND EARS TO HEAR!

The first call of the Beloved is this: O mystic nightingale! Abide not but in the rose-garden of the spirit. O messenger of the Solomon of love! Seek thou no shelter except in the Sheba of the well-beloved, and O immortal phoenix! dwell not save on the mount of faithfulness. Therein is thy habitation, if on the wings of thy soul thou soarest to the realm of the infinite and seekest to attain thy goal.

"Cling, O ye people of Bahá to the cord of servitude unto God, the True One, for thereby your stations shall be made manifest, your names written and preserved, your ranks raised and your memory exalted in the Preserved Tablet." (Bahá'u'lláh: The Kitab-i-Aqdas, Page: 62)

"O ye that have minds to know! Raise up your suppliant hands to the heaven of the one God, and humble yourselves and be lowly before Him, and thank Him for this supreme endowment, and implore Him to succor us until, in this present age, godlike impulses may radiate from the conscience of mankind, and this divinely kindled fire which has been entrusted to the human heart may never die away." ('Abdu'l-Bahá: Secret of Divine Civilization, Page: 2)

"It is easy to read the Holy Scriptures, but it is only with a clean heart and a pure mind that one may understand their true meaning. Let us ask God's help to enable us to understand the Holy Books. Let us pray for eyes to see and ears to hear, and for hearts that long for peace." ('Abdu'l-Bahá: Paris Talks*, Pages: 56-57)

"He that hath ears to hear, let him hear." (Bible MAT 11:15)

"Son of man, thou dwellest in the midst of a rebellious house, which have eyes to see, and see not; they have ears to hear, and hear not: for they are a rebellious house." (Bible EZE 12:2)

The first call of the Beloved is this:
"I testify that no sooner had the First Word proceeded, through the potency of Thy will and purpose, out of His mouth, and the First Call gone forth from His lips than the whole creation was revolutionized, and all that are in the heavens and all that are on earth were stirred to the depths. (Bahá'u'lláh: Prayers and Meditations, Page: 295)

O mystic nightingale! Abide not but in the rose-garden of the spirit.
"Even should the day of the Mystic Nightingale draw to its close, who would ever lend his ear to the raven's croak, or the cawing of the crow?" ('Abdu'l-Bahá: Selections ... 'Abdu'l-Bahá , Page: 219)

"Now doth the mystic nightingale carol its odes, and buds of inner meaning are bursting into blossoms delicate and fair." ('Abdu'l-Bahá: Selections ... 'Abdu'l-Bahá , Page: 255)

"I am the rose of Sharon, and the lily of the valleys." (Bible Son 2:1)

"The wilderness and the solitary place shall be glad for them; and the desert shall rejoice, and blossom as the rose. It shall blossom abundantly, and rejoice even with joy and singing: the glory of Lebanon shall be given unto it, the excellency of Carmel and Sharon, they shall see the glory of the LORD, and the excellency of our God." (Bible ISA 35:1:2)

"And in another connection He saith: 'The wilderness and the solitary place shall be glad for them; and the desert shall rejoice, and blossom as the rose. It shall blossom abundantly, and rejoice even with joy and singing: the glory of Lebanon shall be given unto it, the splendor of Carmel and Sharon, they shall see the glory of the Lord, and the splendor of our God.'" (Bahá'u'lláh: Epistle to the Son of the Wolf,

Page: 146)

"Hear Me, ye mortal birds! In the Rose Garden of changeless splendor a Flower hath begun to bloom, compared to which every other flower is but a thorn, and before the brightness of Whose glory the very essence of beauty must pale and wither." (Bahá'u'lláh: Gleanings, Pages: 320-321)

"The cloud of the Loved One's mercy raineth only on the garden of the spirit," (Bahá'u'lláh: Seven Valleys and Four Valleys, Page: 38)

"On the outspread tablet of this world, ye are the verses of His singleness; and atop lofty palace towers, ye are the banners of the Lord. In His bowers are ye the blossoms and sweet-smelling herbs, in the rose garden of the spirit the nightingales that utter plaintive cries. Ye are the birds that soar upward into the firmament of knowledge, the royal falcons on the wrist of God." ('Abdu'l-Bahá: Selections ... 'Abdu'l-Bahá , Page: 266)

O messenger of the Solomon of love!
"Solomon in all his majesty circles in adoration around Me in this day, uttering this most exalted word: `I have turned my face towards Thy face, O Thou omnipotent Ruler of the world! I am wholly detached from all things pertaining unto me, and yearn for that which Thou dost possess.'" (Shoghi Effendi: World Order of Bahá'u'lláh, Page: 105)

"..... he called his name Solomon: and the LORD loved him." (Bible 2SA 12:24)

Seek thou no shelter except in the Sheba of the well-beloved,
"And when the queen of Sheba heard of the fame of Solomon concerning the name of the LORD, she came to prove him with hard

questions." (Bible 1KI 10:1)

"She (Sheba) said, 'O my Lord! I have sinned against my own soul, and I resign myself, with Solomon, to God the Lord of the Worlds.'" (Qur'án The Ant 45 An-Naml)

"In flower-spangled meadows hath the divine springtime pitched its tents, and the spiritual are inhaling sweet scents from the Sheba of the spirit, carried their way by the east wind. Now doth the mystic nightingale carol its odes, and buds of inner meaning are bursting into blossoms delicate and fair." ('Abdu'l-Bahá : Selections ... 'Abdu'l-Bahá , Page: 255)

O immortal phoenix! dwell not save on the mount of faithfulness.
"The Phoenix of the realms above crieth out from the immortal Branch: 'The glory of all greatness belongeth to God, the Incomparable, the All-Compelling!'" (Bahá'u'lláh: Gleanings, Pages: 35-36)

"Shouldst thou attain to a drop of the ocean of the inner meaning of these words, thou wouldst surely forsake the world and all that is therein, and, as the Phoenix wouldst consume thyself in the flames of the undying Fire." (Bahá'u'lláh: The Kitab-i-Iqan, Page: 131)

"Sacrifices in the path of one's religion produce always immortal results, `Out of the ashes rises the phoenix'." (Multiple Authors: Lights of Guidance, Page: 604)

Therein is thy habitation, if on the wings of thy soul thou soarest to the realm of the infinite and seekest to attain thy goal.
"Regarding the "two wings" of the soul: These signify wings of ascent. One is the wing of knowledge, the other of faith, as this is the means of the ascent of the human soul to the lofty station of divine

perfections." ('Abdu'l-Bahá: Bahá'í World Faith*, Page: 382)

"For with human feet thou canst never hope to traverse these immeasurable distances, nor attain thy goal." (Bahá'u'lláh: The Kitab-i-Iqan, Page: 43)

"Nor shall the seeker reach his goal unless he sacrifice all things. That is, whatever he hath seen, and heard, and understood, all must he set at naught, that he may enter the realm of the spirit, which is the City of God." (Bahá'u'lláh: Seven Valleys and Four Valleys, Page: 7)

2. O SON OF SPIRIT!

The bird seeketh its nest; the nightingale the charm of the rose; whilst those birds, the hearts of men, content with transient dust, have strayed far from their eternal nest, and with eyes turned towards the slough of heedlessness are bereft of the glory of the divine presence. Alas! How strange and pitiful; for a mere cupful, they have turned away from the billowing seas of the Most High, and remained far from the most effulgent horizon.

The bird seeketh its nest; the nightingale the charm of the rose;
"Wherefore, O friend, give up thy self that thou mayest find the Peerless One, pass by this mortal earth that thou mayest seek a home in the nest of heaven." (Bahá'u'lláh: Seven Valleys and Four Valleys, Pages: 9-10)

"The Spirit of truth is soaring on the Supreme Apex, like unto a bird, in order that it may discover a severed heart and alight therein and make its nest." ('Abdu'l-Bahá: Tablets of 'Abdu'l-Bahá Vol 3*, Page: 554)

whilst those birds, the hearts of men, content with transient dust, have strayed far from their eternal nest, and with eyes turned towards the

slough of heedlessness are bereft of the glory of the divine presence.
"Satisfied with the croaking of the crow and enamoured with the visage of the raven, they have renounced the melody of the nightingale and the charm of the rose." (Bahá'u'lláh: The Kitab-i-Iqan, Page: 189)

"Content with transient dust, these people have turned their face unto it, and cast behind their backs Him Who is the Lord of Lords." (Bahá'u'lláh: The Kitab-i-Iqan, Page: 189)

"And whosoever shall not receive you, nor hear your words, when ye depart out of that house or city, shake off the dust of your feet."(Bible MAT 10:14)

"Those whom you find receptive to your call, share with them the epistles and tablets We have revealed for you, that, perchance, these wondrous words may cause them to turn away from the slough of heedlessness, and soar into the realm of the Divine presence." (Nabil-i-Azam: The Dawn-Breakers, Pages: 85-86)

"The Great Being saith: The Tongue of Wisdom proclaimeth: He that hath Me not is bereft of all things." (Bahá'u'lláh: Tablets of Bahá'u'lláh, Page: 169)

Alas! How strange and pitiful; for a mere cupful, they have turned away from the billowing seas of the Most High, and remained far from the most effulgent horizon.
"We cleave to no knowledge but His Knowledge, and set our hearts on naught save the effulgent glories of His light." (Bahá'u'lláh: The Kitab-i-Iqan, Page: 188)

3. O FRIEND!
In the garden of thy heart plant naught but the rose of love, and from

the nightingale of affection and desire loosen not thy hold. Treasure the companionship of the righteous and eschew all fellowship with the ungodly.

<u>In the garden of thy heart plant naught but the rose of love, and from the nightingale of affection and desire loosen not thy hold</u>.

"In the same way, my answers will serve as rain showers and dew, to bestow on those spiritual plants that have blossomed in the garden of thy heart more freshness and delicate beauty than words can tell." ('Abdu'l-Bahá: Selections ... 'Abdu'l-Bahá, Page: 181)

"Glad-tidings unto thee for that by reason of which the spring of knowledge hath flowed out in the garden of thy heart, inundated thy tongue and made thee utter the name of thy Lord and call the people to the Kingdom of thy God!" ('Abdu'l-Bahá: Tablets of 'Abdu'l-Bahá Vol 2*, Page: 258)

"O God, my God! Aid Thou Thy trusted servants to have loving and tender hearts." ('Abdu'l-Bahá: Selections ... 'Abdu'l-Bahá, Page: 22)

"Close association and loving service affects the hearts; and when the heart is affected, then the spirit can enter. It is the Holy Spirit that quickens, and the Friends must become channels for its diffusion." (Shoghi Effendi: Guidelines for Teaching, Page: 324)

"The LORD hath appeared of old unto me, saying, Yea, I have loved thee with an everlasting love: therefore with loving kindness have I drawn thee." (Bible JER 31:3)

"Let none, in this Day, hold fast to aught save that which hath been manifested in this Revelation. Such is the decree of God, afore time and hereafter - a decree wherewith the Scriptures of the Messengers of old have been adorned." (Bahá'u'lláh: The Kitab-i-Aqdas, Pages: 68-69)

"We have indeed made clear the signs unto any people who hold firmly to faith (in their hearts)." (Qur'án The Cow 118 Al-Baqarah)

Treasure the companionship of the righteous and eschew all fellowship with the ungodly.
"He should treasure the companionship of them that have renounced the world, and regard avoidance of boastful and worldly people a precious benefit." (Bahá'u'lláh: Gleanings, Page: 265)

"He that walketh with wise men shall be wise: but a companion of fools shall be destroyed." (Bible PRO 13:20)

"In the passage "eschew all fellowship with the ungodly", Bahá'u'lláh means that we should shun the company of those who disbelieve in God and are wayward. The word "ungodly" is a reference to such perverse people. The words "Be thou as a flame of fire to My enemies and a river of life eternal to My loved ones" should not be taken in their literal sense. Bahá'u'lláh's advice is that again we should flee from the enemies of God, and instead seek the fellowship of His lovers." (Shoghi Effendi: Dawn of a New Day, Page: 200)

4. O SON OF JUSTICE! Whither can a lover go but to the land of his beloved? and what seeker findeth rest away from his heart's desire? To the true lover reunion is life, and separation is death. His breast is void of patience and his heart hath no peace. A myriad lives he would forsake to hasten to the abode of his beloved. (Bahá'u'lláh: Persian Hidden Words, Pages: 3-4)

Whither can a lover go but to the land of his beloved?
"I am come to thee, O land of the heart's desire, with tidings from God, and announce to thee His gracious favor and mercy, and greet

and magnify thee in His name." (Bahá'u'lláh: Gleanings, Pages: 121-122)

"Then set thy foot into the land of the lovers." (Bahá'u'lláh: Seven Valleys and Four Valleys, Page: 11)

"And We said thereafter to the Children of Israel, 'Dwell securely in the land (of promise)'" (Qur'án Children of Israel 104 Al-Isra)

"And all nations shall call you blessed: for ye shall be a delightsome land, saith the LORD of hosts." (Bible MAL 3:12)

"I am come to thee, O land of the heart's desire, with tidings from God, and announce to thee His gracious favor and mercy, and greet and magnify thee in His name." (Bahá'u'lláh: Gleanings, Pages: 121-122)

and what seeker findeth rest away from his heart's desire?
"May Bahá'u'lláh's almighty arms surround you and fulfill your hearts' desire." (Shoghi Effendi: Light of Divine Guidance Vol.1, Page: 35)

"Thou hast given him his heart's desire, and hast not withholden the request of his lips." (Bible PSA 21:2)

To the true lover reunion is life, and separation is death.
"For when the true lover and devoted friend reacheth to the presence of the Beloved, the sparkling beauty of the Loved One and the fire of the lover's heart will kindle a blaze and burn away all veils and wrappings." (Bahá'u'lláh: Seven Valleys and Four Valleys, Page: 36)

"The universe is pregnant with these manifold bounties, awaiting the hour when the effects of Its unseen gifts will be made manifest in this world, when the languishing and sore athirst will attain the living Kawthar of their Well-Beloved, and the erring wanderer, lost in the wilds of remoteness and nothingness, will enter the tabernacle of life, and attain reunion with his heart's desire." (Bahá'u'lláh: The Kitab-i-Iqan, Pages: 60-61)

His breast is void of patience and his heart hath no peace.

"We lack patience in tests and in long-suffering; permit us to attain the lights of oneness." ('Abdu'l-Bahá: Promulgation of Universal Peace*, Page: 275)

"For the poor can find no refuge unless he knocketh at the door of Thy wealth, and the outcast can find no peace until he be admitted to the court of Thy favor." (Bahá'u'lláh: Prayers and Meditations, Page: 176)

"Peace unto you for that ye persevered in patience! Now how excellent is the final Home!" (Qur'án The Thunder 24 Ar-Rad)
"But that on the good ground are they, which in an honest and good heart, having heard the word, keep it, and bring forth fruit with patience." (Bible LUK 8:15)

A myriad lives he would forsake to hasten to the abode of his beloved.

"Should the greatness of this Day be revealed in its fullness, every man would forsake a myriad lives in his longing to partake, though it be for one moment, of its great glory - how much more this world and its corruptible treasures!" (Bahá'u'lláh: Gleanings, Page: 197)

"Would that a myriad lives were mine, would that I possessed the riches of the whole earth and its glory, that I might resign them all freely and joyously in Thy path." (Nabil-i-Azam: The

Dawn-Breakers, Page: 572)

"Did ye but know it, ye would renounce the world, and would hasten with your whole hearts to the presence of the Well-Beloved." (Bahá'u'lláh: The Kitab-i-Aqdas, Page: 39)

"Hasten ye then (at once) to God: I am from Him a warner to you, clear and open!" (Qur'án The Winds 50 Adh-Dhariyat)

5. O SON OF DUST!
Verily I say unto thee: Of all men the most negligent is he that disputeth idly and seeketh to advance himself over his brother. Say, O brethren! Let deeds, not words, be your adorning.

<u>Verily I say unto thee: Of all men the most negligent is he that disputeth idly and seeketh to advance himself over his brother.</u>
"What, O people! Do ye worship the dust, and turn away from your Lord, the Gracious, the All-Bountiful?" (Bahá'u'lláh: Gleanings, Page: 104)

"But warn them of the Day of Distress, when the matter will be determined: for (behold), they are negligent and they do not believe!" (Qur'án Mary 39 Maryam)

"My sons, be not now negligent: for the LORD hath chosen you to stand before him, to serve him, and that ye should minister unto him, and burn incense." (Bible2CH 29:11)

"Man is he who forgets his own interests for the sake of others. His own comfort he forfeits for the well-being of all. Nay, rather, his own life must he be willing to forfeit for the life of mankind. Such a man is the honor of the world of humanity. Such a man is the glory of the world of mankind. Such a man is the one who wins eternal bliss. Such a man is near to the threshold of God. Such a man is the very manifestation of eternal happiness. Otherwise, men are like animals, exhibiting the same proclivities and propensities as the world of animals. What distinction is there? What prerogatives, what perfections? None whatever! Animals are better even -- thinking only of themselves and negligent of the needs of others." ('Abdu'l-Bahá, Foundations of World Unity, p. 42)

"Wish not for others what ye wish not for yourselves; fear God, and be not of the prideful. Ye are all created out of water, and unto dust shall ye return." (Bahá'u'lláh: The Kitab-i-Aqdas, Page: 73)

"Blessed is he who preferreth his brother before himself." (Bahá'u'lláh: Tablets of Bahá'u'lláh, Page: 71)

"..... they prefer them before themselves, though poverty be their own lot. And with such as are preserved from their own covetousness shall it be well." (Qur'án The Gathering 10 Al-Hashr)

"Then came Peter to him, and said, Lord, how oft shall my brother sin against me, and I forgive him? till seven times? Jesus saith unto him, I say not unto thee, Until seven times: but, Until seventy times seven." (Bible MAT 18:21&22)

Say, O brethren! Let deeds, not words, be your adorning.
"But he that doeth truth cometh to the light, that his deeds may be made manifest, that they are wrought in God." (Bible JOH 3:21)

"Now is the time to show forth the true signs of God, to rend asunder the veils of idle fancy, to promote the Word of God, and to sacrifice ourselves in His path. Let deeds, not words, be our adorning!" ('Abdu'l-Bahá: Memorials of the Faithful, Page: 201)

"People have grown weary and impatient of rhetoric and discourse, of preaching and sermonizing. In this day, the one thing that can deliver the world from its travail and attract the hearts of its peoples is deeds, not words; example, not precept; saintly virtues, not statements and charters issued by governments and nations on socio-political affairs." (Shoghi Effendi: A Chaste and Holy Life, Page: 62)

"Deeds not words are what they demand, and no amount of fervour in the use of expressions of loyalty and adulation will compensate for failure to live in the spirit of the teachings. (Shoghi Effendi: Living the Life, Page: 4)

6. O SON OF EARTH!
Know, verily, the heart wherein the least remnant of envy yet lingers, shall never attain My everlasting dominion, nor inhale the sweet savors of holiness breathing from My kingdom of sanctity.

"And now have we stablished you on the earth, and given you therein the supports of life." (Qur'án The Heights 9 Al-Araf)

"O peoples of the earth! Haste ye to do the pleasure of God," (Bahá'u'lláh: Epistle to the Son of the Wolf, Page: 24)

<u>Know, verily, the heart wherein the least remnant of envy yet lingers, shall never attain My everlasting dominion, nor inhale the sweet savors of holiness breathing from My kingdom of sanctity.</u>
"Such is the outcome of envy, the chief reason why men turn aside from the Straight Path. So hath it occurred, and will occur, in this great Cause." ('Abdu'l-Bahá: Selections ... 'Abdu'l-Bahá, Page: 163)

"It is attachment to the world, avarice, envy, love of luxury and comfort, haughtiness and self-desire; this is the dust which prevents reflection of the rays of the Sun of Reality in the mirror." ('Abdu'l-

Bahá : Promulgation of Universal Peace*, Page: 244)

"A sound heart is the life of the flesh: but envy the rottenness of the bones." (Bible PRO 14:30)

"Many of the people of the Book desire to bring you back to unbelief after ye have believed, out of selfish envy, even after the truth hath been clearly shewn them." (Qur'án The Cow 103 Al-Baqarah)

"Woe unto you, ye congregation of the malicious and envious! Hearken unto My speech, and tarry not though it be for less than a moment." (Bahá'u'lláh: Gleanings, Page: 257)

7. O SON OF LOVE!
Thou art but one step away from the glorious heights above and from the celestial tree of love. Take thou one pace and with the next advance into the immortal realm and enter the pavilion of eternity. Give ear then to that which hath been revealed by the pen of glory.

Thou art but one step away from the glorious heights above and from the celestial tree of love.
"Likewise, these souls, through the potency of the Divine Elixir, traverse, in the twinkling of an eye, the world of dust and advance into the realm of holiness; and with one step cover the earth of limitations and reach the domain of the Placeless." (Bahá'u'lláh: The Kitab-i-Iqan, Page: 157)

Take thou one pace and with the next advance into the immortal realm and enter the pavilion of eternity. Give ear then to that which hath been revealed by the pen of glory.
"O my brother! Take thou the step of the spirit, so that, swift as the twinkling of an eye, thou mayest flash through the wilds of remoteness

and bereavement, attain the Ridvan of everlasting reunion, and in one breath commune with the heavenly Spirits. For with human feet thou canst never hope to traverse these immeasurable distances, nor attain thy goal. Peace be upon him whom the light of truth guideth unto all truth, and who, in the name of God, standeth in the path of His Cause, upon the shore of true understanding." (Bahá'u'lláh : The Kitab-i-Iqan, Page: 43)

"Take thou good heed that ye may all, under the leadership of Him Who is the Source of Divine Guidance, be enabled to direct thy steps aright upon the Bridge (sirat), which is sharper than the sword and finer than a hair, so that perchance the things which from the beginning of thy life till the end thou hast performed for the love of God, may not, all at once and unrealized by thyself, be turned to acts not acceptable in the sight of God. Verily God guideth whom He will into the path of absolute certitude." (The Báb: Selections from the Báb, Page: 96)

8. O SON OF GLORY!
Be swift in the path of holiness, and enter the heaven of communion with Me. Cleanse thy heart with the burnish of the spirit, and hasten to the court of the Most High.

Be swift in the path of holiness, and enter the heaven of communion with Me.

"This most great, this fathomless and surging Ocean is near, astonishingly near, unto you. Behold it is closer to you than your life-vein! Swift as the twinkling of an eye ye can, if ye but wish it, reach and partake of this imperishable favor, this God-given grace, this incorruptible gift, this most potent and unspeakably glorious bounty." (Bahá'u'lláh: Gleanings, Page: 326)

"It was We who created man and We know what dark suggestions his

soul makes to him: for We are nearer to him than (his) jugular vein."
(Taken from Yusuf translation)(Qur'án Qaf 16 Qaf)

"We created man: and we know what his soul whispereth to him, and we are closer to him than his neck-vein." (Taken from Rodwell translation) (Qur'án Qaf 15 Qaf)

Cleanse thy heart with the burnish of the spirit, and hasten to the court of the Most High.

"Hearken ye to the Call of this wronged One, and magnify ye the name of the one true God, and adorn yourselves with the ornament of His remembrance, and illumine your hearts with the light of His love. This is the key that unlocketh the hearts of men, the burnish that shall cleanse the souls of all beings. He that is careless of what hath poured out from the finger of the Will of God liveth in manifest error." (Bahá'u'lláh: Gleanings, Page: 205)

"O My Brother! A pure heart is as a mirror; cleanse it with the burnish of love and severance from all save God, that the true sun may shine within it and the eternal morning dawn. Then wilt thou clearly see the meaning of 'Neither doth My earth nor My heaven contain Me, but the heart of My faithful servant containeth Me.'" (Bahá'u'lláh: Seven Valleys and Four Valleys, Pages: 21-22)

"Now hath God been gracious to the faithful, when he raised up among them an apostle out of their own people, to rehearse unto them his signs, and to cleanse them, and to give them knowledge of the Book and of Wisdom: for before they were in manifest error." (Qur'án The Family of Imran 158 Al-Imran)

9. O FLEETING SHADOW!
Pass beyond the baser stages of doubt and rise to the exalted heights of certainty. Open the eye of truth, that thou mayest behold the

veilless Beauty and exclaim: Hallowed be the Lord, the most excellent of all creators!

"How can utter nothingness gallop its steed in the field of preexistence, or a fleeting shadow reach to the everlasting sun?" (Bahá'u'lláh: Seven Valleys and Four Valleys, Page: 23)

"Whoever gazeth this day on My signs will distinguish truth from falsehood as the sun from shadow, and will be made cognizant of the goal." (Bahá'u'lláh: Epistle to the Son of the Wolf, Page: 88)

"For we are strangers before thee, and sojourners, as were all our fathers: our days on the earth are as a shadow, and there is none abiding." (Bible 1CH 29:15)

Pass beyond the baser stages of doubt and rise to the exalted heights of certainty.

"It is evident that nothing short of this mystic transformation could cause such spirit and behaviour, so utterly unlike their previous habits and manners, to be made manifest in the world of being. For their agitation was turned into peace, their doubt into certitude, their timidity into courage. Such is the potency of the Divine Elixir, which, swift as the twinkling of an eye, transmuteth the souls of men!" (Bahá'u'lláh: The Kitab-i-Iqan, Pages: 156-157)

"Blessed are they who, on the wings of certitude, have flown in the heavens which the Pen of thy Lord, the All-Merciful, hath spread." (Bahá'u'lláh : Gleanings, Page: 242)

"Only when the lamp of search, of earnest striving, of longing desire, of passionate devotion, of fervid love, of rapture, and ecstasy, is kindled within the seeker's heart, and the breeze of His loving-kindness is wafted upon his soul, will the darkness of error be dispelled, the mists of doubts and misgivings be dissipated, and the lights of knowledge and certitude envelop his being." (Bahá'u'lláh: Gleanings, Page: 267)

"So also did We show Abraham the power and the laws of the heavens and the earth, that he might (with understanding) have certitude." (Qur'án The Cattle 75 Al-Anam)

"That I might make thee know the certainty of the words of truth; that thou mightest answer the words of truth to them that send unto thee?" (Bible PRO 22:21)

<u>*Open the eye of truth, that thou mayest behold the veilless Beauty and exclaim: Hallowed be the Lord, the most excellent of all creators!*</u>
"Therefore do the lovers of the Abhá Beauty wish for no other recompense but to reach that station where they may gaze upon Him in the Realm of Glory, and they walk no other path save over desert sands of longing for those exalted heights." ('Abdu'l-Bahá: Selections ... 'Abdu'l-Bahá, Page: 184)

"Therefore, we must endeavor with heart and soul in order that the veil covering the eye of inner vision may be removed, that we may behold the manifestations of the signs of God, discern His mysterious graces and realize that material blessings as compared with spiritual bounties are as nothing." ('Abdu'l-Bahá: Promulgation of Universal Peace*, Page: 90)

"This is the Decree of God, concealed ere now within the veil of impenetrable mystery. We have disclosed it in this Revelation, and have thereby rent asunder the veils of such as have failed to recognize that which the Book of God set forth and who were numbered with the heedless." (Bahá'u'lláh: The Kitab-i-Aqdas, Page: 37)

10. O SON OF DESIRE!

Give ear unto this: Never shall mortal eye recognize the everlasting beauty, nor the lifeless heart delight in aught but in the withered bloom. For like seeketh like, and taketh pleasure in the company of its kind.

"Give ear unto God's holy Voice, and heed thou His sweet and immortal melody." (Bahá'u'lláh The Kitab-i-Iqan, Page: 215)

"Give ear unto the verses of God which He Who is the sacred Lote-Tree reciteth unto you. They are assuredly the infallible balance, established by God, the Lord of this world and the next. Through them the soul of man is caused to wing its flight towards the Dayspring of Revelation, and the heart of every true believer is suffused with light. Such are the laws which God hath enjoined upon you, such His commandments prescribed unto you in His Holy Tablet; obey them with joy and gladness, for this is best for you, did ye but know." (Bahá'u'lláh: The Kitab-i-Aqdas, Page: 73)

Never shall mortal eye recognize the everlasting beauty,
"He that was hidden from mortal eyes is come! His all-conquering sovereignty is manifest; His all-encompassing splendor is revealed." (Bahá'u'lláh: Gleanings, Page: 16)

"If thou desirest that God may open thy (spiritual) eye, thou must supplicate unto God, pray to and commune with Him at midnight," ('Abdu'l-Bahá : Tablets of 'Abdu'l-Bahá Vol 3*, Page: 676)

nor the lifeless heart delight in aught but in the withered bloom.
"It behooveth him to prize this food that cometh from heaven, that perchance, through the wondrous favours of the Sun of Truth, the dead may be brought to life, and withered souls be quickened by the infinite Spirit." (Bahá'u'lláh: The Kitab-i-Iqan, Page: 23)

For like seeketh like, and taketh pleasure in the company of its kind.
"He should treasure the companionship of them that have renounced the world, and regard avoidance of boastful and worldly people a precious benefit." (Bahá'u'lláh: Gleanings, Page: 265)

"Unto you be that which ye desire and unto us that which we desire. Wretched indeed is the plight of the ungodly." (Bahá'u'lláh: Tablets of Bahá'u'lláh, Page: 186)

"Then spake Jesus to the multitude, and to his disciples, Saying The scribes and the Pharisees sit in Moses' seat: All therefore whatsoever they bid you observe, that observe and do; but do not ye after their works: for they say, and do not." (Bible Mat: 23:1:2:3)

11. O SON OF DUST!
Blind thine eyes, that thou mayest behold My beauty; stop thine ears, that thou mayest hearken unto the sweet melody of My voice; empty thyself of all learning, that thou mayest partake of My knowledge; and sanctify thyself from riches, that thou mayest obtain a lasting share from the ocean of My eternal wealth. Blind thine eyes, that is, to all save My beauty; stop thine ears to all save My word; empty thyself of all learning save the knowledge of Me; that with a clear vision, a pure heart and an attentive ear thou mayest enter the court of My holiness.

"The eyes are blind; thine eyes became bright by beholding the lights. The ears are deaf; thou hast heard the voice of the Merciful One." ('Abdu'l-Bahá: Tablets of 'Abdu'l-Bahá Vol 3*, Page: 536)

"Have they not journeyed through the land? Have they not hearts to understand with, or ears to hear with? It is not that to these sights their eyes are blind, but the hearts in their breasts are blind!"

(Qur'án The Pilgrimage 45 Al-Hajj)

"Then the eyes of the blind shall be opened, and the ears of the deaf shall be unstopped." (Bible ISA 35:5)

"These two sorts of persons resemble the blind and deaf, and the seeing and hearing: shall these be compared as alike? Ah! do ye not comprehend?" (Qur'án Hud 26 Hud)

"Let them alone: they be blind leaders of the blind. And if the blind lead the blind, both shall fall into the ditch." (Bible MAT 15:14)

empty thyself of all learning save the knowledge of Me;
"I beg Thee to forgive me, O my Lord, for every mention but the mention of Thee, and for every praise but the praise of Thee, and for every delight but delight in Thy nearness, and for every pleasure but the pleasure of communion with Thee, and for every joy but the joy of Thy love and of Thy good-pleasure, and for all things pertaining unto me which bear no relationship unto Thee, O Thou Who art the Lord of lords, He Who provideth the means and unlocketh the doors." (Compilations, Bahá'í Prayers, p. 79)

"This reed is a Perfect Man Who is likened to a reed, and the manner of its likeness is this: when the interior of a reed is empty and free from all matter, it will produce beautiful melodies; and as the sound and melodies do not come from the reed, but from the flute player who blows upon it, so the sanctified heart of that blessed Being is free and emptied from all save God, pure and exempt from the attachments of all human conditions, and is the companion of the Divine Spirit. Whatever He utters is not from Himself, but from the real flute player, and it is a divine inspiration." ('Abdu'l-Bahá: Some Answered Questions, Page: 45) *that with a clear vision, a pure heart and an attentive ear thou mayest enter the court of My holiness.*

"We have decreed, O people, that the highest and last end of all learning be the recognition of Him Who is the Object of all knowledge; and yet, behold how ye have allowed your learning to shut you out, as by a veil, from Him Who is the Day Spring of this Light, through Whom every hidden thing hath been revealed." (Bahá'u'lláh: Gleanings, Page: 199)

"Because thou sayest, I am rich, and increased with goods, and have need of nothing; and knowest not that thou art wretched, and miserable, and poor, and blind, and naked:" (Bible REV 3:17)

12. O MAN OF TWO VISIONS!
Close one eye and open the other. Close one to the world and all that is therein, and open the other to the hallowed beauty of the Beloved.
"We have created thine eyes to behold the light of My countenance, thine ears to hearken unto the melody of My words, thy body to pay homage before My throne." (Bahá'u'lláh: Bahiyyih Khanum, Page: 3)

"Night and day endeavor to attain perfect harmony; be thoughtful concerning your own spiritual developments and close your eyes to the shortcomings of one another." ('Abdu'l-Bahá: Tablets of 'Abdu'l-Bahá Vol 1*, Page: 23)

"Open thine eyes, that thou mayest behold this glorious Vision, and recognize Him Whom thou invokest in the daytime and in the night season, and gaze on the Light that shineth above this luminous Horizon." (Bahá'u'lláh: The Kitab-i-Aqdas, Page: 51)

"He that seeketh to be a helper of God in this Day, let him close his eyes to whatever he may possess, and open them to the things of God."

(Bahá'u'lláh: Gleanings, Page: 272)

"Hearts have they with which they understand not, and eyes have they with which they see not, and ears have they with which they hearken not." (Qur'án The Heights 178 Al-Araf)

13. O MY CHILDREN!
I fear lest, bereft of the melody of the dove of heaven, ye will sink back to the shades of utter loss, and, never having gazed upon the beauty of the rose, return to water and clay.

"You are all my children, my spiritual children. Spiritual children are dearer than physical children, for it is possible for physical children to turn away from the Spirit of God, but you are spiritual children and, therefore, you are most beloved." ('Abdu'l-Bahá: Promulgation of Universal Peace*, Page: 92)

"O my children! truly God hath chosen a religion for you; so die not unless ye be also Muslims." (Qur'án The Cow 126 Al-Baqarah)

"The Spirit itself beareth witness with our spirit, that we are the children of God:" (Bible ROM 8:16)

I fear lest, bereft of the melody of the dove of heaven, ye will sink back to the shades of utter loss, and, never having gazed upon the beauty of the rose, return to water and clay.
"And if a place be shut away from the light, as by walls or a roof, it will be entirely bereft of the splendor of the light, nor will the sun shine thereon." (Bahá'u'lláh: Seven Valleys and Four Valleys, Page: 19)

"Say: Let not your hearts be perturbed, O people, when the glory of My Presence is withdrawn, and the ocean of My utterance is stilled.

In My presence amongst you there is a wisdom, and in My absence there is yet another, inscrutable to all but God, the Incomparable, the All-Knowing. Verily, We behold you from Our realm of glory, and shall aid whosoever will arise for the triumph of Our Cause with the hosts of the Concourse on high and a company of Our favoured angels." (Bahá'u'lláh : The Kitab-i-Aqdas, Page: 39)

"When the ocean of My presence hath ebbed and the Book of My Revelation is ended, turn your faces toward Him Whom God hath purposed, Who hath branched from this Ancient Root." (Bahá'u'lláh: The Kitab-i-Aqdas, Page: 63)

"At the close of His strenuous Western tours, which had called forth the last ounce of His ebbing strength, He had written: 'Friends, the time is coming when I shall be no longer with you. I have done all that could be done. I have served the Cause of Bahá'u'lláh to the utmost of My ability. I have labored night and day all the years of My life. O how I long to see the believers shouldering the responsibilities of the Cause!... My days are numbered, and save this there remains none other joy for me.'" (Shoghi Effendi: God Passes By, Page: 309)

"Remember, whether or not I be on earth, My presence will be with you always." (Shoghi Effendi: God Passes By, Page: 309)

"Muhammad is no more than an Apostle: many were the Apostles that passed away before him. If he died or were slain, will ye then turn back on your heels?" (Qur'án The Family of Imran 144 Al-Imran)

"And I say also unto thee, That thou art Peter, and upon this rock I will build my church;" (Bible MAT 16:18)

14. O FRIENDS!

Abandon not the everlasting beauty for a beauty that must die, and set not your affections on this mortal world of dust.

"For whereas in days past every lover besought and searched after his Beloved, it is the Beloved Himself Who now is calling His lovers and is inviting them to attain His presence. Take heed lest ye forfeit so precious a favor; beware lest ye belittle so remarkable a token of His grace. Abandon not the incorruptible benefits, and be not content with that which perisheth." (Bahá'u'lláh : Gleanings, Page: 320)

"It is for this reason that, in every age, when a new Manifestation hath appeared and a fresh revelation of God's transcendent power was vouchsafed unto men, they that misbelieved in Him, deluded by the appearance of the peerless and everlasting Beauty in the garb of mortal men, have failed to recognize Him." (Bahá'u'lláh: Gleanings, Page: 72)

"You must die to self and live in God." (Multiple Authors: Lights of Guidance, Page: 214)

"May you all be born again from this mortal world into the realm of the Kingdom." ('Abdu'l-Bahá: Promulgation of Universal Peace*, Page: 333)

"O God! Make me ablaze, like unto the fire of Thy love, and make me free from attachment to this mortal world, until I find the peace of soul and the rest of conscience." ('Abdu'l-Bahá : Tablets of 'Abdu'l-Bahá Vol 1*, Page: 196)

"The source of all majesty is God's, the Object of the adoration of all that is in the heavens and all that is on the earth. Such forces as have their origin in this world of dust are, by their very nature, unworthy of consideration." (Bahá'u'lláh: Gleanings, Page: 341)

"These are the people who buy the life of this world at the price of the Hereafter; their penalty shall not be lightened, nor shall they be helped." (Qur'án The Cow 86 Al-Baqarah)

15. O SON OF SPIRIT!
The time cometh, when the nightingale of holiness will no longer unfold the inner mysteries and ye will all be bereft of the celestial melody and of the voice from on high.

"O My brother! When a true seeker determineth to take the step of search in the path leading unto the knowledge of the Ancient of Days, he must, before all else, cleanse his heart, which is the seat of the revelation of the inner mysteries of God, from the obscuring dust of all acquired knowledge, and the allusions of the embodiments of satanic fancy." (Bahá'u'lláh: Gleanings, Page: 264)

"The first station, which is related to His innermost reality, representeth Him as One Whose voice is the voice of God Himself... The second station is the human station, exemplified by the following verses: 'I am but a man like you.'" (Bahá'u'lláh: Aqdas: Notes, Page: 233)

"Say: Let not your hearts be perturbed, O people, when the glory of My Presence is withdrawn, and the ocean of My utterance is stilled. In My presence amongst you there is a wisdom, and in My absence there is yet another, inscrutable to all but God, the Incomparable, the All-Knowing. Verily, We behold you from Our realm of glory, and shall aid whosoever will arise for the triumph of Our Cause with the hosts of the Concourse on high and a company of Our favoured angels." (Bahá'u'lláh : The Kitab-i-Aqdas, Page: 39)

16. O ESSENCE OF NEGLIGENCE!
Myriads of mystic tongues find utterance in one speech, and myriads of hidden mysteries are revealed in a single melody; yet, alas, there is no ear to hear, nor heart to understand.

"Shake off, O heedless ones, the slumber of negligence, that ye may behold the radiance which His glory hath spread through the world." (Bahá'u'lláh: Gleanings, Page: 103)

"All the people of the world are, as thou dost observe, in the sleep of negligence. They have forgotten God altogether. They are all busy in war and strife. They are undergoing misery and destruction." ('Abdu'l-Bahá: Bahá'í World Faith*, Page: 384)

Myriads of mystic tongues find utterance in one speech,
"Methinks people's sense of taste hath, alas, been sorely affected by the fever of negligence and folly, for they are found to be wholly unconscious and deprived of the sweetness of His utterance." (Bahá'u'lláh: Tablets of Bahá'u'lláh, Pages: 173-174)

and myriads of hidden mysteries are revealed in a single melody;
"With this vision clearly set before us, and fortified by the knowledge of the gracious aid of Bahá'u'lláh and the repeated assurances of 'Abdu'l-Bahá , let us first strive to live the life and then arise with one heart, one mind, one voice, to reinforce our numbers and achieve our end." (Shoghi Effendi: Bahá'í Administration, Pages: 68-69)

17. O COMRADES!
The gates that open on the Placeless stand wide and the habitation of the loved one is adorned with the lovers' blood, yet all but a few remain bereft of this celestial city, and even of these few, none but the smallest handful hath been found with a pure heart and sanctified spirit.

The gates that open on the Placeless stand wide

"I beseech Thee, by Thy name that hath unlocked the gates of Heaven and filled with ecstasy the Concourse on high, to enable me to serve Thee, in this Day, and to strengthen me to observe that which Thou didst prescribe in Thy Book." (Bahá'u'lláh: Gleanings, Page: 59)

"The gates of heaven are open; blessed are they who see! The hosts of angels are standing in battle order; what a joy to those who gain the victory!" ('Abdu'l-Bahá: Tablets of 'Abdu'l-Bahá Vol 3*, Page: 621)

"This is because the spirit has no place; it is placeless; and for the spirit the earth and the heaven are as one since it makes discoveries in both." ('Abdu'l-Bahá: Some Answered Questions, Page: 241)

"This sovereignty must needs be revealed and established either in the lifetime of every Manifestation of God or after His ascension unto His true habitation in the realms above...." (Bahá'u'lláh: Gleanings, Page: 26)

O My friends that dwell upon the dust! Haste forth unto your celestial habitation. Announce unto yourselves the joyful tidings: 'He Who is the Best-Beloved is come! He hath crowned Himself with the glory of God's Revelation, and hath unlocked to the face of men the doors of His ancient Paradise.' Let all eyes rejoice, and let every ear be gladdened, for now is the time to gaze on His beauty, now is the fit time to hearken to His voice." (Bahá'u'lláh: Gleanings, Pages: 319-320)

and the habitation of the loved one is adorned with the lovers' blood,

"How vast the number of those sanctified beings, those symbols of certitude, who, in their great love for thee, have laid down their lives and sacrificed their all for thy sake!" (Bahá'u'lláh: Gleanings, Page:

109)

<u>*none but the smallest handful hath been found with a pure heart and sanctified spirit.*</u>
"Only a few have as yet quaffed from this peerless, this soft-flowing grace of the Ancient King. These occupy the loftiest mansions of Paradise, and are firmly established upon the seats of authority." (Bahá'u'lláh: Gleanings, Page: 107)

"For many are called, but few are chosen." (Bible MAT 22:14)

"The parable of those who spend their substance in the way of God is that of a grain of corn: it groweth seven ears, and each ear hath a hundred grains. God giveth manifold increase to whom He pleaseth; and God careth for all and He knoweth all things." (Qur'án The Cow 261 Al-Baqarah)

"With unswerving vision, with pure heart, and sanctified spirit, consider attentively what God hath established as the testimony of guidance for His people in His Book, which is recognized as authentic by both the high and lowly." (Bahá'u'lláh: The Kitab-i-Iqan, Page: 202)

18. O YE DWELLERS IN THE HIGHEST PARADISE!
Proclaim unto the children of assurance that within the realms of holiness, nigh unto the celestial paradise, a new garden hath appeared, round which circle the denizens of the realm on high and the immortal dwellers of the exalted paradise. Strive, then, that ye may attain that station, that ye may unravel the mysteries of love from its wind-flowers and learn the secret of divine and consummate wisdom from its eternal fruits. Solaced are the eyes of them that enter and abide therein!

"Glorified art Thou, O Lord my God! Thou hast, in Thine all highest Paradise, assigned unto Thy servants such stations that if any one of them were to be unveiled to men's eyes all who are in heaven and all who are on earth would be dumbfounded." (Bahá'u'lláh: Prayers and Meditations, Page: 209)

Proclaim unto the children of assurance that within the realms of holiness,

"The herald of peace, reformation, love and reconciliation is the Religion of the Blessed Beauty which has pitched its tent on the apex of the world and proclaimed its summons to the people." ('Abdu'l-Bahá, Bahá'í World Faith - 'Abdu'l-Bahá Section, p. 216)

"And he said unto me: ' He proclaims unto thee peace in the name of the world to come;" (Other Apocrypha, 15 The Book of Enoch)

"And he said, I will make all my goodness pass before thee, and I will proclaim the name of the LORD before thee; and will be gracious to whom I will be gracious, and will shew mercy on whom I will shew mercy." (Bible EXO 33:19).

"All the divine Manifestations have proclaimed the oneness of God and the unity of mankind." ('Abdu'l-Bahá, Bahá'í World Faith - 'Abdu'l-Bahá Section, p. 245)

"Anger, passion, ignorance, prejudice, greed, envy, covetousness, jealousy and suspicion prevent man from ascending to the realms of holiness, imprisoning him in the claws of self and the cage of egotism." (Compilations, Bahá'í Scriptures, p. 546)

nigh unto the celestial paradise,

"Hadst thou faithfully obeyed the Decree of God, all the inhabitants of thy land would have followed thee, and would have themselves entered into the celestial Paradise, content with the good-pleasure of God for evermore." (The Báb, Selections from the Writings of the Báb, p. 32)

"THIS Religion is indeed, in the sight of God, the essence of the Faith of Muhammad; haste ye then to attain the celestial Paradise and the all-highest Garden of His good-pleasure in the presence of the One True God, could ye but be patient and thankful before the evidences of the signs of God." (The Báb, Selections from the Writings of the Báb, p. 71)

<u>*a new garden hath appeared, round which circle the denizens of the realm on high and the immortal dwellers of the exalted paradise.*</u>
"Let the people of certainty know that a new Garden has appeared near the Ridvan in the Open Court of Holiness, and that all the people of the Heights, and the temples of the Exalted Heaven, are around it." (Compilations, Bahá'í Scriptures, p. 177)

"Whatsoever people is graciously favoured therewith by God, its name shall surely be magnified and extolled by the Concourse from on high, by the company of angels, and the denizens of the Abhá Kingdom." ('Abdu'l-Bahá, Selections from the Writings of 'Abdu'l-Bahá, p. 27)

"Upon them be the glory of God, the glory of all that is in the heavens and all that is on the earth, and the glory of the inmates of the most exalted Paradise, the heaven of heavens." (Bahá'u'lláh, Gleanings from the Writings of Bahá'u'lláh, p. 197)

<u>*Strive, then, that ye may attain that station, that ye may unravel the mysteries of love from its wind-flowers and learn the secret of divine and consummate wisdom from its eternal fruits.*</u>
"Sanctify your souls, O ye peoples of the world, that haply ye may

attain that station which God hath destined for you and enter thus the tabernacle which, according to the dispensations of Providence, hath been raised in the firmament of the Bayan." (Bahá'u'lláh, The Kitab-i-Iqan, p. 3)

"I testify before God that each one of these Manifestations hath been sent down through the operation of the Divine Will and Purpose, that each hath been the bearer of a specific Message, that each hath been entrusted with a divinely-revealed Book and been commissioned to unravel the mysteries of a mighty Tablet." (Bahá'u'lláh, Gleanings from the Writings of Bahá'u'lláh, p. 74)

"They who have believed, and fled their homes, and striven with their substance and with their persons on the path of God, shall be of highest grade with God: and these are they who shall be happy!" (Qur'án Repentance 20 At-Taubah)

19. O MY FRIENDS!

Have ye forgotten that true and radiant morn, when in those hallowed and blessed surroundings ye were all gathered in My presence beneath the shade of the tree of life, which is planted in the all-glorious paradise? Awe-struck ye listened as I gave utterance to these three most holy words: O friends! Prefer not your will to Mine, never desire that which I have not desired for you, and approach Me not with lifeless hearts, defiled with worldly desires and cravings. Would ye but sanctify your souls, ye would at this present hour recall that place and those surroundings, and the truth of My utterance should be made evident unto all of you.

<u>Have ye forgotten that true and radiant morn, when in those hallowed and blessed surroundings ye were all gathered in My presence beneath the shade of the tree of life, which is planted in the all-glorious paradise?</u>

"O people of the Bayán! Have ye forgotten My exhortations, which My Pen hath revealed and My tongue hath uttered? Have ye bartered away My certitude in exchange for your idle fancies and My Way for your selfish desires? Have ye cast away the precepts of God and His remembrance and have ye forsaken His laws and ordinances?" (Bahá'u'lláh: Tablets of Bahá'u'lláh, Page: 104)

"And remember We took your covenant and We raised above you (the towering height) of Mount (Sinai) (saying): 'Hold firmly to what We have given you and bring (ever) to remembrance what is therein, perchance ye may fear God.'"(Qur'án The Cow 63 (Al-Baqarah)

"The plain of your hearts hath been illumined by the lights of the Lord of the Kingdom and ye have been led to the straight path, have marched along the road that leadeth to the Kingdom, have entered the Abhá Paradise, and have secured a portion and share of the fruit of the Tree of Life." ('Abdu'l-Bahá, Selections from the Writings of 'Abdu'l-Bahá, p. 29)

"Enter, then, the holy paradise of the good-pleasure of the All-Merciful. Sanctify your souls from whatsoever is not of God, and taste ye the sweetness of rest within the pale of His vast and mighty Revelation, and beneath the shadow of His supreme and infallible authority." (Bahá'u'lláh: Gleanings, Page: 143)

"The contingent beings are the branches of the tree of life while the Messenger of God is the root of that tree." ('Abdu'l-Bahá, Bahá'í World Faith - 'Abdu'l-Bahá Section, p. 364)

"This Tree of Life is the Book of the Covenant." ('Abdu'l-Bahá, Bahá'í World Faith - 'Abdu'l-Bahá Section, p. 429)

Awe-struck ye listened as I gave utterance to these three most holy words: O friends! Prefer not your will to Mine, never desire that which I have not desired for you, and approach Me not with lifeless hearts, defiled with worldly desires and cravings.

"Leave all thought of self, and strive only to be obedient and submissive to the Will of God." ('Abdu'l-Bahá, Paris Talks, p. 54)

"Be content, O people, with that which God hath desired for you and predestined unto you." (Bahá'u'lláh, Gleanings from the Writings of Bahá'u'lláh, p. 103)

"Love gives life to the lifeless. Love lights a flame in the heart that is cold. Love brings hope to the hopeless and gladdens the hearts of the sorrowful." ('Abdu'l-Bahá, Paris Talks, p. 179)

"and the bird of thy soul shall recall the holy sanctuaries of preexistence and soar on the wings of longing in the heaven of 'walk the beaten paths of thy Lord," (Qur'án 16:71 (Bahá'u'lláh, The Seven Valleys, p. 3)

In the eighth of the most holy lines, in the fifth Tablet of Paradise, He saith:

20. *O YE THAT ARE LYING AS DEAD ON THE COUCH OF HEEDLESSNESS!*
Ages have passed and your precious lives are well-nigh ended, yet not a single breath of purity hath reached Our court of holiness from you. Though immersed in the ocean of misbelief, yet with your lips ye profess the one true faith of God. Him whom I abhor ye have loved, and of My foe ye have made a friend. Notwithstanding, ye walk on My earth complacent and self-satisfied, heedless that My earth is weary of you and everything within it shunneth you. Were ye but to open your eyes, ye would, in truth, prefer a myriad griefs unto this joy, and would count death itself better than this life.

O YE THAT ARE LYING AS DEAD ON THE COUCH OF HEEDLESSNESS!

"Notwithstanding, they are still oblivious of this truth, and in the sleep of heedlessness, are pursuing the vanities of the world, and are occupied with thoughts of vain and earthly leadership." (Bahá'u'lláh: The Kitab-i-Iqan, Page: 228)

Ages have passed and your precious lives are well-nigh ended, yet not a single breath of purity hath reached Our court of holiness from you.
"Should God punish men for their perverse doings, He would not leave on earth a moving thing! But to an appointed term doth He respite them...." (Bahá'u'lláh, The Seven Valleys, p. 21)

"Night hath succeeded day, and day hath succeeded night, and the hours and moments of your lives have come and gone, and yet none of you hath, for one instant, consented to detach himself from that which perisheth. Bestir yourselves, that the brief moments that are still yours may not be dissipated and lost. Even as the swiftness of lightning your days shall pass, and your bodies shall be laid to rest beneath a canopy of dust. What can ye then achieve? How can ye atone for your past failure?" (Bahá'u'lláh: Gleanings, Page: 321)

"O Son of Man! Many a day hath passed over thee whilst thou hast busied thyself with thy fancies and idle imaginings. How long art thou to slumber on thy bed? Lift up thine head from slumber, for the Sun hath risen to the zenith; haply it may shine upon thee with the light of beauty." (Bahá'u'lláh: The Kitab-i-Iqan, Page: 228)

Though immersed in the ocean of misbelief, yet with your lips ye profess the one true faith of God. Him whom I abhor ye have loved, and of My foe ye have made a friend.
"O ye who believe! take not my foe and your foe for friends, shewing

them kindness, although they believe not that truth which hath come to you: they drive forth the Apostles and yourselves because ye believe in God your Lord!" (The Qur'án (Rodwell tr), Sura 60 - She Who is Tried)

<u>*Notwithstanding, ye walk on My earth complacent and self-satisfied, heedless that My earth is weary of you and everything within it shunneth you.*</u>
"Ye have loved that which hateth Me, and ye have taken My foe to be your friend. Ye are walking with mirth and pleasure upon My earth, heedless that it detests you, and that the things of the earth are fleeing from you." (Compilations, Bahá'í Scriptures, p. 177)

"They should conduct themselves in such manner that the earth upon which they tread may never be allowed to address to them such words as these: 'I am to be preferred above you. For witness, how patient I am in bearing the burden which the husbandman layeth upon me. I am the instrument that continually imparteth unto all beings the blessings with which He Who is the Source of all grace hath entrusted me. Notwithstanding the honor conferred upon me, and the unnumbered evidences of my wealth - a wealth that supplieth the needs of all creation - behold the measure of my humility, witness with what absolute submissiveness I allow myself to be trodden beneath the feet of men...." (Bahá'u'lláh: Gleanings, Pages: 7-8)

"Fain would they put out God's light with their mouths: but God only desireth to perfect His light, albeit the Infidels abhor it." (Repentance 32 At-Taubah)

<u>*Were ye but to open your eyes, ye would, in truth, prefer a myriad griefs unto this joy, and would count death itself better than this life.*</u>
"The life of man is useful if he attains the perfections of man. If he becomes the center of the imperfections of the world of humanity,

death is better than life, and nonexistence better than existence." ('Abdu'l-Bahá, The Promulgation of Universal Peace)

"But those that seek my soul, to destroy it, shall go into the lower parts of the earth." (King James Bible, Psalms 63:9)

21. O MOVING FORM OF DUST!
I desire communion with thee, but thou wouldst put no trust in Me. The sword of thy rebellion hath felled the tree of thy hope. At all times I am near unto thee, but thou art ever far from Me. Imperishable glory I have chosen for thee, yet boundless shame thou hast chosen for thyself. While there is yet time, return, and lose not thy chance.

"One heart may possess the capacity of the polished mirror; another be covered and obscured by the dust and dross of this world." ('Abdu'l-Bahá, Bahá'í World Faith - 'Abdu'l-Bahá Section, p. 218)

"When the human soul soareth out of this transient heap of dust and riseth into the world of God, then veils will fall away, and verities will come to light, and all things unknown before will be made clear, and hidden truths be understood." ('Abdu'l-Bahá, Selections from the Writings of 'Abdu'l-Bahá, p. 177)

<u>The sword of thy rebellion hath felled the tree of thy hope.</u>
"They did not realize that the Tree of Truth cannot be felled by any material ax." (Dr. J. E. Esslemont, Bahá'u'lláh and the New Era, p. 18)

" And the likeness of a bad word is as a bad tree, which is felled from above the earth, and has no staying place." (The Qur'án (E.H. Palmer tr), Sura 14 - Abraham)

At all times I am near unto thee, but thou art ever far from Me. Imperishable glory I have chosen for thee, yet boundless shame thou hast chosen for thyself.

"The one true God is My witness! This most great, this fathomless and surging ocean is near, astonishingly near, unto you. Behold it is closer to you than your life vein! Swift as the twinkling of an eye ye can, if ye but wish it, reach and partake of this imperishable favor, this God-given grace, this incorruptible gift, this most potent and unspeakably glorious bounty." (Shoghi Effendi: The Promised Day is Come, Page: 16)

"It was We who created man and We know what dark suggestions his soul makes to him: for We are nearer to him than (his) jugular vein." (Qur'án Qaf 16 Qaf)

"Meditate on what the poet hath written: 'Wonder not, if my Best-Beloved be closer to me than mine own self; wonder at this, that I, despite such nearness, should still be so far from Him.'... Considering what God hath revealed, that 'We are closer to man than his life-vein,' the poet hath, in allusion to this verse, stated that, though the revelation of my Best-Beloved hath so permeated my being that He is closer to me than my life-vein, yet, notwithstanding my certitude of its reality and my recognition of my station, I am still so far removed from Him. By this he meaneth that his heart, which is the seat of the All-Merciful and the throne wherein abideth the splendor of His revelation, is forgetful of its Creator, hath strayed from His path, hath shut out itself from His glory, and is stained with the defilement of earthly desires." (Bahá'u'lláh: Gleanings, Page: 185)

While there is yet time, return, and lose not thy chance.
"Every single cup hath been borne round by the hand of the Well-Beloved. Draw near, and tarry not, though it be for one short

moment." (Bahá'u'lláh, Gleanings from the Writings of Bahá'u'lláh, p. 34)

"While there is yet time, and the blessed Lote-Tree is still calling aloud amongst men, suffer not thyself to be deprived." (Bahá'u'lláh, Epistle to the Son of the Wolf, p. 114)

22. O SON OF DESIRE!
The learned and the wise have for long years striven and failed to attain the presence of the All-Glorious; they have spent their lives in search of Him, yet did not behold the beauty of His countenance. Thou without the least effort didst attain thy goal, and without search hast obtained the object of thy quest. Yet, notwithstanding, thou didst remain so wrapt in the veil of self, that thine eyes beheld not the beauty of the Beloved, nor did thy hand touch the hem of His robe. Ye that have eyes, behold and wonder.

<u>The learned and the wise have for long years striven and failed to attain the presence of the All-Glorious; they have spent their lives in search of Him, yet did not behold the beauty of His countenance.</u>
"The eye of My loving-kindness weepeth sore over you, inasmuch as ye have failed to recognize the One upon Whom ye have been calling in the daytime and in the night season, at even and at morn. Advance, O people, with snow-white faces and radiant hearts, unto the blest and crimson Spot, wherein the Sadratu'l-Muntaha is calling: 'Verily, there is none other God beside Me, the Omnipotent Protector, the Self-Subsisting!'" (Bahá'u'lláh: The Kitab-i-Aqdas, Page: 56)

<u>Thou without the least effort didst attain thy goal, and without search hast obtained the object of thy quest.</u>
"If thou seekest another than Me, yea, if thou searchest the universe for evermore, thy quest will be in vain." (Bahá'u'lláh, The Arabic Hidden Words 15)

"For with human feet thou canst never hope to traverse these immeasurable distances, nor attain thy goal." (Bahá'u'lláh, The Kitab-i-Iqan, p. 43)

<u>Yet, notwithstanding, thou didst remain so wrapt in the veil of self, that thine eyes beheld not the beauty of the Beloved, nor did thy hand touch the hem of His robe. Ye that have eyes, behold and wonder.</u>
"He is indeed as one dead who, at the wondrous dawn of this Revelation, hath failed to be quickened by its soul-stirring breeze. He is indeed a captive who hath not recognized the Supreme Redeemer, but hath suffered his soul to be bound, distressed and helpless, in the fetters of his desires." (Bahá'u'lláh: Gleanings, Page: 169)

"The Most Great Name beareth Me witness! How sad if any man were, in this Day, to rest his heart on the transitory things of this world! Arise, and cling firmly to the Cause of God. Be most loving one to another. Burn away, wholly for the sake of the Well-Beloved, the veil of self with the flame of the undying Fire, and with faces joyous and beaming with light, associate with your neighbor." (Bahá'u'lláh, Gleanings from the Writings of Bahá'u'lláh, p. 316)

23. O DWELLERS IN THE CITY OF LOVE!
Mortal blasts have beset the everlasting candle, and the beauty of the celestial Youth is veiled in the darkness of dust. The chief of the monarchs of love is wronged by the people of tyranny and the dove of holiness lies prisoned in the talons of owls. The dwellers in the pavilion of glory and the celestial concourse bewail and lament, while ye repose in the realm of negligence, and esteem yourselves as of the true friends. How vain are your imaginings!

"Let all strive to grow in the light of the Sun of Truth, and reflecting this luminous love on all men, may their hearts become so united that they may dwell evermore in the radiance of the limitless love." ('Abdu'l-Bahá, Paris Talks, p. 37)

<u>Mortal blasts have beset the everlasting candle, and the beauty of the celestial Youth is veiled in the darkness of dust.</u>
"....oblivious of the truth that no earthly water can quench the flames of Divine wisdom, nor mortal blasts extinguish the lamp of everlasting dominion. Nay, rather, such water cannot but intensify the burning of the flame, and such blasts cannot but ensure the preservation of the lamp, were ye to observe with the eye of discernment, and walk in the way of God's holy will and pleasure...." (Bahá'u'lláh: Gleanings, Page: 19)

Behold a candle how it gives its light. It weeps its life away drop by drop in order to give forth its flame of light. (H.M. Balyuzi, 'Abdu'l-Bahá - The Centre of the Covenant, p. 73)

From the peoples of the world, against the Candle of the Covenant discordant winds do beat and blow. ('Abdu'l-Bahá, Selections from the Writings of 'Abdu'l-Bahá, p. 9)

<u>The chief of the monarchs of love is wronged by the people of tyranny and the dove of holiness lies prisoned in the talons of owls. The dwellers in the pavilion of glory and the celestial concourse bewail and lament, while ye repose in the realm of negligence, and esteem yourselves as of the true friends. How vain are your imaginings!</u>
"But a myriad times alas for the wayward who are like unto dried-up leaves fallen upon the dust. Ere long mortal blasts shall carry them away to the place ordained for them. Ignorant did they arrive, ignorant did they linger and ignorant did they retire to their abodes." (Bahá'u'lláh : Tablets of Bahá'u'lláh, Pages: 257-258)

"Though beset with countless afflictions, We summon the people unto

God, the Lord of names. Say, strive ye to attain that which ye have been promised in the Books of God, and walk not in the way of the ignorant. My body hath endured imprisonment that ye may be released from the bondage of self. Set your faces then towards His countenance and follow not the footsteps of every hostile oppressor. Verily, He hath consented to be sorely abased that ye may attain unto glory, and yet, ye are disporting yourselves in the vale of heedlessness." (Bahá'u'lláh: Tablets of Bahá'u'lláh, Pages: 11-12)

24. O YE THAT ARE FOOLISH, YET HAVE A NAME TO BE WISE!

Wherefore do ye wear the guise of shepherds, when inwardly ye have become wolves, intent upon My flock? Ye are even as the star, which riseth ere the dawn, and which, though it seem radiant and luminous, leadeth the wayfarers of My city astray into the paths of perdition.

"O ye followers of this Wronged One! Ye are the shepherds of mankind; liberate ye your flocks from the wolves of evil passions and desires, and adorn them with the ornament of the fear of God. This is the firm commandment which hath, at this moment, flowed out from the Pen of Him Who is the Ancient of Days." (Bahá'u'lláh: Epistle to the Son of the Wolf, Page: 29)

"O ye Men of Justice! Be ye, in the realm of God, shepherds unto His sheep and guard them from the ravening wolves that have appeared in disguise, even as ye would guard your own sons." (Bahá'u'lláh: The Kitab-i-Aqdas, Page: 38)

"O my Lord! they have indeed led astray many among mankind: he then who follows my (ways) is of me, and he that disobeys me - but thou art indeed Oft-Forgiving, Most Merciful." (Qur'án Abraham 36 Ibrahim)

"Her princes in the midst thereof are like wolves ravening the prey, to shed blood, and to destroy souls, to get dishonest gain. (Bible EZE 22:27)

"Beware of false prophets, which come to you in sheep's clothing, but inwardly they are ravening wolves." (Bible MAT 7:15)

"Behold, I send you forth as sheep in the midst of wolves: be ye therefore wise as serpents, and harmless as doves." (Bible MAT 10:16)

"O faithless ones! Why do ye outwardly claim to be shepherds, while inwardly ye have become the wolves of My sheep? Your likeness is like unto the star before the morning, which is apparently bright and luminous, but really causeth the misguidance and destruction of the caravans of My city and country." ('Abdu'l-Bahá: A Traveler's Narrative, Page: 68)

**Ye are even as the star, which riseth ere the dawn, and which, though it seem radiant and luminous, leadeth the wayfarers of My city astray into the paths of perdition.**
"Your likeness is like unto the star before the morning, which is apparently bright and luminous, but really causeth the misguidance and destruction of the caravans of My city and country." ('Abdu'l-Bahá, A Travelers's Narrative, p. 68)

"The Jews were expecting the coming of the Messiah, lamenting day and night, saying: "O God, send to us our deliverer!" But as they walked in the path of dogmas, rather than reality, when the Messiah appeared they denied him." ('Abdu'l-Bahá, Divine Philosophy, p. 153)

"Enter not into the path of the wicked, and go not in the way of evil men." (Bible PRO 4:14)

"We shall leave him in the path he has chosen, and land him in Hell, what an evil refuge?." Qur'án Women (An-Nisa)

25. O YE SEEMING FAIR YET INWARDLY FOUL!

Ye are like clear but bitter water, which to outward seeming is crystal pure but of which, when tested by the divine Assayer, not a drop is accepted. Yea, the sun beam falls alike upon the dust and the mirror, yet differ they in reflection even as doth the star from the earth: nay, immeasurable is the difference!

<u>Ye are like clear but bitter water, which to outward seeming is crystal pure but of which, when tested by the divine Assayer, not a drop is accepted.</u>

"O outwardly fair and inwardly faulty! Thy likeness is like unto clear bitter water, wherein outwardly the utmost sweetness and purity is beheld, but when it falleth into the assaying hands of the taste of the [Divine] Unity He doth not accept a single drop thereof. The radiance of the sun is on the earth and on the mirror alike; but regard the difference as from the guard-stars to the earth; nay, between them is a limitless distance." ('Abdu'l-Bahá: A Traveler's Narrative, Pages: 68-69)

"These people have imagined that the flow of God's all-encompassing grace and plenteous mercies, the cessation of which no mind can contemplate, has been halted. From every side they have risen and girded up the loins of tyranny, and exerted the utmost endeavor to quench with the bitter waters of their vain fancy the flame of God's Burning Bush, oblivious that the globe of power shall, within its own mighty stronghold, protect the Lamp of God...." (Bahá'u'lláh: Gleanings, Page: 24)

"Whenever discord prevails instead of unity, wherever hatred and antagonism take the place of love and spiritual fellowship, Antichrist reigns instead of Christ. Who is right in these controversies and hatreds between the sects? Did Christ command them to love or to hate each other? He loved even His enemies and prayed in the hour of His crucifixion for those who killed Him. Therefore, to be a Christian is not merely to bear the name of Christ and say, 'I belong to a Christian government.' To be a real Christian is to be a servant in His Cause and Kingdom, to go forth under His banner of peace and love toward all mankind, to be self-sacrificing and obedient, to become quickened by the breaths of the Holy Spirit, to be mirrors reflecting the radiance of the divinity of Christ, to be fruitful trees in the garden of His planting, to refresh the world by the water of life of His teachings - in all things to be like Him and filled with the spirit of His love." ('Abdu'l-Bahá: Promulgation of Universal Peace*, Page: 6)

"It seems both strange and pitiful that the Church and clergy should always, in every age, be the most bitter opponents of the very Truth they are continually admonishing their followers to be prepared to receive! They have become so violently attached to the form that the substance itself eludes them!" (Multiple Authors: Lights of Guidance, Page: 420)

"Ye shall certainly be tried and tested in your possessions and in your personal selves; and ye shall certainly hear much that will grieve you, from those who received the Book before you and from those who worship many gods. But if ye persevere patiently, and guard against evil, then that will be a determining factor in all affairs." (Qur'án The Family of Imran 186 Al-Imran)

Yea, the sun beam falls alike upon the dust and the mirror, yet differ they in reflection even as doth the star from the earth: nay, immeasurable is the difference!
"This people draweth nigh unto me with their mouth, and honoureth me with their lips; but their heart is far from me." (Bible Mat 15:8)

"Behold how the sun shines upon all creation, but only surfaces that are pure and polished can reflect its glory and light. The darkened soul has no portion of the revelation of the glorious effulgence of reality; and the soil of self, unable to take advantage of that light, does not produce growth. The eyes of the blind cannot behold the rays of the sun; only pure eyes with sound and perfect sight can receive them." ('Abdu'l-Bahá: Promulgation of Universal Peace*, Page: 148)

26. O MY FRIEND IN WORD!
Ponder awhile. Hast thou ever heard that friend and foe should abide in one heart? Cast out then the stranger, that the Friend may enter His home.

"Bahá'u'lláh proclaims in the Hidden Words that God inspires His servants and is revealed through them. He says, 'Thy heart is My home; sanctify it for My descent. Thy spirit is My place of revelation; cleanse it for My manifestation.' Therefore, we learn that nearness to God is possible through devotion to Him, through entrance into the Kingdom and service to humanity; it is attained by unity with mankind and through loving-kindness to all; it is dependent upon investigation of truth, acquisition of praiseworthy virtues, service in the cause of universal peace and personal sanctification. In a word, nearness to God necessitates sacrifice of self, severance and the giving up of all to Him. Nearness is likeness." ('Abdu'l-Bahá: Promulgation of Universal Peace*, Page: 148)

"Say, O brethren! Let deeds, not words, be your adorning." (Bahá'u'lláh: Persian Hidden Words, Page: 5)

"The essence of faith is fewness of words and abundance of deeds; he whose words exceed his deeds, know verily his death is better than his life." (Bahá'u'lláh: Tablets of Bahá'u'lláh, Page: 156)

"For thus the Master of the house hath appeared within His home, and all the pillars of the dwelling are ashine with His light." (Bahá'u'lláh: Seven Valleys and Four Valleys, Page: 22)

"Return, then, and cleave wholly unto God, and cleanse thine heart from the world and all its vanities, and suffer not the love of any stranger to enter and dwell therein. Not until thou dost purify thine heart from every trace of such love can the brightness of the light of God shed its radiance upon it, for to none hath God given more than one heart. This, verily, hath been decreed and written down in His ancient Book. And as the human heart, as fashioned by God, is one and undivided, it behoveth thee to take heed that its affections be, also, one and undivided." (Bahá'u'lláh: Gleanings, Pages: 237-238)

"Is one whose heart God has opened to Islam, so that he has received enlightenment from God, (no better than one hard-hearted)? Woe to those whose hearts are hardened against celebrating the praises of God! They are manifestly wandering (in error)!" (Qur'án The Crowds 22 Az-Zumar)

"No man can serve two masters: for either he will hate the one, and love the other; or else he will hold to the one, and despise the other. Ye cannot serve God and mammon." (Bible MAT 6:24)

27. O SON OF DUST!
All that is in heaven and earth I have ordained for thee, except the human heart, which I have made the habitation of My beauty and glory; yet thou didst give My home and dwelling to another than Me; and whenever the manifestation of My holiness sought His own abode, a stranger found He there, and, homeless, hastened unto the sanctuary of the Beloved. Notwithstanding I have concealed thy secret and desired not thy shame.

"By thy life, O my beloved! if thou didst know what God had ordained for thee, thou wouldst fly with delight and thy happiness, gladness and joy would increase every hour. El-Bahá be upon thee!" ('Abdu'l-Bahá: Bahá'í World Faith*, Page: 363)

"Among them is this saying: 'Earth and heaven cannot contain Me; what can alone contain Me is the heart of him that believeth in Me, and is faithful to My Cause.' How often hath the human heart, which is the recipient of the light of God and the seat of the revelation of the All-Merciful, erred from Him Who is the Source of that light and the Well Spring of that revelation. It is the waywardness of the heart that removeth it far from God, and condemneth it to remoteness from Him." (Bahá'u'lláh: Gleanings, Page: 186)

"O banished and faithful friend! Quench the thirst of heedlessness with the sanctified waters of My grace, and chase the gloom of remoteness through the morning-light of My Divine presence. Suffer not the habitation wherein dwelleth My undying love for thee to be destroyed through the tyranny of covetous desires, and overcloud not the beauty of the heavenly Youth with the dust of self and passion. Clothe thyself with the essence of righteousness, and let thine heart be afraid of none except God. Obstruct not the luminous spring of thy soul with the thorns and brambles of vain and inordinate affections, and impede not the flow of the living waters that stream from the fountain of thine heart. Set all thy hope in God, and cleave tenaciously to His unfailing mercy." (Bahá'u'lláh: Gleanings, Page: 323)

"Nor do I absolve my own self (of blame): the (human soul) is certainly prone to evil, unless my Lord do bestow His Mercy: but surely certainly my Lord is Oft-Forgiving, Most Merciful." (Qur'án Joseph 53 Yusuf)

"A man's heart deviseth his way: but the LORD directeth his steps." (Bible PRO 16:9)

"There are many devices in a man's heart; nevertheless the counsel of the LORD, that shall stand." (Bible PRO 19:21)

28. O ESSENCE OF DESIRE!

At many a dawn have I turned from the realms of the Placeless unto thine abode, and found thee on the bed of ease busied with others than Myself. Thereupon, even as the flash of the spirit, I returned to the realms of celestial glory and breathed it not in My retreats above unto the hosts of holiness.

"At the dawn of every day he should commune with God, and, with all his soul, persevere in the quest of his Beloved." (Bahá'u'lláh: Gleanings, Page: 265)

"I beseech Thee, O my God, by the fire of Thy love which drove sleep from the eyes of Thy chosen ones and Thy loved ones, and by their remembrance and praise of Thee at the hour of dawn, to number me with such as have attained unto that which Thou hast sent down in Thy Book and manifested through Thy will." (Bahá'u'lláh: Prayers and Meditations, Page: 292)

"These are the glorious days on the like of which the sun hath never risen in the past. These are the days which the people in bygone times eagerly expected. What hath then befallen you that ye are fast asleep? (The Báb: Selections from the Báb, Page: 161)

"How pitiful, how regrettable, that most men are cleaving fast to, and have busied themselves with, the things they possess, and are unaware of, and shut out as by a veil from, the things God possesseth!"

(Bahá'u'lláh: Epistle to the Son of the Wolf, Page: 12)

"Many a morning hath the effulgence of My grace come unto thy place from the day-spring of the placeless, found thee on the couch of ease busied with other things, and returned like the lightning of the spirit to the bright abode of glory. And I, desiring not thy shame, declared it not in the retreats of nearness to the hosts of holiness."
('Abdu'l-Bahá: A Traveler's Narrative, Page: 69)

29. O SON OF BOUNTY!

Out of the wastes of nothingness, with the clay of My command I made thee to appear, and have ordained for thy training every atom in existence and the essence of all created things. Thus, ere thou didst issue from thy mother's womb, I destined for thee two founts of gleaming milk, eyes to watch over thee, and hearts to love thee. Out of My loving-kindness, 'neath the shade of My mercy I nurtured thee, and guarded thee by the essence of My grace and favor. And My purpose in all this was that thou mightest attain My everlasting dominion and become worthy of My invisible bestowals. And yet heedless thou didst remain, and when fully grown, thou didst neglect all My bounties and occupied thyself with thine idle imaginings, in such wise that thou didst become wholly forgetful, and, turning away from the portals of the Friend didst abide within the courts of My enemy.

"This robe with which the body and soul of man hath been adorned is the very foundation of his well-being and development. Oh, how blessed the day when, aided by the grace and might of the one true God, man will have freed himself from the bondage and corruption of the world and all that is therein, and will have attained unto true and abiding rest beneath the shadow of the Tree of Knowledge!"
(Bahá'u'lláh: Gleanings, Page: 78)

"Beware, beware, lest after me the world's fleeting vanities beguile you. Beware lest you wax haughty and forgetful of God." (Nabil-i-Azam: The Dawn-Breakers, Page: 40)

"Such as took their religion to be mere amusement and play, and were deceived by the life of the world. That day shall We forget them as they forgot the meeting of this day of theirs, and as they were wont to reject Our signs." (Qur'án The Heights 51 Al-Araf)

30. O BOND SLAVE OF THE WORLD!

Many a dawn hath the breeze of My loving-kindness wafted over thee and found thee upon the bed of heedlessness fast asleep. Bewailing then thy plight it returned whence it came.

"The peoples of the world are fast asleep. Were they to wake from their slumber, they would hasten with eagerness unto God, the All-Knowing, the All-Wise. They would cast away everything they possess, be it all the treasures of the earth, that their Lord may remember them to the extent of addressing to them but one word." (Bahá'u'lláh: The Kitab-i-Aqdas, Page: 33)

"Assuredly we are today living in the Days of God. These are the glorious days on the like of which the sun hath never risen in the past. These are the days which the people in bygone times eagerly expected. What hath then befallen you that ye are fast asleep?" (The Báb: Selections from the Báb, Page: 161)

"Then they also which are fallen asleep in Christ are perished." (Bible 1CO 15:18)

"But know this, that if the goodman of the house had known in what watch the thief would come, he would have watched, and would not have suffered his house to be broken up." (Bible MAT 24:43)

"Verily those who plight their fealty to thee do no less than plight their fealty to God: the Hand of God is over their hands: Then anyone who violates His oath, does so to the harm of his own soul, and anyone who fulfills what he has covenanted with God, God will soon grant him a great Reward." (Qur'án The Victory 10 Al-Fath)

31. O SON OF EARTH!
Wouldst thou have Me, seek none other than Me; and wouldst thou gaze upon My beauty, close thine eyes to the world and all that is therein; for My will and the will of another than Me, even as fire and water, cannot dwell together in one heart.

"Return, then, and cleave wholly unto God, and cleanse thine heart from the world and all its vanities, and suffer not the love of any stranger to enter and dwell therein. Not until thou dost purify thine heart from every trace of such love can the brightness of the light of God shed its radiance upon it, for to none hath God given more than one heart. This, verily, hath been decreed and written down in His ancient Book. And as the human heart, as fashioned by God, is one and undivided, it behoveth thee to take heed that its affections be, also, one and undivided." (Bahá'u'lláh: Gleanings, Pages: 237-238)

"O thou who art turning thy face towards God! Close thine eyes to all things else, and open them to the realm of the All-Glorious. Ask whatsoever thou wishest of Him alone; seek whatsoever thou seekest from Him alone. With a look He granteth a hundred thousand hopes, with a glance He healeth a hundred thousand incurable ills, with a nod He layeth balm on every wound, with a glimpse He freeth the hearts from the shackles of grief. He doeth as He doeth, and what recourse have we? He carrieth out His Will, He ordaineth what He pleaseth. Then better for thee to bow down thy head in submission, and put thy trust in the All-Merciful Lord." ('Abdu'l-Bahá:

Selections ...'Abdu'l-Bahá, Page: 51)

"I implore Thee, O my Lord, by Thy name the splendors of which have encompassed the earth and the heavens, to enable me so to surrender my will to what Thou hast decreed in Thy Tablets, that I may cease to discover within me any desire except what Thou didst desire through the power of Thy sovereignty, and any will save what Thou didst destine for me by Thy will." (Bahá'u'lláh: Prayers and Meditations, Page: 241)

"They have hearts wherewith they understand not, eyes wherewith they see not, and ears wherewith they hear not." (Qur'án The Heights 179 Al-Araf)

"For this people's heart is waxed gross, and their ears are dull of hearing, and their eyes they have closed; lest at any time they should see with their eyes and hear with their ears, and should understand with their heart, and should be converted, and I should heal them." (Bible MAT 13:15)

32. O BEFRIENDED STRANGER!
The candle of thine heart is lighted by the hand of My power, quench it not with the contrary winds of self and passion. The healer of all thine ills is remembrance of Me, forget it not. Make My love thy treasure and cherish it even as thy very sight and life.

Neither the candle nor the lamp can be lighted through their own unaided efforts, nor can it ever be possible for the mirror to free itself from its dross. (Bahá'u'lláh, Gleanings from the Writings of Bahá'u'lláh, p. 65)

"By angels is meant the divine confirmations and heavenly powers. Angels are also those holy souls who have severed attachment to the earthly world, who are free from the fetters of self and passion and who have attached their hearts to the Divine Realm and the Merciful Kingdom. They are of the Kingdom, heavenly; they are of the Merciful One, divine. They are the manifestations of the divine grace and the dawns of spiritual bounty." ('Abdu'l-Bahá : Tablets of 'Abdu'l-Bahá Vol 3*, Page: 509)

"Say: God hath made My hidden love the key to the Treasure; would that ye might perceive it! But for the key, the Treasure would to all eternity have remained concealed; would that ye might believe it! Say: This is the Source of Revelation, the Dawning-place of Splendour, Whose brightness hath illumined the horizons of the world. Would that ye might understand! This is, verily, that fixed Decree through which every irrevocable decree hath been established." (Bahá'u'lláh: The Kitab-i-Aqdas, Page: 24)

"Such is God, your real Cherisher and Sustainer: apart from Truth, what (remains) but error? How then are ye turned away?" (Qur'án Jonah 32 Yunus)

"For where your treasure is, there will your heart be also." (Bible MAT 6:21)

33. O MY BROTHER!
Hearken to the delight some words of My honeyed tongue, and quaff the stream of mystic holiness from My sugar-shedding lips. Sow the seeds of My divine wisdom in the pure soil of thy heart, and water them with the water of certitude, that the hyacinths of My knowledge and wisdom may spring up fresh and green in the sacred city of thy heart.

"The Ark of Salvation was made the safe refuge of the righteous, and the holy Tree was hung with bright, immortal fruit, so that the honeyed yield of the love of God is sweet on the lips of His people." (Shoghi Effendi: Bahiyyih Khanum, Page: 209)

"Thus God hath reaffirmed the law of the day of His Revelation, and inscribed it with the pen of power upon the mystic Tablet hidden beneath the veil of celestial glory. Wert thou to heed these words, wert thou to ponder their outward and inner meaning in thy heart, thou wouldst seize the significance of all the abstruse problems which, in this day, have become insuperable barriers between men and the knowledge of the Day of Judgment." (Bahá'u'lláh: The Kitab-i-Iqan, Page: 123)

"All the Prophets have drawn near to God through severance. We must emulate those Holy Souls and renounce our own wishes and desires. We must purify ourselves from the mire and soil of earthly contact until our hearts become as mirrors in clearness and the light of the most great guidance reveals itself in them." ('Abdu'l-Bahá: Promulgation of Universal Peace*, Page: 148)

"For unless the seed is sown, the bounty and blessing will not be attained; until the tree be planted, the fresh fruit will not be produced; unless the candle contact with fire, it will not ignite; and until a light dawn, the darkness will not vanish. Therefore, the beloved of God must sow the seeds and plant the fresh plants in that garden." ('Abdu'l-Bahá: Tablets of 'Abdu'l-Bahá Vol 3*, Pages: 632-633)

"Such are the mysteries of the Word of God, which have been unveiled and made manifest, that haply thou mayest apprehend the morning light of divine guidance, mayest quench, by the power of reliance and renunciation, the lamp of idle fancy, of vain imaginings, of hesitation, and doubt, and mayest kindle, in the inmost chamber of thine heart, the new-born light of divine knowledge and certitude."

(Bahá'u'lláh: The Kitab-i-Iqan, Page: 49)

"So also did We show Abraham the power and the laws of the heavens and the earth, that he might (with understanding) have certitude." (Qur'án The Cattle 76 Al-Anam)

"That thou mightest know the certainty of those things, wherein thou hast been instructed." (Bible LUK 1:4)

34. O DWELLERS OF MY PARADISE!
With the hands of loving-kindness I have planted in the holy garden of paradise the young tree of your love and friendship, and have watered it with the goodly showers of My tender grace; now that the hour of its fruiting is come, strive that it may be protected, and be not consumed with the flame of desire and passion.

"Through the graces of the Beauty of Abhá I cherish the hope that those souls will become sublime emblems and fruitful trees in this Supreme Paradise because a productive man is like unto a tree which is fruitful and of large shadow and so he is the ornament of the garden of Paradise." (Compilations, Japan Will Turn Ablaze)

"In Him I have found my paradise, and in the observance of His law I recognise the ark of my salvation." (Shoghi Effendi, The Dawn-Breakers, p. 509)

"As to those who believe and work righteous deeds, they have, for their
entertainment, the Gardens of Paradise," (Qur'án 107 The Cave Al-Kahf)

"How foolish the bird that builds its nest in a tree that may perish when it could build its nest in an ever-verdant garden of paradise."

('Abdu'l-Bahá, Divine Philosophy, p. 137)

"He that hath an ear, let him hear what the Spirit saith unto the churches; To him that overcometh will I give to eat of the tree of life, which is in the midst of the paradise of God." (Bible REV 2:7)

35. O MY FRIENDS!
Quench ye the lamp of error, and kindle within your hearts the everlasting torch of divine guidance. For ere long the assayers of mankind shall, in the holy presence of the Adored, accept naught but purest virtue and deeds of stainless holiness.

"Take ye good heed lest this calamitous day slacken the flames of your ardor, and quench your tender hopes." ('Abdu'l-Bahá, Bahá'í World Faith - 'Abdu'l-Bahá Section, p. 349)

"Dost thou imagine that thou canst quench the fire which God hath kindled in the horizons?" ('Abdu'l-Bahá, The Promulgation of Universal Peace, p. 398)

"Quench the thirst of heedlessness with the sanctified waters of My grace, and chase the gloom of remoteness through the morning-light of My Divine presence." (Bahá'u'lláh, Gleanings from the Writings of Bahá'u'lláh, p. 323)

"Above all, taking the shield of faith, wherewith ye shall be able to quench all the fiery darts of the wicked." (Bible, Ephesians 6:16)

"Many waters cannot quench love, neither can the floods drown it: if a man would give all the substance of his house for love, it would utterly be contemned." (Bible, Song of Solomon 8:7)

"Quench not thy earthy torch, That it may be a light to lighten mankind." (Mathnavi of Rumi (E.H. Whinfield tr), The Masnavi Vol 1)

"O My Friends! Extinguish the lamp of ignorance and kindle the ever-burning torch of guidance in the heart and mind." (Compilations, Bahá'í Scriptures, p. 179)

"And one who, through His own permission, summoneth to God, and a light-giving torch." (Qur'án The Confederates 45 Al-Ahzab)

For ere long the assayers of mankind shall, in the holy presence of the Adored, accept naught but purest virtue and deeds of stainless holiness.
"For in a short while the Assayers of Being shall accept naught but pure virtue in the portico of the Presence of the Adored One, and will receive none but holy deeds." (Compilations, Bahá'í Scriptures, p. 179)

"Thy likeness is like unto clear bitter water, wherein outwardly the utmost sweetness and purity is beheld, but when it falleth into the assaying hands of the taste of the [Divine] Unity He doth not accept a single drop thereof." ('Abdu'l-Bahá, A Traveller's Narrative, p. 68)

36. O SON OF DUST!
The wise are they that speak not unless they obtain a hearing, even as the cup-bearer, who proffereth not his cup till he findeth a seeker, and the lover who crieth not out from the depths of his heart until he gazeth upon the beauty of his beloved. Wherefore sow the seeds of wisdom and knowledge in the pure soil of the heart, and keep them hidden, till the hyacinths of divine wisdom spring from the heart and not from mire and clay.

The wise are they that speak not unless they obtain a hearing, even as the cup-bearer, who proffereth not his cup till he findeth a seeker, and the lover who crieth not out from the depths of his heart until he gazeth upon the beauty of his beloved..

"Say, O people of the Bayan, speak not according to the dictates of passion and selfish desire." (Bahá'u'lláh, Tablets of Bahá'u'lláh, p. 53)

"Speak not unless thou knowest it is perfectly proper." (Islamic Miscellaneous, Gulistan of Sa'di (Edwin Arnold tr))

"Beseech God to grant unto men hearing ears, and sharp sight, and dilated breasts, and receptive hearts, that haply His servants may attain unto their hearts' Desire, and set their faces towards their Beloved." (Bahá'u'lláh, Epistle to the Son of the Wolf, p. 44)

"Whoever has ears to hear, let him hear." (Other Apocrypha, The Gospel of Thomas)

Wherefore sow the seeds of wisdom and knowledge in the pure soil of the heart, and keep them hidden, till the hyacinths of divine wisdom spring from the heart and not from mire and clay.
"And among the greatest of these attributes of perfection are wisdom and knowledge." ('Abdu'l-Bahá, Selections from the Writings of 'Abdu'l-Bahá, p. 140)

"Say, the beginning of wisdom and knowledge and its origin, is to confess and acknowledge that which God has made manifest -- because through it, order has been firmly established and thus become a coat of mail for the preservation of the body of the world." (Compilations, Bahá'í Scriptures, p. 199)

"Give me now wisdom and knowledge, that I may go out and come in before this people: for who can judge this thy people, that is so great?" (King James Bible, 2 Chronicles 1:10)

"And when he had reached his age of strength, and had become a man, we bestowed on him wisdom and knowledge; for thus do we reward the righteous." (The Qur'án (Rodwell tr), Sura 28 - The Story)

<u>In the first line of the Tablet it is recorded and written, and within the sanctuary of the tabernacle of God is hidden:</u>
"It hath been decreed by Us that the Word of God and all the potentialities thereof shall be manifested unto men in strict conformity with such conditions as have been foreordained by Him Who is the All-Knowing, the All-Wise. We have, moreover, ordained that its veil of concealment be none other except its own Self. Such indeed is Our Power to achieve Our Purpose." (Bahá'u'lláh, Gleanings from the Writings of Bahá'u'lláh, p. 76)

"It has ever been hidden and secluded in its own holiness and sanctity above our comprehending." (Abdu'l-Bahá, Bahá'í World Faith - Abdu'l-Bahá Section, p. 259)

37. O MY SERVANT!
Abandon not for that which perisheth an everlasting dominion, and cast not away celestial sovereignty for a worldly desire. This is the river of everlasting life that hath flowed from the well-spring of the pen of the merciful; well is it with them that drink!

"Beware that ye deny not the favor of God after it hath been sent down unto you. Better is this for you than that which ye possess; for that which is yours perisheth, whilst that which is with God endureth." (Bahá'u'lláh, Epistle to the Son of the Wolf, p. 46)

"This is that blessed and everlasting life that perisheth not: whosoever is quickened thereby shall never die, but will endure as long as His Lord and Creator will endure." (Bahá'u'lláh, Gems of Divine Mysteries)

"Although it is necessary for man to strive for material needs and comforts, his real need is the acquisition of the bounties of God." ('Abdu'l-Bahá, The Promulgation of Universal Peace, p. 335)

"The love of the soul is for wisdom and knowledge, That of the body for houses, gardens, and vineyards; The love of the soul is for things exalted on high, That of the body for acquisition of goods and food." (Mathnavi of Rumi (E.H. Whinfield tr), The Masnavi Vol 3)

38. O SON OF SPIRIT!
Burst thy cage asunder, and even as the phoenix of love soar into the firmament of holiness. Renounce thyself and, filled with the spirit of mercy, abide in the realm of celestial sanctity.

"If thou art desiring divine joy, free thyself from the bands of attachment." ('Abdu'l-Bahá, Tablets of 'Abdu'l-Bahá v3, p. 557)

"Enter thou My presence, that thou mayest behold what the eye of the universe hath never beheld, and hear that which the ear of the whole creation hath never heard, that haply thou mayest free thyself from the mire of vague fancies, and set thy face towards the Most Sublime Station," (Bahá'u'lláh, Epistle to the Son of the Wolf, p. 130)

"To consider that after the death of the body the spirit perishes, is like imagining that a bird in a cage will be destroyed if the cage is broken, though the bird has nothing to fear from the destruction of the cage." ('Abdu'l-Bahá, Bahá'í World Faith - 'Abdu'l-Bahá Section, p. 326)

"Shouldst thou attain to a drop of the ocean of the inner meaning of these words, thou wouldst surely forsake the world and all that is therein, and, as the Phoenix wouldst consume thyself in the flames of the undying Fire." (Bahá'u'lláh, The Kitab-i-Iqan, p. 131)

Renounce thyself and, filled with the spirit of mercy, abide in the realm of celestial sanctity

"I have renounced My desire for Thy desire, O my God, and My will for the revelation of Thy Will." (Bahá'u'lláh, Epistle to the Son of the Wolf, p. 36)

"This is unity, oneness, sanctity; this is glorification whereby we praise and adore God." ('Abdu'l-Bahá Bahá'í World Faith - 'Abdu'l-Bahá Section, p. 259)

"When the soul attaineth the Presence of God, it will assume the form that best befitteth its immortality and is worthy of its celestial habitation." (Bahá'u'lláh: Gleanings, Page: 157)

39. O OFFSPRING OF DUST!

Be not content with the ease of a passing day, and deprive not thyself of everlasting rest. Barter not the garden of eternal delight for the dust-heap of a mortal world. Up from thy prison ascend unto the glorious meads above, and from thy mortal cage wing thy flight unto the paradise of the Placeless.

"Hear Me, ye mortal birds! In the Rose Garden of changeless splendor a Flower hath begun to bloom, compared to which every other flower is but a thorn, and before the brightness of Whose glory the very essence of beauty must pale and wither. Arise, therefore, and, with the whole enthusiasm of your hearts, with all the eagerness of your souls, the full fervor of your will, and the concentrated efforts of your entire being, strive to attain the paradise of His presence, and endeavor to inhale the fragrance of the incorruptible Flower, to breathe the sweet savors of holiness, and to obtain a portion of this perfume of celestial glory. Whoso followeth this counsel will break his chains asunder, will taste the abandonment of enraptured love, will attain unto his heart's desire, and will surrender his soul into the hands of his Beloved. Bursting through his cage, he will, even as the bird of the spirit, wing his flight to his holy and everlasting nest.

Night hath succeeded day, and day hath succeeded night, and the hours and moments of your lives have come and gone, and yet none of you hath, for one instant, consented to detach himself from that which perisheth. Bestir yourselves, that the brief moments that are still yours may not be dissipated and lost. Even as the swiftness of lightning your days shall pass, and your bodies shall be laid to rest beneath a canopy of dust. What can ye then achieve? How can ye atone for your past failure?" (Bahá'u'lláh: Gleanings, Pages: 320-321)

"Every soul shall have a taste of death: and only on the Day of Judgment shall you be paid your full recompense. Only he who is saved far from the fire and admitted to the garden will have attained the object (of life): for the life of this world is but goods and chattels of deception." (Qur'án The Family of Imran (Al-Imran 185)

"Don't practice an ignoble way of life, don't indulge in a careless attitude. Don't follow a wrong view, and don't be attached to the world." (Dhammapada Buddha 167)

40. O MY SERVANT!
Free thyself from the fetters of this world, and loose thy soul from the prison of self. Seize thy chance, for it will come to thee no more.

"'Abdu'l-Bahá said, "Luxuries cut off the freedom of communication.

One who is imprisoned by desires is always unhappy; the children of the Kingdom have unchained themselves from their desires. Break all fetters and seek for spiritual joy and enlightenment; then, though you walk on this earth, you will perceive yourselves to be within the divine horizon. To man alone is this possible. When we look about us we see every other creature captive to his environment." ('Abdu'l-Bahá, 'Abdu'l-Bahá in London, p. 87)

"Angels are also those holy souls who have severed attachment to the earthly world, who are free from the fetters of self and passion and who have attached their hearts to the divine realm and the merciful kingdom. They are of the kingdom, heavenly; they are of the merciful One, divine. They are the manifestations of the divine grace and the dawns of spiritual bounty."
    ('Abdu'l-Bahá, Bahá'í World Faith - 'Abdu'l-Bahá Section, p. 410)

"He is indeed a captive who hath not recognized the Supreme Redeemer, but hath suffered his soul to be bound, distressed and helpless, in the fetters of his desires." (Bahá'u'lláh, Gleanings from the Writings of Bahá'u'lláh, p. 169)

"Or (lest) it should say when it (actually) sees the Penalty: 'If only I had another chance I should certainly be among those who do good!' "(The reply will be) 'Nay, but there came to thee My signs and thou didst reject them: thou wast haughty, and became one of those who reject Faith!'" (Qur'án The Crowds (Az-Zumar 58)

"Soon will our handful of days, our vanishing life, be gone, and we shall pass, empty-handed, into the hollow that is dug for those who speak no more; wherefore must we bind our hearts to the manifest Beauty, and cling to the lifeline that faileth never. We must gird ourselves for service, kindle love's flame, and burn away in its heat.

We must loose our tongues till we set the wide world's heart afire, and with bright rays of guidance blot out the armies of the night, and then, for His sake, on the field of sacrifice, fling down our lives." ('Abdu'l-Bahá, Selections from the Writings of 'Abdu'l-Bahá, p. 267)

"Abandon anger, give up pride, and overcome all fetters. Suffering does not befall him who is without attachment to names and forms, and possesses nothing of his own. 221 (Dhammapada Buddha)

"Rise up from this place, O man, do not fall down, but cast off the fetters of Death which now hold you." (Hindu Vedas 4.)

41. O SON OF MY HANDMAID!
Didst thou behold immortal sovereignty, thou wouldst strive to pass from this fleeting world. But to conceal the one from thee and to reveal the other is a mystery which none but the pure in heart can comprehend.

"Walk ye in such wise that this fleeting world will change into a splendour and this dismal heap of dust become a palace of delights." ('Abdu'l-Bahá, Selections from the Writings of 'Abdu'l-Bahá, p. 280)

"O friend, the heart is the dwelling of eternal mysteries, make it not the home of fleeting fancies; waste not the treasure of thy precious life in employment with this swiftly passing world. Thou comest from the world of holiness—bind not thine heart to the earth; thou art a dweller in the court of nearness—choose not the homeland of the dust." (Bahá'u'lláh, The Seven Valleys, p. 34)

"Beware, beware, lest after me the world's fleeting vanities beguile you. Beware lest you wax haughty and forgetful of God." (Shoghi Effendi, The Dawn-Breakers, p. 40)

"Be that as it may, one who sings the cool rush of the wind of dawn, the scarlet cup of the tulip uplifted in solitary places, the fleeting shadows of the clouds, and the praise of gardens and fountains and fruitful fields, was not likely to forget that even if the world is no more than an intangible reflection of its Creator, the reflection of eternal beauty is in itself worthy to be admired." (Islamic Miscellaneous, Teachings of Hafiz (G. L. Bell tr))

"One day he visited the tomb as usual, and found it covered with snow, and a voice was heard saying, 'The world is fleeting as snow.'" (Mathnavi of Rumi (E.H. Whinfield tr), The Masnavi Vol 4)

"Do not barter away eternal blessing for pleasures of this mortal and fleeting world." (Ali b. Abi Taalib, Letters from Nahjul Balaagh)

"Book that fixeth the term of life. He who desireth the recompense of this world, we will give him thereof; And he who desireth the recompense of the next life, we will give him thereof! And we will certainly reward the thankful. (The Family of Imran (Al-Imran) 139. (Qur'án)

"The life in this world is but a play and pastime; and better surely for men of godly fear will be the future mansion! Will ye not then comprehend?" (Cattle (Al-Anam) 32.(Qur'án)

"For we are strangers before thee, and sojourners, as were all our fathers: our days on the earth are as a shadow, and there is none abiding." (1CH 29:15 Bible)

Man is like to vanity: his days are as a shadow that passeth away. (Bible PSA 144:4"

42. O MY SERVANT!

Purge thy heart from malice and, innocent of envy, enter the divine court of holiness.

"I am well pleased with that which Thou didst ordain for me, and welcome, however calamitous, the pains and sorrows I am made to suffer." (Shoghi Effendi, The World Order of Bahá'u'lláh, p. 118)

"To be kind and merciful is right, while to hate is sinful. Justice is a noble quality and injustice an iniquity. That it is one's duty to be pitiful and harm no one, and to avoid jealousy and malice at all costs." ('Abdu'l-Bahá, Paris Talks, p. 79)

"Other attributes of perfection are to fear God, to love God by loving His servants, to exercise mildness and forbearance and calm, to be sincere, amenable, clement and compassionate; to have resolution and courage, trustworthiness and energy, to strive and struggle, to be generous, loyal, without malice, to have zeal and a sense of honor, to be high-minded and magnanimous, and to have regard for the rights of others." ('Abdu'l-Bahá, The Secret of Divine Civilization, p. 40)

"....that God might test what is in your breasts and purge what is in your hearts: for God knoweth well the secrets of your hearts." (Qur'án The Family of Imran (Al-Imran)

"God doth purify whom He pleases: and God is One Who hears and knows (all things)." (Qur'án) The Light (An-Nur)

"Therefore let us keep the feast, not with old leaven, neither with the leaven of malice and wickedness; but with the unleavened bread of sincerity and truth." (1CO 5:8 (Bible)

"Let all bitterness, and wrath, and anger, and clamour, and evil speaking, be put away from you, with all malice: And be ye kind one to another, tenderhearted, forgiving one another, even as God for Christ's sake hath forgiven you." (EPH 4:31 (Bible)

43. O MY FRIENDS!
Walk ye in the ways of the good pleasure of the Friend, and know that His pleasure is in the pleasure of His creatures. That is: no man should enter the house of his friend save at his friend's pleasure, nor lay hands upon his treasures nor prefer his own will to his friend's, and in no wise seek an advantage over him. Ponder this, ye that have insight!

"This is a Revelation, under which, if a man shed for its sake one drop of blood, myriads of oceans will be his recompense. Take heed, O friends, that ye forfeit not so inestimable a benefit, or disregard its transcendent station." (Bahá'u'lláh, Gleanings from the Writings of Bahá'u'lláh, p. 5)

"O friends! Help ye the one true God, exalted be His glory, by your goodly deeds, by such conduct and character as shall be acceptable in His sight. He that seeketh to be a helper of God in this Day, let him close his eyes to whatever he may possess, and open them to the things of God." (Bahá'u'lláh, Gleanings from the Writings of Bahá'u'lláh, p. 271)

Service to God and mankind is their sole intention; they have neither wish nor desire save that which is in accordance with the good pleasure of God. The good pleasure of God is love for His creatures. ('Abdu'l-Bahá, The Promulgation of Universal Peace, p. 332)

44. O COMPANION OF MY THRONE!
Hear no evil, and see no evil, abase not thyself, neither sigh and weep. Speak no evil, that thou mayest not hear it spoken unto thee, and magnify not the faults of others that thine own faults may not appear

great; and wish not the abasement of anyone, that thine own abasement be not exposed. Live then the days of thy life, that are less than a fleeting moment, with thy mind stainless, thy heart unsullied, thy thoughts pure, and thy nature sanctified, so that, free and content, thou mayest put away this mortal frame, and repair unto the mystic paradise and abide in the eternal kingdom for evermore.

"They must consider every one on the earth as a friend; regard the stranger as an intimate, and the alien as a companion." ('Abdu'l-Bahá, Bahá'í World Faith - 'Abdu'l-Bahá Section, p. 215)
"Make them companions of the holy breezes, in order that they may know the pleasures of the wine of the love of God, and that they may attain to the joy and the happiness of attraction to the Kingdom of Abhá!" (Abdu'l-Bahá, Bahá'í World Faith - 'Abdu'l-Bahá Section, p. 336)

"The glory which proceedeth from God, the Lord of the Throne on High and of the earth below, rest upon you, O people of Bahá, O ye the companions of the Crimson Ark," (Bahá'u'lláh, Tablets of Bahá'u'lláh, p. 97)

<u>*Hear no evil, and see no evil, abase not thyself, neither sigh and weep. Speak no evil, that thou mayest not hear it spoken unto thee, and magnify not the faults of others that thine own faults may not appear great; and wish not the abasement of anyone, that thine own abasement be not exposed.*</u>
"Night and day endeavor to attain perfect harmony; be thoughtful concerning your own spiritual developments and close your eyes to the shortcomings of one another." ('Abdu'l-Bahá, Tablets of 'Abdu'l-Bahá v1, p. 23)

"Whoso keepeth the commandment shall feel no evil thing: and a wise man's heart discerneth both time and judgment." (King James Bible,

Ecclesiastes 8:5)

"Yea, though I walk through the valley of the shadow of death, I will fear no evil: for thou art with me; thy rod and thy staff they comfort me." (King James Bible, Psalms 23:4)

"Breathe not the sins of others so long as thou art thyself a sinner." (Bahá'u'lláh, The Arabic Hidden Words 27)

<u>Live then the days of thy life, that are less than a fleeting moment, with thy mind stainless, thy heart unsullied, thy thoughts pure, and thy nature sanctified, so that, free and content, thou mayest put away this mortal frame, and repair unto the mystic paradise and abide in the eternal kingdom for evermore.</u>
"These shall labor ceaselessly by day and by night, shall heed neither trial nor woe, shall suffer no respite in their efforts, shall seek no repose, shall disregard all ease and comfort and, detached and unsullied, shall consecrate every fleeting moment of their life to the diffusion of the divine fragrance and the exaltation of God's holy Word." ('Abdu'l-Bahá, Bahá'í World Faith - 'Abdu'l-Bahá Section, p. 355)

"Ye are glorified in all the worlds of God because of your relationship to Him Who is the Eternal Truth, but in your lives on this earthly plane, which pass away as a fleeting moment, ye are afflicted with abasement." (Compilations, The Compilation of Compilations vol. I, p. 170)

45. ALAS! ALAS! O LOVERS OF WORLDLY DESIRE!
Even as the swiftness of lightning ye have passed by the Beloved One, and have set your hearts on satanic fancies. Ye bow the knee before your vain imagining, and call it truth. Ye turn your eyes towards the thorn, and name it a flower. Not a pure breath have ye breathed, nor

hath the breeze of detachment been wafted from the meadows of your hearts. Ye have cast to the winds the loving counsels of the Beloved and have effaced them utterly from the tablet of your hearts, and even as the beasts of the field, ye move and have your being within the pastures of desire and passion.

"There can be no doubt whatever that, in consequence of the efforts which every man may consciously exert and as a result of the exertion of his own spiritual faculties, this mirror can be so cleansed from the dross of earthly defilements and purged from satanic fancies as to be able to draw nigh unto the meads of eternal holiness and attain the courts of everlasting fellowship." (Bahá'u'lláh, Gleanings from the Writings of Bahá'u'lláh, p. 262)

"Perplexing and difficult as this may appear, the still greater task of converting satanic strength into heavenly power is one that We have been empowered to accomplish." (Bahá'u'lláh, Gleanings from the Writings of Bahá'u'lláh, p. 200)
"Consume the egotistical veils with the fire of oneness, sincerely for the sake of God, and consort with one another with cheerful and rejoicing faces." (Compilations, Bahá'í Scriptures, p. 134)

"Know verily that Knowledge is of two kinds: Divine and Satanic. The one welleth out from the fountain of divine inspiration; the other is but a reflection of vain and obscure thoughts. The source of the former is God Himself; the motive-force of the latter the whisperings of selfish desire." (Bahá'u'lláh, The Kitab-i-Iqan, p. 68)

"There are two sides to man. One is divine, the other worldly; one is luminous, the other dark; one is angelic, the other diabolic." (Compilations, Bahá'í Scriptures, p. 406)

46. O BRETHREN IN THE PATH!

Wherefore have ye neglected the mention of the Loved One, and kept remote from His holy presence? The essence of beauty is within the peerless pavilion, set upon the throne of glory, whilst ye busy yourselves with idle contentions. The sweet savors of holiness are breathing and the breath of bounty is wafted, yet ye are all sorely afflicted and deprived thereof. Alas for you and for them that walk in your ways and follow in your footsteps!

Therefore all nations and peoples must consider themselves brethren. They are all descendants from Adam. ('Abdu'l-Bahá, 'Abdu'l-Bahá in London, p. 28)

"Make us brethren in Thy love, and cause us to be loving toward all Thy children." ('Abdu'l-Bahá The Promulgation of Universal Peace, p. 302)

<u>Wherefore have ye neglected the mention of the Loved One, and kept remote from His holy presence?</u>
"Yield thanks unto Him with joy and radiance, and follow not such as are remote from the Dawning-place of His nearness." (Bahá'u'lláh, The Kitab-i-Aqdas, p. 46)

"But as they were not detached from the things of this world and could not subdue their self and ego, they remained remote from His bountiful favours." (Adib Taherzadeh, The Revelation of Bahá'u'lláh v 3, p. 404)

<u>The essence of beauty is within the peerless pavilion, set upon the throne of glory, whilst ye busy yourselves with idle contentions.</u>
"In the Rose Garden of changeless splendor a Flower hath begun to bloom, compared to which every other flower is but a thorn, and before the brightness of Whose glory the very #SYMBOL \f

"Symbol"95321#SYMBOL \f "Symbol"95 essence of beauty must pale and wither." (Bahá'u'lláh, Gleanings from the Writings of Bahá'u'lláh, p. 320)

"Give ear unto the Voice calling from this manifest Temple: Verily, there is none other God but Me, the Everlasting, the Peerless, the Ancient of Days." (Bahá'u'lláh, Synopsis and Codification of the Kitab-i-Aqdas, p. 20)

Conflict and contention are categorically forbidden in His Book. This is a decree of God in this Most Great Revelation. It is divinely preserved from annulment and is invested by Him with the splendour of His confirmation. Verily He is the All-Knowing, the All-Wise. (Bahá'u'lláh, Tablets of Bahá'u'lláh, p. 220)

<u>The sweet savors of holiness are breathing and the breath of bounty is wafted, yet ye are all sorely afflicted and deprived thereof. Alas for you and for them that walk in your ways and follow in your footsteps!</u>
"Veiled as they remain within their own selves, the generality of the people have failed to perceive the sweet accents of holiness, inhale the fragrance of mercy, or seek guidance, as bidden by God, from those who are the custodians of the Scriptures". (Bahá'u'lláh, Gems of Divine Mysteries)

"Blessed be the man that directeth his steps toward thee, and visiteth thee. Woe to him that denieth thy right, that turneth away from thee, that dishonoreth thy name, and profaneth thy holiness." Bahá'u'lláh, Gleanings from the Writings of Bahá'u'lláh, p. 113)

"Say: Let truthfulness and courtesy be your adorning. Suffer not yourselves to be deprived of the robe of forbearance and justice, that the sweet savors of holiness may be wafted from your hearts upon all created things. Say: Beware, O people of Bahá, lest ye walk in the ways of them whose words differ from their deeds." (Bahá'u'lláh, Gleanings from the Writings of Bahá'u'lláh, p. 304)

"Fear God, O followers of the Spirit, and walk not in the footsteps of every divine that hath gone far astray." (Bahá'u'lláh, Tablets of Bahá'u'lláh, p. 10)

47. O CHILDREN OF DESIRE!
Put away the garment of vainglory, and divest yourselves of the attire of haughtiness.

"There can be no doubt that whoever is cognizant of this truth, is cleansed and sanctified from all pride, arrogance, and vainglory. Whatever hath been said hath come from God. Unto this, He, verily, hath borne, and beareth now, witness, and He, in truth, is the All-Knowing, the All-Informed." (Bahá'u'lláh, Epistle to the Son of the Wolf, p. 44)

"'Knowledge is the most grievous veil between man and his Creator.' The former bringeth forth the fruit of patience, of longing desire, of true understanding, and love; whilst the latter can yield naught but arrogance, vainglory and conceit." (Bahá'u'lláh, The Kitab-i-Iqan, p. 69)

"The religious doctors of every age have been the cause of preventing the people from the shore of the Sea of Oneness, for the reins of the people were in their control." (Compilations, Bahá'í Scriptures, p. 6)

In the third of the most holy lines writ and recorded in the Ruby Tablet by the pen of the unseen this is revealed:
48. O BRETHREN!
Be forbearing one with another and set not your affections on things

below. Pride not yourselves in your glory, and be not ashamed of abasement. By My beauty! I have created all things from dust, and to dust will I return them again.

"How can the lowly dust ever reach unto Him Who is the Lord of lords?" (Bahá'u'lláh, Gems of Divine Mysteries)

"Forbear ye from concerning yourselves with the affairs of this world and all that pertaineth unto it, or from meddling with the activities of those who are its outward leaders." (Bahá'u'lláh, Gleanings from the Writings of Bahá'u'lláh, p. 241)

"It behoveth, likewise, the loved ones of God to be forbearing towards their fellow-men, and to be so sanctified and detached from all things, and to evince such sincerity and fairness, that all the peoples of the earth may recognize them as the trustees of God amongst men." (Bahá'u'lláh, Gleanings from the Writings of Bahá'u'lláh, p. 241)

49. O CHILDREN OF DUST!
Tell the rich of the midnight sighing of the poor, lest heedlessness lead them into the path of destruction, and deprive them of the Tree of Wealth. To give and to be generous are attributes of Mine; well is it with him that adorneth himself with My virtues.

"Then shall the dust return to the earth as it was: and the spirit shall return unto God who gave it." (King James Bible, Ecclesiastes 12:7)

"And the LORD God formed man of the dust of the ground, and breathed into his nostrils the breath of life; and man became a living soul." (King James Bible, Genesis 2:7)

<u>Tell the rich of the midnight sighing of the poor, lest heedlessness lead them into the path of destruction, and deprive them of the Tree of</u>

Wealth.
"Fear the sighs of the poor and of the upright in heart who, at every break of day, bewail their plight, and be unto them a benignant sovereign. They, verily, are thy treasures on earth." (Bahá'u'lláh, Gleanings from the Writings of Bahá'u'lláh, p. 236)

To give and to be generous are attributes of Mine; well is it with him that adorneth himself with My virtues.
"Strive diligently to acquire virtues befitting your degree and station." ('Abdu'l-Bahá, Bahá'í World Faith - 'Abdu'l-Bahá Section, p. 265)

"All religions teach that we must do good, that we must be generous, sincere, truthful, law-abiding, and faithful; all this is reasonable, and logically the only way in which humanity can progress." ('Abdu'l-Bahá, Paris Talks, p. 141)

"The obligation to obey the injunctions of Christ, to be kind, generous, forgiving, compassionate, devoid of prejudice or partiality, peaceable, is not something imposed by a ruler's decree or an external power; it proceeds from man's own nature." (George Townshend, The Heart of the Gospel, p. 29)

50. O QUINTESSENCE OF PASSION!
Put away all covetousness and seek contentment; for the covetous hath ever been deprived, and the contented hath ever been loved and praised.

"His Holiness Bahá'u'lláh has revoiced and re-established the quintessence of the teachings of all the prophets, setting aside the accessories and purifying religion from human interpretation." ('Abdu'l-Bahá, Bahá'í World Faith - 'Abdu'l-Bahá Section, p. 251)

"For instance, a musical and melodious voice imparteth life to an attracted heart but lureth toward lust those souls who are engulfed in passion and desire." ('Abdu'l-Bahá, Bahá'í World Faith - 'Abdu'l-Bahá Section, p. 366)

"The drunkenness of passion hath perverted most of mankind." (Compilations, Bahá'í Prayers, p. 215)

<u>Put away all covetousness and seek contentment; for the covetous hath ever been deprived, and the contented hath ever been loved and praised.</u>
"Those who speak falsehoods, who covet worldly things and seek to accumulate the riches of this earth are not of me." ('Abdu'l-Bahá, The Promulgation of Universal Peace, p. 456)

"Suffer not the habitation wherein dwelleth My undying love for thee to be destroyed through the tyranny of covetous desires, and overcloud not the beauty of the heavenly Youth with the dust of self and passion." (Bahá'u'lláh, Gleanings from the Writings of Bahá'u'lláh, p. 323)

"Every soul that walketh humbly with its God, in this Day, and cleaveth unto Him, shall find itself invested with the honor and glory of all goodly names and stations." (Bahá'u'lláh, Gleanings from the Writings of Bahá'u'lláh, p. 159)

51. O SON OF MY HANDMAID!
Be not troubled in poverty nor confident in riches, for poverty is followed by riches, and riches are followed by poverty. Yet to be poor in all save God is a wondrous gift, belittle not the value thereof, for in the end it will make thee rich in God, and thus thou shalt know the meaning of the utterance, "In truth ye are the poor," and the holy words, "God is the all-possessing," shall even as the true morn break forth gloriously resplendent upon the horizon of the lover's heart, and abide secure on the throne of wealth.

"Without wealth there would be no poverty," (Bahá'í World Faith - 'Abdu'l-Bahá Section, p. 344)

"O ye that believe! Ye are but paupers in need of God; but God is the All-Possessing, the All-Praised." (Gleanings from the Writings of Bahá'u'lláh, p. 134)

"Having attained the stage of fulfilment and reached his maturity, man standeth in need of wealth," (Tablets of Bahá'u'lláh, p. 34)

52. O CHILDREN OF NEGLIGENCE AND PASSION!

Ye have suffered My enemy to enter My house and have cast out My friend, for ye have enshrined the love of another than Me in your hearts. Give ear to the sayings of the Friend and turn towards His paradise. Worldly friends, seeking their own good, appear to love one the other, whereas the true Friend hath loved and doth love you for your own sakes; indeed He hath suffered for your guidance countless afflictions. Be not disloyal to such a Friend, nay rather hasten unto Him. Such is the daystar of the word of truth and faithfulness, that hath dawned above the horizon of the pen of the Lord of all names. Open your ears that ye may hearken unto the word of God, the Help in peril, the Self-existent.

<u>Ye have suffered My enemy to enter My house and have cast out My friend, for ye have enshrined the love of another than Me in your hearts.</u>
"Thy Paradise is My love; thy heavenly home, reunion with Me." (Bahá'u'lláh, The Arabic Hidden Words 6)

"'A servant is drawn unto Me in prayer until I answer him; and when I have answered him, I become the ear wherewith he heareth....'" For thus the Master of the house hath appeared within His home, and all the pillars of the dwelling are ashine with His light. (Bahá'u'lláh, The

Seven Valleys, p. 22)

"Thy heart is My home; sanctify it for My descent". (Bahá'u'lláh, The Arabic Hidden Words 59)

"Also He says: 'Ye have taken one whom I hate to be thy beloved, and My enemy to be thy friend.'" (Bahá'í World Faith - 'Abdu'l-Bahá Section, p. 434)

Give ear to the sayings of the Friend and turn towards His paradise.
"For this is the station wherein the effulgent glories of the Beloved are revealed to the sincere lover and the resplendent lights of the Friend are cast upon the severed heart that is devoted to Him." (Bahá'u'lláh, Gems of Divine Mysteries p.70)

"Sanctify, then, their eyes, O my God, that they may behold the light of Thy Beauty, and purge their ears, that they may listen to the melodies of the Dove of Thy transcendent oneness." (Prayers and Meditations by Bahá'u'lláh, p. 336)

Worldly friends, seeking their own good, appear to love one the other, whereas the true Friend hath loved and doth love you for your own sakes; indeed He hath suffered for your guidance countless afflictions. Be not disloyal to such a Friend, nay rather hasten unto Him.
"My body hath endured imprisonment that ye may be released from the bondage of self." (Tablets of Bahá'u'lláh, p. 11)

"Verily, He hath consented to be sorely abased that ye may attain unto glory, and yet, ye are disporting yourselves in the vale of heedlessness." (Tablets of Bahá'u'lláh, p. 11)

"Through affliction hath His light shone and His praise been bright unceasingly:" ('Abdu'l-Bahá, A Traveller's Narrative, p. 80)

"The Ancient Beauty hath consented to be bound with chains that mankind may be released from its bondage, and hath accepted to be made a prisoner within this most mighty Stronghold that the whole world may attain unto true liberty. He hath drained to its dregs the cup of sorrow, that all the peoples of the earth may attain unto abiding joy, and be filled with gladness. This is of the mercy of your Lord, the Compassionate, the Most Merciful. We have accepted to be abased, O believers in the Unity of God, that ye may be exalted, and have suffered #SYMBOL \f "Symbol"95100#SYMBOL \f "Symbol"95 manifold afflictions, that ye might prosper and flourish."(Gleanings from the Writings of Bahá'u'lláh, p. 99)

53. O YE THAT PRIDE YOURSELVES ON MORTAL RICHES!

Know ye in truth that wealth is a mighty barrier between the seeker and his desire, the lover and his beloved. The rich, but for a few, shall in no wise attain the court of His presence nor enter the city of content and resignation. Well is it then with him, who, being rich, is not hindered by his riches from the eternal kingdom, nor deprived by them of imperishable dominion. By the Most Great Name! The splendor of such a wealthy man shall illuminate the dwellers of heaven even as the sun enlightens the people of the earth!

"Today, however, most of those who sit at that table are the poor, and this is why Christ hath said blessed are the poor, for riches do prevent the rich from entering the Kingdom; and again, He saith, 'It is easier for a camel to go through the eye of a needle, than for a rich man to enter into the Kingdom of God.' If, however, the wealth of this world, and worldly glory and repute, do not block his entry therein, that rich man will be favoured at the Holy Threshold and accepted by the Lord of the Kingdom." (Selections from the Writings of 'Abdu'l-Bahá p. 195)

54. O YE RICH ONES ON EARTH!
The poor in your midst are My trust; guard ye My trust, and be not intent only on your own ease.

"As the rich man enjoys his life surrounded by ease and luxuries, so the poor man must likewise have a home and be provided with sustenance and comforts commensurate with his needs." (Bahá'í World Faith - 'Abdu'l-Bahá, Section, p. 240)

"Great is the blessedness awaiting the poor that endure patiently and conceal their sufferings, and well is it with the rich who bestow their riches on the needy and prefer them before themselves." (Gleanings from the Writings of Bahá'u'lláh, p. 202)

55. O SON OF PASSION!
Cleanse thyself from the defilement of riches and in perfect peace advance into the realm of poverty; that from the well-spring of detachment thou mayest quaff the wine of immortal life.

"Cleanse thou the rheum from out thine head And breathe the breath of God instead.." (Bahá'u'lláh, The Seven Valleys, p. 20)

"Cast away that which ye possess, and, on the wings of detachment, soar beyond all created things." (Gleanings from the Writings of Bahá'u'lláh, p. 139)

"Though you may be poor here, you are rich in the treasures of the Kingdom."   ('Abdu'l-Bahá in London, p. 85)

"Man's merit lieth in service and virtue and not in the pageantry of wealth and riches." (Tablets of Bahá'u'lláh, p. 138)

56. O MY SON!

The company of the ungodly increaseth sorrow, whilst fellowship with the righteous cleanseth the rust from off the heart. He that seeketh to commune with God, let him betake himself to the companionship of His loved ones; and he that desireth to hearken unto the word of God, let him give ear to the words of His chosen ones.

"Verily I say: The greater the decline of religion, the more grievous the waywardness of the ungodly."(Bahá'u'lláh, Epistle to the Son of the Wolf, p. 28)

"Obey ye My commandments, and follow not the ungodly, they who have been reckoned as sinners in God's Holy Tablet." (Bahá'u'lláh, The Kitab-i-Aqdas, p. 43)

"Bear ye witness unto that whereunto God Himself hath borne witness, that the company of His favoured ones may be illumined by the words that issue from your lips." (Bahá'u'lláh, The Summons of the Lord of Hosts p.31)

57. O SON OF DUST!

Beware! Walk not with the ungodly and seek not fellowship with him, for such companionship turneth the radiance of the heart into infernal fire.

"In the passage 'eschew all fellowship with the ungodly,' Bahá'u'lláh means that we should shun the company of those who disbelieve in God and are wayward. The word 'ungodly' is a reference to such perverse people." (Compilations, Lights of Guidance, p. 483)

58. O SON OF MY HANDMAID!

Wouldst thou seek the grace of the Holy Spirit, enter into fellowship with the righteous, for he hath drunk the cup of eternal life at the hands of the immortal Cup-bearer and even as the true morn doth quicken and illumine the hearts of the dead.

"Therefore we must thank God that He has created for us both material blessings and spiritual bestowals. He has given us material gifts and spiritual graces, outer sight to view the lights of the sun and inner vision by which we may perceive the glory of God." (Bahá'í World Faith, p. 266)

"O My servants! Whoso hath tasted of this Fountain hath attained unto everlasting Life, and whoso hath refused to drink therefrom is even as the dead." (Gleanings from the Writings of Bahá'u'lláh, p. 168)

"With all his heart he should avoid fellowship with evil-doers, and pray for the remission of their sins." (Gleanings from the Writings of Bahá'u'lláh, p. 265)

59. O HEEDLESS ONES!
Think not the secrets of hearts are hidden, nay, know ye of a certainty that in clear characters they are engraved and are openly manifest in the holy Presence.

"Think not the deeds ye have committed have been blotted from My sight. By My beauty! All your doings hath My Pen graven with open characters upon tablets of chrysolite." (Gleanings from the Writings of Bahá'u'lláh, p. 209)

"Naught in the heavens or on the earth can escape His knowledge, and He, verily, perceiveth all things." (Bahá'u'lláh, Gems of Divine Mysteries, p.68)

60. O FRIENDS!

Verily I say, whatsoever ye have concealed within your hearts is to Us open and manifest as the day; but that it is hidden is of Our grace and favor, and not of your deserving.

"No vision taketh in Him, but He taketh in all vision, and He is the Subtile, the All-Informed!" (Bahá'u'lláh, Epistle to the Son of the Wolf, p. 13)

"Verily, thy Lord is aware of that which lieth concealed within the breasts of the unbelievers." (Bahá'u'lláh, The Summons of the Lord of Hosts, p. 153)

"Thus have We informed thee of that which lieth concealed within the hearts of men." (Bahá'u'lláh, The Summons of the Lord of Hosts, p. 181)

61. O SON OF MAN!

A dewdrop out of the fathomless ocean of My mercy I have shed upon the peoples of the world, yet found none turn thereunto, inasmuch as every one hath turned away from the celestial wine of unity unto the foul dregs of impurity, and, content with mortal cup, hath put away the chalice of immortal beauty. Vile is that wherewith he is contented.

"Alas, alas, for my waywardness, and my shame, and my sinfulness, and my wrong-doing that have withheld me from the depths of the ocean of Thy unity and from fathoming the sea of Thy mercy." (Bahá'u'lláh, Epistle to the Son of the Wolf, p. 3)

"How often hast Thou sent down the food of Thine utterance out of the heaven of Thy bounty, and I denied it; and how numerous the occasions on which Thou hast summoned me to the soft flowing waters of Thy mercy, and I have chosen to turn away therefrom, by reason of my having followed my own wish and desire!" (Bahá'u'lláh, Epistle to the Son of the Wolf, p. 7)

62. O SON OF DUST!
Turn not away thine eyes from the matchless wine of the immortal Beloved, and open them not to foul and mortal dregs. Take from the hands of the divine Cup-bearer the chalice of immortal life, that all wisdom may be thine, and that thou mayest hearken unto the mystic voice calling from the realm of the invisible. Cry aloud, ye that are of low aim! Wherefore have ye turned away from My holy and immortal wine unto evanescent water?

"Follow not the promptings of your own desires, nor the whisperings of the Evil One in your souls." (Bahá'u'lláh, The Summons of the Lord of Hosts, p. 207)

"Hearken, now, unto the notes of the Birds of Wisdom upraised in the Most Sublime Paradise. They verily will acquaint thee with things of which thou wert wholly unaware. Give ear unto that which the Tongue of Might and Power hath spoken in the Books of God, the Desire of every understanding heart." (Epistle to the Son of the Wolf, p. 140)

63. O YE PEOPLES OF THE WORLD!
Know, verily, that an unforeseen calamity followeth you, and grievous retribution awaiteth you. Think not that which ye have committed hath been effaced in My sight. By My beauty! All your doings hath My pen graven with open characters upon tablets of chrysolite.

"Should God punish men for their perverse doings, He would not leave on earth a moving thing! But to an appointed term doth He respite them...." (The Seven Valleys, p. 21)

"And when the appointed hour is come, there shall suddenly appear that which shall cause the limbs of mankind to quake." (Gleanings from the Writings of Bahá'u'lláh, p. 118)

"A tempest, unprecedented in its violence, unpredictable in its course, catastrophic in its immediate effects, unimaginably glorious in its ultimate consequences, is at present sweeping the face of the earth." (The Promised Day is Come, p. vi)

"The promised day is come, the day when tormenting trials will have surged above your heads, and beneath your feet, saying: 'Taste ye what your hands have wrought!'" (The Promised Day is Come, p. 3)

64. O OPPRESSORS ON EARTH!
Withdraw your hands from tyranny, for I have pledged Myself not to forgive any man's injustice. This is My covenant which I have irrevocably decreed in the preserved tablet and sealed with My seal.

"Justice is, in this day, bewailing its plight, and Equity groaneth beneath the yoke of oppression. The thick clouds of tyranny have darkened the face of the earth, and enveloped its peoples. (Gleanings from the Writings of Bahá'u'lláh, p. 92)

65. O REBELLIOUS ONES!
My forbearance hath emboldened you and My long-suffering hath made you negligent, in such wise that ye have spurred on the fiery charger of passion into perilous ways that lead unto destruction. Have ye thought Me heedless or that I was unaware?

"Thou seest, O my God! how my long-suffering, my forbearance and silence have increased their cruelty, their arrogance and their pride." (The Will and Testament, p. 23)

"Meditate, that thou mayest be made aware of thine act, O heedless outcast! Erelong will the breaths of chastisement seize thee, as they seized others before thee." (Epistle to the Son of the Wolf, p. 100)

66. O EMIGRANTS!
The tongue I have designed for the mention of Me, defile it not with detraction. If the fire of self overcome you, remember your own faults and not the faults of My creatures, inasmuch as every one of you knoweth his own self better than he knoweth others.

"Ye have been and are the dawnings of affection and the daysprings of divine grace: defile not the tongue with cursing or execration of anyone, and guard the eye from that which is not seemly. ('Abdu'l-Bahá, A Traveller's Narrative, p. 83)

"Verily I say unto you, the tongue is for the mention of good; defile it not with unseemly words." (Mirza Abu'l-Fadl, The Brilliant Proof, p. 32)

"No soul must interfere with another and no one must find fault with the rest." (Bahá'í World Faith - 'Abdu'l-Bahá Section, p. 408)

"If any differences arise amongst you, behold Me standing before your face, and overlook the faults of one another for My name's sake and as a token of your love for My manifest and resplendent Cause. (Gleanings from the Writings of Bahá'u'lláh, p. 315)

67. O CHILDREN OF FANCY!
Know, verily, that while the radiant dawn breaketh above the horizon of eternal holiness, the satanic secrets and deeds done in the gloom of night shall be laid bare and manifest before the peoples of the world.

"The Dawn hath broken, yet the people understand not." (Tablets of

Bahá'u'lláh, p. 75)

"Shall we not free ourselves from the horror of satanic gloom, and hasten towards the rising light of the heavenly Beauty?" (Bahá'u'lláh, The Kitab-i-Iqan, p. 38)

68. O WEED THAT SPRINGETH OUT OF DUST!

Wherefore have not these soiled hands of thine touched first thine own garment, and why with thine heart defiled with desire and passion dost thou seek to commune with Me and to enter My sacred realm? Far, far are ye from that which ye desire.

"We have forsaken the path of God; we have given up attention to the divine Kingdom; we have not severed the heart from worldly attractions; we have become defiled with qualities which are not praiseworthy in the sight of God; we are so completely steeped in material issues and tendencies that we are not partakers of the virtues of humanity." ('Abdu'l-Bahá, The Promulgation of Universal Peace, p. 187)

"And there shall ye remember your ways, and all your doings, wherein ye have been defiled; and ye shall lothe yourselves in your own sight for all your evils that ye have committed.." (King James Bible, Ezekiel 20:43)

69. O CHILDREN OF ADAM!

Holy words and pure and goodly deeds ascend unto the heaven of celestial glory. Strive that your deeds may be cleansed from the dust of self and hypocrisy and find favor at the court of glory; for ere long the assayers of mankind shall, in the holy presence of the Adored One, accept naught but absolute virtue and deeds of stainless purity. This is the daystar of wisdom and of divine mystery that hath shone above the horizon of the divine will. Blessed are they that turn thereunto.

"Say: O men! This is a matchless Day. Matchless must, likewise, be the tongue that celebrateth the praise of the Desire of all nations, and matchless the deed that aspireth to be acceptable in His sight." (Gleanings from the Writings of Bahá'u'lláh, p. 38)

"The fruits of the tree of man have ever been and are goodly deeds and a praiseworthy character." (Bahá'u'lláh, Epistle to the Son of the Wolf, p. 25)

"The days when idle worship was deemed sufficient are ended. The time is come when naught but the purest motive, supported by deeds of stainless purity, can ascend to the throne of the Most High and be acceptable unto Him." (Shoghi Effendi, The Dawn-Breakers, p. 93)

70. O SON OF WORLDLINESS!
Pleasant is the realm of being, wert thou to attain thereto; glorious is the domain of eternity, shouldst thou pass beyond the world of mortality; sweet is the holy ecstasy if thou drinkest of the mystic chalice from the hands of the celestial Youth. Shouldst thou attain this station, thou wouldst be freed from destruction and death, from toil and sin.

"Verily, verily, the dawn of a new Day has broken. The promised One is enthroned in the hearts of men. In His hand He holds the mystic cup, the chalice of immortality. Blessed are they who drink therefrom!" (Shoghi Effendi, The Dawn-Breakers, p. 69)

71. O MY FRIENDS!
Call ye to mind that covenant ye have entered into with Me upon Mount Paran, situate within the hallowed precincts of Zaman. I have taken to witness the concourse on high and the dwellers in the city of eternity, yet now none do I find faithful unto the covenant. Of a

certainty pride and rebellion have effaced it from the hearts, in such wise that no trace thereof remaineth. Yet knowing this, I waited and disclosed it not.

"References in the Bible to "Mt. Paran" and "Paraclete" refer to Muhammad's Revelation." (Shoghi Effendi, Letters from the Guardian to Australia and New Zealand, p. 41)

"As for the reference in The Hidden Words regarding the Covenant entered into on Mount Paran, this signifieth that in the sight of God the past, the present and the future are all one and the same -- whereas, relative to man, the past is gone and forgotten, the present is fleeting, and the future is within the realm of hope." (Selections from the Writings of 'Abdu'l-Bahá, p. 207)

"For according to the irrefutable texts, He has taken from us a firm covenant that we may live and act in accord with the divine exhortations, commands and lordly teachings." (Bahá'í World Faith - 'Abdu'l-Bahá Section, p. 401)

"Follow not, therefore, your earthly desires, and violate not the Covenant of God, nor break your pledge to Him. With firm determination, with the whole affection of your heart, and with the full force of your words, turn ye unto Him, and walk not in the ways of the foolish." (Gleanings from the Writings of Bahá'u'lláh, p. 328)

72. O MY SERVANT!

Thou art even as a finely tempered sword concealed in the darkness of its sheath and its value hidden from the artificer's knowledge. Wherefore come forth from the sheath of self and desire that thy worth may be made resplendent and manifest unto all the world.

"O My Servant! Thou art like unto a jeweled sword concealed in a dark sheath, by reason of which its value is unknown to the jewelers. Then come forth from the sheath of self and desire, that thy jewels may become open and manifest to the people of the world." (Compilations, Bahá'í Scriptures, p. 182)

73. O MY FRIEND!
Thou art the daystar of the heavens of My holiness, let not the defilement of the world eclipse thy splendor. Rend asunder the veil of heedlessness, that from behind the clouds thou mayest emerge resplendent and array all things with the apparel of life.

"Ye are the stars of the heaven of understanding, the breeze that stirreth at the break of day, the soft-flowing waters upon which must depend the very life of all men, the letters inscribed upon His sacred scroll." (Gleanings from the Writings of Bahá'u'lláh, p. 196)

74. O CHILDREN OF VAINGLORY!
For a fleeting sovereignty ye have abandoned My imperishable dominion, and have adorned yourselves with the gay livery of the world and made of it your boast. By My beauty! All will I gather beneath the one-colored covering of the dust and efface all these diverse colors save them that choose My own, and that is purging from every color.

"Whither are gone the proud and their palaces? Gaze thou into their tombs, that thou mayest profit by this example, inasmuch as We made it a lesson unto every beholder." (Bahá'u'lláh, Epistle to the Son of the Wolf, p. 56)

"Night hath succeeded day, and day hath succeeded night, and the hours and moments of your lives have come and gone, and yet none of you hath, for one instant, consented to detach himself from that which perisheth. Bestir yourselves, that the brief moments that are still yours may not be dissipated and lost. Even as the swiftness of lightning your days shall pass, and your bodies shall be laid to rest beneath a canopy of dust. What can ye then achieve? How can ye atone for your past failure?" (Gleanings from the Writings of Bahá'u'lláh, p. 320)

75. O CHILDREN OF NEGLIGENCE!
Set not your affections on mortal sovereignty and rejoice not therein. Ye are even as the unwary bird that with full confidence warbleth upon the bough; till of a sudden the fowler Death throws it upon the dust, and the melody, the form and the color are gone, leaving not a trace. Wherefore take heed, O bondslaves of desire!

"Life in this mortal world will quickly come to an end, and this earthly glory, wealth, comfort and happiness will soon vanish and be no more." (Bahá'í World Faith - 'Abdu'l-Bahá Section, p. 216)

"I know not how long they shall ride the steed of desire and wander erringly in the desert of heedlessness and error." ('Abdu'l-Bahá, A Traveller's Narrative, p. 80)

76. O SON OF MY HANDMAID!
Guidance hath ever been given by words, and now it is given by deeds. Every one must show forth deeds that are pure and holy, for words are the property of all alike, whereas such deeds as these belong only to Our loved ones. Strive then with heart and soul to distinguish yourselves by your deeds. In this wise We counsel you in this holy and resplendent tablet.

"The fruits of the tree of man have ever been and are goodly deeds and a praiseworthy character." (Bahá'u'lláh, Epistle to the Son of the Wolf, p. 25)

"Say: Beware, O people of Bahá, lest ye walk in the ways of them whose words differ from their deeds." (Gleanings from the Writings of Bahá'u'lláh, p. 305)

"The essence of faith is fewness of words and abundance of deeds; he whose words exceed his deeds, know verily his death is better than his life." (Tablets of Bahá'u'lláh, p. 156)

77. O SON OF JUSTICE!

In the night-season the beauty of the immortal Being hath repaired from the emerald height of fidelity unto the Sadratu'l-Muntaha, and wept with such a weeping that the concourse on high and the dwellers of the realms above wailed at His lamenting. Whereupon there was asked, Why the wailing and weeping? He made reply: As bidden I waited expectant upon the hill of faithfulness, yet inhaled not from them that dwell on earth the fragrance of fidelity. Then summoned to return I beheld, and lo! certain doves of holiness were sore tried within the claws of the dogs of earth. Thereupon the Maid of heaven hastened forth unveiled and resplendent from Her mystic mansion, and asked of their names, and all were told but one. And when urged, the first letter thereof was uttered, whereupon the dwellers of the celestial chambers rushed forth out of their habitation of glory. And whilst the second letter was pronounced they fell down, one and all, upon the dust. At that moment a voice was heard from the inmost shrine: "Thus far and no farther." Verily We bear witness to that which they have done and now are doing.

"The sovereignty, power, names and attributes of God are eternal, ancient".

('Abdu'l-Bahá, Foundations of World Unity, p. 102)

"Accordingly all these attributes, names, praises and eulogies apply to the Places of Manifestation; and all that we imagine and suppose beside them is mere imagination, for we have no means of comprehending that which is invisible and inaccessible." ('Abdu'l-Bahá, Some Answered Questions, p. 148)

"God in His Essence and in His own Self hath ever been unseen, inaccessible, and unknowable. By Presence, therefore, is meant the Presence of the One Who is His Viceregent amongst men." (Bahá'u'lláh, Epistle to the Son of the Wolf, p. 118)

"The angelic company of the celestial Concourse have joined in a call that hath rung throughout the universe, all loudly and mightily acclaiming: 'Hail, O City of God!'" (Bahá'í World Faith - 'Abdu'l-Bahá Section, p. 350)

"Say: Step out of Thy holy chamber, O Maid of Heaven, inmate of the Exalted Paradise! Drape thyself in whatever manner pleaseth Thee in the silken Vesture of Immortality, and put on, in the name of the All-Glorious, the broidered Robe of Light." (Gleanings from the Writings of Bahá'u'lláh, p. 282)

"Cry out before the gaze of the dwellers of heaven and of earth: I am the Maid of Heaven, the Offspring begotten by the Spirit of Bahá." (Gleanings from the Writings of Bahá'u'lláh, p. 283)

78. O SON OF MY HANDMAID!
Quaff from the tongue of the merciful the stream of divine mystery, and behold from the dayspring of divine utterance the unveiled splendor of the daystar of wisdom. Sow the seeds of My divine wisdom in the pure soil of the heart, and water them with the waters of certitude, that the hyacinths of knowledge and wisdom may spring up fresh and green from the holy city of the heart.

"Should he discover a pure soil, let him sow the seed of the Word of

God, otherwise it would be preferable to observe silence." (Tablets of Bahá'u'lláh, p. 242)

"The seas of Divine wisdom and divine utterance have risen under the breath of the breeze of the All-Merciful. Hasten to drink your fill, O men of understanding!" (Gleanings from the Writings of Bahá'u'lláh, p. 331)

79. O SON OF DESIRE!
How long wilt thou soar in the realms of desire? Wings have I bestowed upon thee, that thou mayest fly to the realms of mystic holiness and not the regions of satanic fancy. The comb, too, have I given thee that thou mayest dress My raven locks, and not lacerate My throat.

"Finally, the 'wings' and the 'comb' mentioned in the following verse are both interpreted by 'Abdu'l-Bahá as the Covenant of Bahá'u'lláh." (Adib Taherzadeh, The Revelation of Bahá'u'lláh v 1, p. 81)

"How long shall we drift on the wings of passion and vain desire; how long shall we spend our days like barbarians in the depths of ignorance and abomination?" ('Abdu'l-Bahá, The Secret of Divine Civilization, p. 3)

"Wherefore, O My servants, defile not your wings with the clay of waywardness and vain desires, and suffer them not to be stained with the dust of envy and hate, that ye may not be hindered from soaring in the heavens of My divine knowledge." (Gleanings from the Writings of Bahá'u'lláh, p. 327)

80. O MY SERVANTS! Ye are the trees of My garden; ye must give forth goodly and wondrous fruits, that ye yourselves and others may

beside them is mere imagination, for we have no means of comprehending that which is invisible and inaccessible." ('Abdu'l-Bahá, Some Answered Questions, p. 148)

"God in His Essence and in His own Self hath ever been unseen, inaccessible, and unknowable. By Presence, therefore, is meant the Presence of the One Who is His Viceregent amongst men." (Bahá'u'lláh, Epistle to the Son of the Wolf, p. 118)

"The angelic company of the celestial Concourse have joined in a call that hath rung throughout the universe, all loudly and mightily acclaiming: 'Hail, O City of God!'" (Bahá'í World Faith - 'Abdu'l-Bahá Section, p. 350)

"Say: Step out of Thy holy chamber, O Maid of Heaven, inmate of the Exalted Paradise! Drape thyself in whatever manner pleaseth Thee in the silken Vesture of Immortality, and put on, in the name of the All-Glorious, the broidered Robe of Light." (Gleanings from the Writings of Bahá'u'lláh, p. 282)

"Cry out before the gaze of the dwellers of heaven and of earth: I am the Maid of Heaven, the Offspring begotten by the Spirit of Bahá." (Gleanings from the Writings of Bahá'u'lláh, p. 283)

78. O SON OF MY HANDMAID!
Quaff from the tongue of the merciful the stream of divine mystery, and behold from the dayspring of divine utterance the unveiled splendor of the daystar of wisdom. Sow the seeds of My divine wisdom in the pure soil of the heart, and water them with the waters of certitude, that the hyacinths of knowledge and wisdom may spring up fresh and green from the holy city of the heart.

"Should he discover a pure soil, let him sow the seed of the Word of

God, otherwise it would be preferable to observe silence." (Tablets of Bahá'u'lláh, p. 242)

"The seas of Divine wisdom and divine utterance have risen under the breath of the breeze of the All-Merciful. Hasten to drink your fill, O men of understanding!" (Gleanings from the Writings of Bahá'u'lláh, p. 331)

79. O SON OF DESIRE!
How long wilt thou soar in the realms of desire? Wings have I bestowed upon thee, that thou mayest fly to the realms of mystic holiness and not the regions of satanic fancy. The comb, too, have I given thee that thou mayest dress My raven locks, and not lacerate My throat.

"Finally, the 'wings' and the 'comb' mentioned in the following verse are both interpreted by 'Abdu'l-Bahá as the Covenant of Bahá'u'lláh." (Adib Taherzadeh, The Revelation of Bahá'u'lláh v 1, p. 81)

"How long shall we drift on the wings of passion and vain desire; how long shall we spend our days like barbarians in the depths of ignorance and abomination?" ('Abdu'l-Bahá, The Secret of Divine Civilization, p. 3)

"Wherefore, O My servants, defile not your wings with the clay of waywardness and vain desires, and suffer them not to be stained with the dust of envy and hate, that ye may not be hindered from soaring in the heavens of My divine knowledge." (Gleanings from the Writings of Bahá'u'lláh, p. 327)

80. O MY SERVANTS!
Ye are the trees of My garden; ye must give forth goodly and wondrous fruits, that ye yourselves and others may

profit therefrom. Thus it is incumbent on every one to engage in crafts and professions, for therein lies the secret of wealth, O men of understanding! For results depend upon means, and the grace of God shall be all-sufficient unto you. Trees that yield no fruit have been and will ever be for the fire.

"Everyone should have some trade, or art or profession, be he rich or poor, and with this he must serve humanity. This service is acceptable as the highest form of worship." ('Abdu'l-Bahá in London, p. 93)

"We have graciously exalted your engagement in such work to the rank of worship unto God, the True One." (Tablets of Bahá'u'lláh, p. 26)

81. O MY SERVANT!

The basest of men are they that yield no fruit on earth. Such men are verily counted as among the dead, nay better are the dead in the sight of God than those idle and worthless souls.

"Waste not your time in idleness and sloth. Occupy yourselves with that which profiteth yourselves and others. Thus hath it been decreed in this Tablet from whose horizon the day-star of wisdom and utterance shineth resplendent." (Tablets of Bahá'u'lláh, p. 26)

82. O MY SERVANT!

The best of men are they that earn a livelihood by their calling and spend upon themselves and upon their kindred for the love of God, the Lord of all worlds.

"The best of men are those who serve the people; the worst of men are those who harm the people." ('Abdu'l-Bahá, The Secret of Divine Civilization, p. 103)

The mystic and wondrous Bride, hidden ere this beneath the veiling of utterance, hath now, by the grace of God and His divine favor, been made manifest even as the resplendent light shed by the beauty of the Beloved. I bear witness, O friends! that the favor is complete, the argument fulfilled, the proof manifest and the evidence established. Let it now be seen what your endeavors in the path of detachment will reveal. In this wise hath the divine favor been fully vouchsafed unto you and unto them that are in heaven and on earth. All praise to God, the Lord of all Worlds.

The End

www.ingramcontent.com/pod-product-compliance
Lightning Source LLC
Chambersburg PA
CBHW080331170426
43194CB00014B/2521